The Cultural Context of Human Resource Development

The Cultural Context of Human Resource Development

Edited by

Carol D. Hansen
Associate Professor, Georgia State University, USA

and

Yih-teen Lee
Assistant Professor, IESE Business School, Spain

First published 2009 by
PALGRAVE MACMILLAN

Palgrave Macmillan in the UK is an imprint of Macmillan Publishers Limited,
registered in England, company number 785998, of Houndmills, Basingstoke,
Hampshire RG21 6XS.

Palgrave Macmillan in the US is a division of St Martin's Press LLC,
175 Fifth Avenue, New York, NY 10010.

Palgrave Macmillan is the global academic imprint of the above companies
and has companies and representatives throughout the world.

Palgrave® and Macmillan® are registered trademarks in the United States,
the United Kingdom, Europe and other countries.

ISBN-13: 978-0-230-55134-3   hardback
ISBN-10: 0-230-55134-3   hardback

This book is printed on paper suitable for recycling and made from fully
managed and sustained forest sources. Logging, pulping and manufacturing
processes are expected to conform to the environmental regulations of the
country of origin.

A catalogue record for this book is available from the British Library.

A catalog record for this book is available from the Library of Congress.

10 9 8 7 6 5 4 3 2 1
18 17 16 15 14 13 12 11 10 09

Printed and bound in Great Britain by
CPI Antony Rowe, Chippenham and Eastbourne

Contents

Figures

Tables

Preface

Purpose

The aim of this book is to broaden our knowledge of human resource development (HRD)—a key issue in the workplace that helps people achieve optimum personal and organizational improvement. One way to advance knowledge is to explore the boundaries of existing theories, or more precisely, to put them into context. This book is distinctive in that it provides an insight into the understanding of HRD in various cultural contexts. Although it is generally recognized that a universal approach to management entails serious limitations, few books in HRD have explicitly addressed this issue.

Culture, as a set of beliefs, frames our expectations for what is appropriate and inappropriate behavior. It is a powerful determinant in how human performance problems are perceived and in how their solutions are formed, implemented, and evaluated. As a lens, we emphatically believe that cultural frames color both the role and the importance of our field as a scholarly endeavor and as a professional area of practice.

We, as the editors of this book, were born and raised in different parts of the world: North America and Asia. However, we have both lived and worked in a variety of international and organizational settings. We first met at a conference in Budapest, where dinner conversations were stimulated by differences in how we viewed the means and the ends of developing human resources. We found ourselves wondering if colleagues in other settings had similar questions. We knew that culture as a variable plays a role in our scholarship and in our practice. However, we knew little of the content of these differences nor of the evolution of their historical context. Over a period of several years, our inquiry grew, which fostered our decision to offer a descriptive voice in the hope that we may all better understand the substance of varying beliefs patterns and their substantive impact on our field.

We recognize that all members of a professional area belong to more than one culture at any given time. For example, Hansen is not only an American, she is a woman, she is an academic, and she is a member of a given scholarly field. We invited key scholars and practitioners to help us address the following questions.

1. Why is the contextual fabric of culture important to HRD? Why is it important to understand the construct of culture as more than an independent variable but instead to identify and to describe the actual content of a given set of beliefs?
2. How does the national or societal culture in which an organization is founded and sustained influence the role and strategies of HRD? For example, is there anything in the societal culture that might explain why Americans spend far more on management development than other cultures? Likewise, for example, why does the German approach to HRD emphasize technical training and assessment centers?
3. Does an individual organizational culture affect the support and strategic power of employee development interventions? In addition, do HRD specialists see their field in the same way as the decision-makers at the executive level? How might cultural differences in decision-making power impact the strategic role of the field?

Chapter content

The book is organized into three key parts. Each part is written and sequenced to address the three sets of focus questions that frame this book.

In Part One, Gary McLean sets the stage for us to consider the fundamental question of why the field of anthropology is paramount to our cultural comprehension of HRD. Anthropology in general, and cultural ethnography in particular, help us to understand patterns of thought and behavior. It is these unwritten and often unconscious behavioral rules that condition people's interpretation of performance problems and solutions.

Next, Wei-Wen Chang builds upon McLean's argument for the grounding of our inquiry in anthropology by explaining the emic approach to the understanding of HRD from the insider's point of view; that is, what are the specific distinctions in how a given culture uniquely defines its concept of HRD? Far too often, in contrast, an etic approach, which is the outsiders' perspective, is used to standardize approaches that have little meaning to those within the culture that we seek to serve.

Part Two consists of six chapters that view HRD from six different societal cultures. These contributions are specifically written both to remind us that our fundamental belief about work, relationships, and development are first formed at home. Scholars such as Alder, d'Iribarne, and Hofstede speak to the power of the societal culture in which we are raised. In fact, Hofstede suggests that these fundamental beliefs are formed by the time we reach puberty.

Hansen begins this part of the book by focusing on the anthropological power of professional myths. She offers a cross-cultural study of how cultural myths vary in three different continents. Data collected in Germany and in the Côte d'Ivoire are contrasted with those myths that first formed professional models of HRD in the United States, as developed by well-known contributors such as Len Nadler and Patricia McLagan.

Susan Lynham, Fredrick Nafukho, and Peter Cunningham describe the changing nature of South Africa's multicultural political power base, which despite twentieth century tension has retained its dominant and very humane worldview of *ubuntu*. This concept reflects the interconnection and interdependence of human beings. It is this philosophy that frames a sense of collective learning which guides the current construction of the country's view of HRD.

Sylvie Chevrier focuses on the concept of empowerment by using anthropological symbolism and metaphors again to compare differences between the United States and, in this case, her home country—France. These metaphors not only describe current differences in definitions and perceptions of need for employee empowerment, but their evolution is also grounded in the historical background of the two countries.

Austrian culture is the subject of the next chapter by Astrid Reichel, Wolfgang Mayrhofer, and Katharina Chudzikowski. Focusing on management development, they describe the strong context of Austria's cultural evolution, beginning with the Habsburgs and taking us past World War II, the Cold War, and the country's entry into the European Union. They describe the present-day workplace as collective, loyal, and systematic, which presents some tension and multicultural concern in welcoming an influx of twenty-first century immigrants.

Javier Quintanilla, Mª Jesús Belizón, Lourdes Susaeta, and Rocío Sánchez-Mangas provide a rich history to explain Spain's recent economic growth and large influx of foreign investment. They concentrate on the lack of previous concern for employee development in large enterprise; in particular, those firms that are now subsidiaries of American multinationals. Given this lack of tradition, the authors find a kind of malleability in Spanish firms that causes companies to copy what appears to be successful in American firms, suggesting that Spain is only beginning to define and customize its own sense of HRD.

Looking to the East, Lee and Hansen conclude this part of the book by questioning what has become a career path for upwardly mobile, high-potential employees in many Western societies. They turn to ancient oriental philosophy to argue that a linear progression may not always be the most fruitful nor the most strategic form of career development. They call this new concept the Tao of reversalism.

Thirdly, we seek to examine the context of organizational life. The remaining seven chapters, in Part Three, focus on particular functions of HRD within the context of a given organization. Given the background of these authors, and given their access to illustrative data, the context of their concerns and their arguments are embedded in the sociocultural context of the American model of HRD and the American firm.

Sheila Margolis explores the strategic role of HRD in helping organizations better understand their core identity and core beliefs. This model can help any work setting better understand the likelihood of alignment between its mission and the degree to which employees may be willing to adopt their work style to the overall needs of the organization. Each element of the model reflects the specific and unique cultural beliefs that guide a given organization's core purpose, philosophy, and priorities.

Ava Wilensky offers a contrast in the role and influence of HRD in for-profit and nonprofit organizations. By focusing on nonprofit organizations, she illustrates how a focus point on funding and the temporal nature of a volunteer work force constrains the perception of what employee development measures can and should do. Although HRD in today's nonprofit organizations typically plays a small and secondary role, current research suggests that our field should be more powerful in fostering and retaining volunteers.

Saul Carliner addresses the dilemma of demonstrating the value of HRD. He explains the cultural tension that exists between those who have the ad hoc responsibility of a training function and those who have been professionally trained to design and deliver instruction. For those who identify with the field of HRD through their own professional education, there is a greater emphasis on linking the worth of HRD to organizational performance. His research data conclude that those who are members of the HRD culture see training as a means of *improving* performance whereas those who are not a part of the field tend to see it as a means to *impart* skills.

The influence of organizational culture on training effectiveness is the subject of Kay Bunch's contribution. In general, she describes how an organization's culture and subcultures may play a role in the failure of our work by denying the necessary resources and power to guide the development of training interventions professionally. She reminds the reader that ultimately we must secure the cultural support of top decision-makers and we must work to improve HRD's professional image.

The cultural context of performance management is explored in a case study of a large company in the food and beverage industry by Kimberly Magee. She contrasts administrative and developmental purposes of performance management, and strongly suggests that HRD professionals have a strategic role to play in ensuring the developmental use of such systems. The subject of cultural alignment is raised to guarantee the effectiveness and the learning potential of this device.

Lori Fancher focuses on the succession planning process, including executive development, by defining it as one of the most important responsibilities that HRD leaders have when contributing to strategic business success. She illustrates this point with data from a case study of a package delivery company. She found that participants had difficulties articulating and offering a clear rationale for the process and its pathways, which underscores the cultural power of those who have the authority to determine their own successors.

Acknowledgments

Thanks to our many colleagues who contributed to this book. Their collaboration in sharing their knowledge and research allowed an in-depth and unique understanding of culture and its impact on our field. I greatly appreciate their patience in addressing all of my various comments and questions. Most of all, I appreciate their willingness to collaborate with Yih-teen and me in philosophy, tone, and commonality of purpose. We all learned from the experience and I am honored to write with this wonderful group of scholars.

Likewise, I am grateful to my co-editor, Yih-teen Lee. It is thanks to his encouragement that we decided to create this book. His tenacity and sense of excellence guided our efforts. It is his energy and fascination with culture that fuels my own inquiry.

I extend a special thank you to my research assistant, Travis Wright, whose tireless efforts in reading and commenting on all of the drafts made such a huge difference in bringing this book to print. I am especially grateful for his assistance in coordinating and organizing the authors' contributions. His work went far beyond our expectations. Travis is a wonderful writer and editor whose participation was a true gift to us, the authors, and whose partnership we will value forever.

Finally, many thanks to my department, family, and friends for their patience and support.

—Carol

Thank you, my dear friend, co-author, and co-editor, Carol. You guided and accompanied me on the road of learning about culture from a doctoral student to a scholar and faculty member. Thanks to all of you, the authors of the book, without whose contributions this book would not have seen the light of day. Thank you, Travis, for your great and reliable assistance in preparing this manuscript. Thanks to my colleagues at IESE, who provided me with a wonderful environment for growth and self-development.

Thank you, my dear wife, Bih-Chyi, and son, Yunn-tien, for your continuous support over the years despite the geographical distance that temporarily separates us.

—Yih-teen

Notes on Contributors

Mª Jesús Belizón is a research assistant in the Department of Managing People in Organizations at IESE Business School, University of Navarra (Spain). Her research focuses on the transfer of human resource policies in multinational organizations.

Kay Bunch is an instructor of management in the J. Mack Robinson College of Business at Georgia State University. She has published several academic papers and made numerous presentations. Her research interests include gender, organizational culture, employment law, and leadership.

Saul Carliner is an associate professor of educational technology at Concordia University in Montreal. His research interests include emerging forms of online communication and training for the workplace; means of assessing the productivity, effectiveness, and business performance of workplace content; and transferring research results to practice. He has received research funding from the Social Sciences and Humanities Research Council, Canadian Council on Learning, Hong Kong University Grants Council, and Society for Technical Communication. Also an industry consultant, he performs strategic planning, project evaluation, executive and management coaching, and facilitation for clients such as Chubb Insurance, Cossette Communications, IBM, Microsoft Corporation, Montreal Holocaust Memorial Centre, ST Microelectronics, Wachovia, and several Canadian and US government agencies.

Wei-Wen Chang is an associate professor of international human resource development at National Taiwan Normal University. She received her Ph.D. in adult learning from University of Wisconsin-Madison. Her research focuses on multinational HRD, intercultural training, and cross-cultural competence, and her work has been published in journals such as the *Adult Education Quarterly*, *Human Resource Development Quarterly*, *Human Resource Development International*, and *Human Resource Development Review*.

Sylvie Chevrier is professor of human resource management at the Université de Paris-Est (France). She obtained her Ph.D. from the University of Québec at Montréal (Canada). Her main research activities focus on cross-cultural management. She also works as a consultant for several international organizations including corporations as well as non-governmental organizations.

Katharina Chudzikowski works as research assistant at the Department of Management at the Wirtschaftsuniversitaet Wien (WU Wien, Austria). She received her master's degree in business administration, majoring in management and organizational behavior from the WU Wien. Her research focuses on career research, organizational behavior, intercultural management, and career management.

Peter W. Cunningham D Phil (UPE), DipSoc (Kent), accredited consultant: SAP R/3 Human Resources and Business Information Warehouse (BIW), Head of department and Programme Head Sociology and Anthropology, Nelson Mandela Metropolitan University, South Africa. Educated in South Africa and Britain, he has been involved in HRM international keynote conference presentations, public presentations, executive management training, and consultation for more than 30 years. He has published widely in leading international and national journals. He is the only SAP-certified consultant in HRM and BIW at a South African academic institution, his major areas of research, training, and consultation are SAP (HR), HRD, electronic HRM and organizational behavior. He has co-authored several books, the latest in organizational behavior. As a research specialist, he is a referee for various publications, examiner of master's and doctoral degrees, and an editorial board member of several international management and sustainable development journals.

Lori P. Fancher is a partner and owner of C2C Consulting, LLC in Atlanta, Georgia, USA. She received her Ph.D. in HRD at Georgia State University. She has approximately 15 years experience as an HRD practitioner, having served in various strategic roles including: training and development, performance improvement, leadership development and organizational effectiveness. In these various roles, she has sought to bridge HRD research with the current needs of business. Her primary interest is in change management, including the alignment of strategy with organizational culture and HR processes.

Carol D. Hansen is an associate professor of HRD at Georgia State University. She studies the cultural and cross-cultural frames that shape belief systems and employee and organizational development. She has taught and conducted research with universities in Europe and Africa, and she was a Fulbright scholar to India. She also served as an HRD branch chief at the United States Department of State.

Yih-teen Lee is assistant professor at IESE Business School, University of Navarra (Spain). His recent research topics include the cross-cultural comparative study of person–environment fit, dynamic models of inter-cultural competences, work design and well-being, and performance determinants of auditors. He has taught cross-cultural management, strategic human resource management, and leadership in MBA and executive programs in Europe, Asia, and the USA.

Susan A. Lynham is an associate professor in qualitative research methods and organizational performance and change in the School of Education at Colorado State University in the USA, and a research associate at the Nelson Mandela Metropolitan University in South Africa. She has 18+ years experience as a human resources/development professional. Her scholarship focuses on strategic HRD, leadership in complex and diverse environments, and applied theory building and research methods. A past board member of the Academy of Human Resource Development, Susan serves on the editorial boards of *Human Resource Development International*, the *International Journal of Servant Leadership*, *New Horizons in Adult Education and HRD*, and is the associate editor-in-chief of *Advances in Developing Human Resources*. She obtained her Ph.D. from the University of Minnesota, USA, in May 2000.

Kimberly C. Magee is a senior human resource leader in the consumer products industry. She has worked both in the US and abroad. Her expertise is in organization effectiveness and development. She earned a Ph.D. from The Andrew Young School of Policy Studies at Georgia State University. Her research interests include the intersection of human resource practices and organizational culture. She is also adjunct faculty at Georgia State's Robinson College of Business.

Sheila L. Margolis is president of the Workplace Culture Institute. She is quoted in newspapers and magazines including *The Wall Street Journal*, *The Washington Post* and *The Atlanta Journal-Constitution*. Sheila is the author of *"Building a Culture of Distinction: Activities and Tools to Lead Organizational Change"* and *"Building a Culture of Distinction: Participant Workbook."* Additionally, she is co-author of *"There Is No Place Like Work: Seven Leadership Insights for Creating a Workplace to Call Home."* Sheila is a professional member of the National Speakers Association and speaks regularly on her principles of core culture and change.

Wolfgang Mayrhofer is professor of business administration and holds a chair for management and organizational behavior at WU Wirtschaftsuniversität Wien, Austria. Previously, he held teaching and research positions at German universities. His research interests focus on international comparative research in human resource management and leadership and on careers. He has co-edited, co-authored, and authored 23 books and more than 100 book chapters and peer-reviewed articles. He regularly conducts training for public and private organizations, especially in the area of outdoor training. He has taught in various international programs.

Gary N. McLean is senior professor and executive director of international human resource development programs at Texas A&M University, and former professor and coordinator of HRD and adult education at the University of Minnesota, St. Paul. He has served as President of the Academy of Human Resource Development and the International Management Development Association. As an organizational development practitioner in McLean Global Consulting, Inc., he works extensively globally. His research interests are broad and diverse, focusing primarily on organization development and international HRD.

Fredrick M. Nafukho is an associate professor and program chair for human resource development, Department of Educational Administration and Human Resource Development, College of Education and Human Development at Texas A&M University. His research focus is on investment in human capital development, international and cross-cultural HRD, and use of ICTs in higher education and training in Africa. He has taught and conducted research in universities in Africa and in the USA. He is a member of the executive board of the Academy of Human Resource Development and serves as a member of the editorial boards of *Human Resource Development Quarterly*, *Advances in Developing Human Resource Development*, *Human Resource Development International*, and editor (North America) for the *Journal of European Industrial Training*. He was a Fulbright Scholar to the USA.

Javier Quintanilla is an associate professor at IESE Business School, University of Navarra (Spain). His current research interests are the management of professional service firms and international human resource management, subjects on which he has published widely.

Astrid Reichel works as an assistant professor at the Department of Management at the Vienna University of Economics and Business Administration. She received her master's and doctoral degrees in business administration from the University of Vienna. Her research focuses on international and comparative human resource management, the human resource management–performance link, women in HRM, and career management.

Rocío Sánchez-Mangas is an assistant professor in the Department of Economic Analysis: Quantitative Economis at Universidad Autónoma de Madrid, Spain. She specializes in the field of econometrics, both theoretical and applied. She has conducted research in different economic fields with several universities and institutions in Europe and the USA. Currently, she is working with the IESE Business School, University of Navarra (Spain) in an international research project focused on the diffusion of human resource practices in multinational firms.

Lourdes Susaeta is a researcher in the Department of Managing People in Organizations at IESE Business School, University of Navarra (Spain), and an associate professor of Management at Complutense University of Madrid. She is currently investigating workforce diversity in multinational companies for her doctoral thesis. Her research area is the study of the transfer of human resource policies in multinational organizations.

Ava S. Wilensky, Ph.D. is co-founder of CORE InSites, a management consulting firm specializing in helping organizational leaders leverage their workplace cultures to establish optimum strategic direction, negotiate creative change, and identify and retain valued employees. Her research and publications focus on executive leadership, organizational culture, and nonprofit organizations. She speaks and conducts workshops throughout North America. She serves as an adjunct professor at Georgia State University.

Part I

1
Anthropology: A Foundation for Human Resource Development

Gary N. McLean

Over the years, there has been considerable interest in the foundational areas of human resource development (HRD). Swanson (1995, 1999) has argued for a restricted number of foundational areas (economics, psychology, systems), whereas McLean (1998, 1999) has argued for a greatly extended set of foundational areas, including anthropology. Yet, searches of databases for "anthropology" and "HRD," combined, yielded only two articles, neither of which was of much use in writing this chapter. All other results of the searches, including my articles, simply listed anthropology as one of many possible additional foundation areas to those offered by Swanson.

It is important, then, that the contributions of anthropology to the theory and practice of HRD be explored. In this chapter, I explore how anthropology is increasingly being used in a business context and suggest several contributions that anthropology makes to the three most common aspects of HRD, as originally identified by McLagan (1989): training and development, organization development, and career development.

What is anthropology?

From its Greek roots, anthropology is simply the study of humans. This is far too broad, however, as such a definition also incorporates sociology, history, psychology, and all of the other human sciences. In their attempt to differentiate anthropology from other human sciences, Ember & Ember (1999) decided that, ultimately, it was different from the other human sciences in that "anthropologists are curious about the typical characteristics of human populations—how and why such populations and their characteristics have varied throughout the ages" (p. 3). They went on to classify the field into two broad areas—biological (physical) anthropology and cultural anthropology. For our purposes, we are more concerned with the foundational impact of cultural anthropology on the field of HRD.

"Cultural anthropologists," according to Ember & Ember (1999), "are interested in how populations or societies vary in their cultural features" (p. 5). This branch of anthropology also forces us to confront the need to define culture. There are many such definitions. One of the most familiar to those in HRD is that of Schein (1985), who defined culture as,

> basic assumptions and beliefs that are shared by members of an organization, that operate unconsciously, and that define in a basic "taken-for-granted" fashion an organization's view of itself and its environment. These assumptions and beliefs are learned responses to a group's problems. They come to be taken for granted because they solve those problems repeatedly and reliably.
>
> (pp. 6–7)

Schein's metaphors of culture as an iceberg or onion are also familiar. In such models, Schein described the visible portion of the iceberg or the onion as the behaviors or artifacts of culture. He claimed that just beneath the surface the beliefs or values of a culture can be found. Deep in the water, or at the core of the onion, are the assumptions of a culture, or those aspects that control one's behavior but one seldom explores and simply takes for granted.

Others have defined culture differently from Schein. Out of the myriad definitions of culture, Jordan (2003) offered this definition: "an integrated system of shared ideas (thoughts, ideals, attitudes), behaviors (actions), and material artifacts (objects) that characterize a group" (p. 40).

Ember & Ember (1999) defined culture as "the customary ways of thinking and behaving of a particular population or society" as incorporating "language, religious beliefs, food, preferences, music, work habits, gender roles, how they rear their children, how they construct their houses, and many other learned behaviors and ideas that have come to be widely shared or customary among the group" (p. 5). Within cultural anthropology, they identify three branches: archeology, anthropological linguistics, and ethnology. Ethnology, "the study of existing and recent cultures" (p. 5) is the area of greatest relevance to HRD.

According to Ember & Ember (1999),

> ethnologists seek to understand how and why peoples today and in the recent past differ in their customary ways of thinking and

acting . . . [It] is concerned with patterns of thought and behavior . . . [They] also study the dynamics of culture—that is, how various cultures develop and change. In addition, they are also interested in the relationship between beliefs and practices within a culture.

(p. 7)

Ethnology also provides HRD with the primary tools used in doing needs assessments and evaluations through observation, interviews, and the study of artifacts, which would also include secondary data in the HRD field. Although not as prominent, surveys are also used by ethnologists, though usually they are developed after the other three approaches have been applied so that the surveys reflect the context of the respondents: their beliefs, priorities, definitions, and so on. In this way, respondents can better understand and value the questions being asked. Thus, all four of the approaches to assessment and evaluation specified by McLean (2006) are included within the ethnology tool-kit.

What is human resource development?

There are continuing struggles to define HRD (McLean & McLean, 2001; Swanson, 1995; Watkins & Marsick, 1996), and the emerging subspecialties of HRD, including organization development (McLean, 2006), national HRD (Lynham, Paprock, & Cunningham, 2006; McLean, Osman-Gani, & Cho, 2004), and international HRD (Wang & McLean, 2007). Each of these efforts has emerged out of a specific cultural context with specific assumptions, values, and beliefs. That is, anthropological processes are necessary to understand why such definitions vary and the sources from which they are derived.

Let us look at just the basic definition of HRD. Watkins & Marsick (1996) come out of a background of of adult education. From this perspective, it is not surprising that their emphasis in defining HRD is on *learning*. Swanson (1995), in contrast, comes from a background of industrial education, in which the emphasis has been on efficiency and effectiveness of systems and people, thus leading in his definition to an emphasis on *performance*. McLean & McLean (2001) reflect a value system of inclusion and ambiguity in a cross-cultural setting. Both have dual citizenships (Canada and the USA) and both have traveled and worked extensively in international contexts. It should not come as a surprise to know that their definition emerged out of the use of basic anthropological tools of observation and interviews of people from a broad array of countries. Their definition, and the one used in this chapter, is, with some minor modifications, based on additional insights:

> Human Resource Development is any process or activity that, either initially or over the long term, has the potential to develop . . . knowledge, expertise, productivity, [safety, security, spirituality,] and satisfaction, whether for personal or group/team gain, or for the benefit of an organization, community, nation, or, ultimately, the whole of humanity.
>
> (McLean & McLean, 2001, p. 322)

This definition, like that of anthropology, has been criticized as being too broad and encompassing too much of the human experience. Should it be limited to adults? Should it be limited to the workplace? And, as with the definitions of Swanson or Watkins and Marsick, should it be limited to performance or to learning? Or, as with the argument of Lee (2001), should it be defined at all? Variance in definitions is to be expected. As Spradley (1979) suggested, language is the greatest vehicle for communicating culture. Thus, how one answers these questions is not a matter of being right or wrong. Rather, it is a matter of understanding the cultural context in which one is working and recognizing why diversity exists in our attempts to define the field of HRD—just as anthropologists and those in many of the human sciences have had to struggle in understanding and defining their fields.

How and why is anthropology being used in business?

Increasing attention is being given to the practical application of anthropology, or a field called "applied anthropology" (Ember & Ember, 1999, p. 10). At an even more specific level, Jordan (2003) has written an entire book on business anthropology. According to Ember & Ember (1999), "one out of two anthropologists in this country is now employed outside of academia" (p. xii). Weise (1999) estimated that there were over two thousand anthropologists working as business anthropologists. Miller (2005) indicated that Microsoft Corp. employs at least seven anthropologists, and it is looking to hire more. Other companies that use anthropologists include Pitney Bowes, Inc., Battelle, GM, Nynex, and Intel Corp.

Ember & Ember (1999) enumerated several locations in which anthropologists might be employed in applied settings: "government agencies, international development agencies, private consulting firms, business, public health organizations, medical schools, law offices, community development agencies, and charitable foundations" (p. 11)—all places in which HRD is practiced. They went on to enumerate places where ethnologists might be employed—"community development, urban planning, health care, and agricultural improvement to personnel and organizational management and assessment of the impact of change programs on people's lives" (p. 11)—directly linking the practice of anthropology to organization development. Corporations have used anthropologists in the past to study their customers and how their workers put products together. Anthropologists are used to help companies understand cultures in other countries, and they help different corporate "cultures" or departments understand each other, too (Miller, 2005).

Ember & Ember (1999) argued that anthropology is more and more a practical and applied behavioral science. This is largely so because its purpose is in *"what* humans were and are like," and in *"why* humans are the way they are, why they got to be that way, and why they vary" (p. xii). Kane (1996) explained that the popularity of anthropological applications in business is because "companies are convinced that the tools of ethnographic research—minute observation, subtle interviewing, systematic documentation—can answer questions about organizations and markets that traditional research tools can't" (p. 60). Crain (cited in Kane, 1996) "believes the field's 'holistic' approach—one that draws on evolutionary, cultural, linguistic, and biological perspectives—matches the growing complexity of business itself" (p. 61).

With this understanding of anthropology, it is not surprising that anthropology and its related concepts are widely used in business and, especially, in HRD. Anthropology is clearly a core foundation for the theory and practice of HRD.

The application of anthropology to training and development

Around the world, as definitions of HRD vary, training and development are found to be present almost universally. Thus, we start the application section of this chapter with a few examples of how anthropology has contributed to the manner in which HRD addresses important concepts in training and development.

Lifelong and self-directed learning

Both of these concepts are included together as they emerged from a US perspective of adult education. The premise of both concepts is that learning is a lifelong process that begins at birth and ends at death.

Much of this learning is informal beyond early adulthood but is primarily self-directed, as the individual decides both what is going to be learned and how it is to be learned. Our understanding of this process is due primarily to the work of anthropologists observing the way in which people continue to learn throughout their lifetimes. What one chooses to learn, and the emphasis put on such learning, is also reflective of the culture in which one was raised and lives.

Employing organizations take advantage of both of these concepts in applying the ongoing development of work-related expertise. However, in many cultures, these ideas apply to volunteer work, hobbies, parenting and grandparenting, civic work, and simply self-development for its own sake. Each of these concepts is influenced by the culture in which one lives and the values that have been developed during a person's lifetime. Within the context of the definition of HRD that was provided earlier in this chapter, the concepts, even when applied broadly, fit aptly.

Task analysis

One of the key components of the ADDIE model (Swanson, 1995) is analysis (followed by design, development, implementation, and evaluation). There are many ways of analyzing training needs. One of the more popular forms is task analysis. In this, the HRD professional will often need to observe very carefully how experts perform a given task, to identify the steps that are followed in performing that task. There are actually two purposes of such an analysis: first, as will be expanded on later, one is to improve the process; the second is to use the expertise of these workers to determine what should be included in the training curriculum for new workers. This analysis leads directly into the subsequent phases of the ADDIE model.

As with other training and development interventions discussed in this section, the observational tools required for successful task analysis come directly from anthropological methods. A well-trained observer is essential to this process.

Cross-cultural training

As Jordan (2003) explained,

> Anthropologists are interested in understanding group behavior and culture. They look at the ways the customs and beliefs of a people are interrelated (holism), compare groups of people around the world and across cultures to get a larger understanding of human behavior

(cross-cultural comparison), and try to understand behavior from the participant's point of view rather than their own personal one (cultural relativism).

(p. 2)

Having gained such a global perspective, it is then relatively easy for an HRD practitioner to assist organizations working in multiple countries to understand the employees and consumers in these countries in a behavioral way. They can then impart this information to management and expatriates who want to be more effective in such a cross-cultural context. This is an example in which HRD practitioners learn directly from the information developed by anthropologists and from HRD researchers using anthropological methods.

In fact, one cannot talk about cross-cultural issues without referencing the work of Edward T. Hall. Hall was an anthropologist whose work became extremely important in business and in cross-cultural HRD. Hall's writing focused on communication, emphasizing the need for it to be understood in a cultural context (Hall, 1981). He later also wrote about the importance of space and time in understanding cultures. As a simple example, many cultures such as Korea or Thailand do not have past or future tenses in their languages. This influences not just the language, but also how these cultures think about the past and the future. These constructs are still widely used in cross-cultural training today.

Leadership development

What one understands leadership to mean, how it is differentiated from management, and how HRD attempts to develop leadership will all be influenced by the culture in which one is working. Efforts to apply Bass's (1990) concepts of transformational and transactional leadership in other parts of the world (Saetang & McLean (2003) in Thailand) have met with varying degrees of success. This is true of many instruments that have been developed in a US context. Some aspects of the concepts seem to apply somewhat universally, but others often have to be adapted or indigenized to make sense within a specific cultural context. The concepts of universalism, adaptive cultures, and culture specific all come from anthropology.

The application of anthropology to organization development

As with so many other aspects of HRD, there is no universal or even widely accepted definition of organization development. McLean (2006) defined it, consistent with the McLean and McLean (2001) definition of HRD, as:

- any process or activity, based on the behavioral sciences,
- that, either initially or over the long term,
- has the potential to develop in an organizational setting,
- enhanced knowledge, expertise, productivity, satisfaction, income, interpersonal relationships, and other desired outcomes,
- whether for personal or group/team gain, or for the benefit of an organization, community, nation, region, or, ultimately, the whole of humanity.

(p. 9)

The interdisciplinary nature of this definition fits nicely with the equally interdisciplinary nature of anthropology. Within the context of the definition, there are dozens of interventions designed to fulfill the goals implied in it. Although it is probable that a connection to anthropology can be made for almost all of these interventions, those that follow will serve as examples of how critical anthropological content and methods are to the understanding and practice of HRD.

Organizational culture assessment

Interest in what was originally called corporate culture, but what is now referred to as organizational culture, bloomed in the 1980s with the publication of several books on Japanese management, in particular with Deal and Kennedy's (1982) *Corporate Cultures*. Even today, few organization-wide interventions would be considered without first doing an organizational cultural audit or assessment.

Ethnographic methods are critical in performing these assessments. Observation comes into play from the first exposure to the client organization. When I enter a facility, I watch for how employees and visitors are treated when they arrive. How long are people allowed to wait before their hosts greet them? How are people dressed? How are they greeted? Do visitors sign in? All of these questions suggest something about the culture of the organization. Such observations can even begin as early as the parking lot. How many spots are allocated to visitors? Are there parking spots reserved for managers and executives? How far from the entrance are the parking spots? These questions can also give clues about the hierarchy of the organization and the reward system that exists. Triangulation of methods occurs through the additional use of interviews, surveys, and a review of secondary data and artifacts—all ethnographic methods.

Mergers and acquisitions

Many authors (Orsini, 2006; Schmidt, 2002; Weber, Oded, & Raveh, 1996) have emphasized the importance of cultural fit when companies merge or are acquired. With failure rates estimated to exceed 70 percent in the USA, and even higher internationally (Schmidt, 2002), the importance of examining cultures should be at the forefront, especially during the pre-deal and due-diligence stages. In spite of what appears to be obvious evidence, companies continue to emphasize financial and legal aspects of mergers and acquisitions and often ignore the people and cultural components.

Orsini (2006) stressed how important culture is to the success of a merger and acquisition. He highlighted how fast a good deal can go sour with poor cultural integration. He also noted that cultural due diligence is often missed because of the difficulty of grasping and managing culture. Here, again, we have evidence of the need for an understanding of anthropological concepts and methods for the effective practice of organization development.

Globalization

Outsourcing, mobility for education, mobility of workers, technology, supply chains, continuing high levels of refugees, legal and illegal immigration—all of these factors are influencing how business is being conducted today and challenging cultural descriptions that have existed in the past. Anthropological descriptions based primarily on country borders have much reduced validity in today's world with increasing mixes of cultures within country borders. For example, the EU (European Union) has dramatically influenced the cultures of its countries. By 2007, Galway, in Ireland, had a preponderance of workers from Poland, though this is again changing with the 2008 economic downturn. HRD theorists and practitioners are being confronted with the need to redefine the cultures with which they are likely to be working as companies continue to expand and spread across the globe—not just from the more traditional country cultures, but from the new, emerging diversities of cultures that the movement of people around the world is creating. Jordan (2003) concluded, "the cultural landscape is a complex web of interacting cultural groups and individual humans who fit into multiple cultural groups" (p. 42). This challenges HRD to avoid the simplistic characterizations used in the past (such as Hofstede (2001) and Trompenaars (1994)), to focus on a much more complex approach to culture and to the implications of globalization in how we do our business.

Process improvement

Anthropology's contributions to observation become critical, but not without contributions from other disciplines, as well, in process improvements in organizations. A commitment to continuous improvement is present in most organizations, whether for-profit or not-for-profit. Certainly, in today's world, there are many statistical tools and problem-solving approaches that are used in identifying suggestions for process improvement. Nevertheless, observation remains one of the critical components for it.

How successfully observations for process improvement will be implemented will also depend on the culture in which the organization is functioning. For example, a suggestion made in a high-power distance hierarchy may be ignored if the suggestion does not come from top management, whereas it might be readily accepted in a low-power distance, egalitarian work environment. Anthropological methods can help us to determine how such suggestions are most likely to be implemented within different cultural contexts.

Diversity

In some cultural contexts, interest in diversity has long been a high priority. Creating equal opportunities for people regardless of race, gender, age, national origin, religion, sexual orientation, disabilities, political affiliation, and so on, has received significant attention and financial resources in many organizations in the USA, Canada, and other countries. In some countries, there has been commitment to eliminating discrimination based on some of these factors. Increasingly, with the migration of workers across national boundaries, the importation of foreign brides, the aging of many countries, and shifting value systems, organizations around the world are beginning to address some, if not all, of these factors.

How these issues get addressed, and the extent to which they are addressed, will vary based on the culture. I have been involved in a longitudinal study in Thailand with a colleague (Virakul & McLean, 2000), and in process) in which we have been exploring how Thai companies deal with employees with AIDS/HIV, and what efforts they put into helping their employees understand the source of the disease and how to prevent infection. We have found that the companies are extremely reluctant even to discuss the issue; they fear that, if their name appears in a study related to AIDS/HIV (despite promises of anonymity), customers will stop buying their products. Because of the fear and subsequent secrecy associated with this disease, obvious forms of discrimination continue to be practiced. It is our hope that, through anthropological methods of observation, interviews, review of secondary data, and surveys, we can bring the issue out into the open where it can be explored and decisions made about how to reduce such discrimination and the pain that it brings to those affected.

Demographic studies, also associated with anthropology, are proving very useful in countries with dramatically changing demographics. Countries like Italy, for example, face a drastic reduction in population. Although many countries have an older (maturing) population, others, such as Saudi Arabia, face an overwhelming number of their population below the age of 25. Countries that have had enforced population controls, with abortions permitted, and a preference for male children, are confronted with an unimaginable imbalance between men and women, such as is found in China, Korea, and Taiwan. These cultures are finding that they must import foreign brides as local females become too highly educated, and thus unacceptable within the cultural traditions, for the males. Alternatively, females do not wish to marry farmers, so brides are brought in who are willing to make such marriages.

Each of these examples creates enormous challenges for HRD—not only at the organizational level, but also at local and national levels. Anthropological methods, again, are important as we begin to get an understanding of what the cultural implications are of these demographic changes and what must be done to respond appropriately to the challenges that are created.

Organizational change

Unfortunately, we seem to understand much more about describing the organization's culture than we do about creating the changes desired in it. Perhaps we have stopped short with the observational method by not determining how to be effective in translating the assessment into change.

One of the most famous (and controversial) experiments in organizational change was conducted in the Western Electric Hawthorne Works, a manufacturing plant in Chicago. Elton Mayo, an Australian psychiatrist, became director of the project designed to explore reasons for changes in levels of productivity. He brought in W. Lloyd Werner, a US anthropologist. Using qualitative, anthropological tools, the team observed the workers and discovered that, no matter what the condition, performance improved. They concluded that productivity was a factor of management's interest in the workers (Jordan, 2003). Jordan (2003) claimed that it was from research such as this conducted by industrial anthropologists that the human relations school was born. This case is of further interest as it helps to elucidate the evolution of traditional anthropology (observe and describe) to applied and then business anthropology. In business anthropology, the skills and tools of the science are used to create change holistically and intuitively, something traditionalists would find abhorrent (Pant & Alberti, 1997).

Systems thinking

Although popularized by Senge (1990), systems thinking has its roots in the anthropological perspective of holism. As Jordan (2003) explained, "One of the anthropologists' great strengths is a holistic perspective, by which I mean the ability to understand the big picture" (p. 8). She went on to define holism—"pulling back from the specific problem, event, or situation under study and putting it in a larger context. Anthropologists are trained to look at larger questions than the one they are being asked to answer" (p. 108). Although Jordan made the claim that *only* anthropologists can take such a holistic view, this is exactly what well-trained HRD professionals do. In fact, Swanson (1995) pictured systems as one of only three foundations for HRD. Yet, conceptually, systems thinking is a subset of one of the basic premises of anthropology.

Small group behavior

The ability to observe and describe the behavior of individuals in groups as they interact may also have its origins in anthropology. Jordan (2003), for example, described the development of interactional analysis developed by Chapple and Arensberg to quantify "interactive human behavior through specific measurements of interactions" (p. 11). The use of observation is widely applied in organization development (OD), resulting in the concept of process consultation, whereby a third party reflects back to a group his or her observations about their interactions, with the intent of improving them. Sociograms are specific tools that are used to allow a team to see how frequently its members interact with each other. These often serve the purpose of triangulation, whereby these so-called objective measures can be used to verify or challenge our subjective observations.

In addition, just as traditional anthropologists were often mistrusted as spies, the same can be true of both our subjective and objective observations of small groups—we can often be seen as corporate spies, and the members of the organization may try hard to camouflage their true beliefs and behaviors—which is, of course, a limitation to the anthropologist's approach.

Others

By no means is this an exhaustive list of the OD functions of HRD. Almost every aspect of OD can be traced in some respect to its origins or influence from anthropology or anthropological methods. Room simply does not allow an exhaustive development of every aspect of these connections.

The application of anthropology to career development

Much less has been written about the career development (CD) component of HRD than is the case with the other two components (training and development (T&D) and OD). Nevertheless, there are several areas in which anthropological understanding and methods become critical to the effective application of CD. Many of these concepts could have been included in the section on OD, but they have been identified for this section as they are somewhat more relevant to CD than to OD.

As with each of the other aspects of HRD, it is not possible in the restrictions of a chapter to provide a comprehensive description of the contributions of anthropology to career development. What follows is simply an example of a few such interventions.

Performance appraisal/management

Providing performance reviews or appraisals has been a struggle for many organizations. We have moved from forced rankings to behaviorally anchored ratings (BARs) to management-by-objectives (MBOs) to 360-degree or multi-rater feedback—all to little avail, as no system seems to provide what the organization is looking for. Some of the factors involved are cultural. In egalitarian or collectivist societies, it is not acceptable to highlight the expertise of one or two individuals over their co-workers. It may not be considered appropriate for a subordinate to rank or grade his or her superior. In some cultures, trading of evaluations goes on—where individuals agree to score an individual highly in return for a reciprocal scoring. As humans, we simply lack the ability to know the impact of another person's behavior, we do not always understand the impact of the system on an individual's performance, and we cannot observe another person all of the time.

In another work (McLean, 1997), I argued that the most effective form of performance appraisal is immediate feedback—whether negative or positive—followed by the necessary coaching of the individual for how the task should be performed, if the feedback was negative. Even though McLean (1997) believes that this is the best approach, it is by no means perfect. In some cultures, it is considered a loss of face if a supervisor has to correct an individual. Certainly, care must be taken how and where such correction occurs. Public correction, in most cultures, would be seen as unacceptable. Even then, the perception of being constantly watched reduces the sense of autonomy that workers in many cultures prefer.

So, once again, anthropology comes into play. What is the culture and how do individuals react to receiving feedback? For that matter, how do individuals react to giving feedback? What is the purpose of performance appraisal and what options would the group find most acceptable, given the limitations that exist in all forms of performance appraisal? These are questions that anthropological tools in the hands of HRD professionals can help to answer.

Career ladders or promotions

A career ladder refers to the expected steps that a person might go through during a career. For example, a university professor in the USA may move from an assistant professor to associate professor to professor, and perhaps even to department chair, dean, and on into higher administrative levels.

The role of promotions in an individual's career development will be largely influenced by the cultural meanings attached to promotions and to the financial, geographic, and other benefits that accrue to the individual, either instead of or in addition to the promotion. Organizational structure comes into play in analyzing this situation. The more layers in the organization, the greater the opportunities for promotion. Conversely, the flatter the organization, the fewer the opportunities for promotion. In cultures where promotion (and the subsequent new title) carries with it prestige, some people might actually prefer to take the promotion rather than a salary increase. Conversely, if the promotion requires a move to a new location or where opportunities for additional income are lost, a person might actually decline a promotion. Consider, for example, a two-income family in the USA. One spouse might receive a wonderful promotional opportunity, but it is to a location in which it would be difficult or impossible for the other spouse to find a job. Depending on the cultural context, and the need for the additional income, the couple may decide to take the promotion anyway, or they may choose to turn it down. In Thailand, recently, I heard of a hotel doorman who had been in his job for over 20 years. He was so effective that he was offered a promotion into management—not for the first time. Once again, he turned it down. When queried, he answered that he made more than five times his salary from tips, and management would offer a lower overall compensation with more responsibilities.

The use of anthropological methods would allow the HRD professional to determine the factors affecting promotions within the organization and to design promotional packages that would be most attractive to those whom management has decided need to be in a higher rank.

Succession planning

One form of career development occurs through an organizational process of succession planning. Succession planning, when done well, provides a pool of people who are qualified to move into a higher level in the organization when vacancies are caused by retirement, relocation, death or illness, or separation from the company, either voluntarily or involuntarily. The idea is to identify high potential employees and to provide them with special developmental opportunities to ensure that they are ready for promotion when the opportunity occurs.

This sounds like a very positive approach to career and organizational planning. However, there are problems, often associated with the culture of the organization. What message is sent to those who are not selected as high potential employees, and how do these employees react to their being passed over? Will they leave, will their morale be negatively affected, and will their commitment and productivity diminish? What is the reaction of a high potential employee when a vacancy occurs and he or she is not selected for it? After all, the organization will want a pool larger than the number of potential vacancies so that there will be choices for the vacancies when they do occur. In response to these concerns, organizations often try to keep quiet or secret about who has been selected or even that there is a selection process in place. It is difficult, however, for anyone to fail to notice when certain individuals' names consistently show up on special project teams, or when they are given special assignments, or when they are sent to special training.

Understanding the factors that are involved in such approaches to succession planning is the first step undertaken by HRD professionals, using the tools of anthropology. Having understood the factors, the

HRD professional can then assist the organization in creating a system that is acceptable to employees, while, at the same time, meeting the needs of the organization.

Coaching and mentoring

Reference was made earlier to the importance of coaching in providing workers with performance feedback. Coaching has increasingly come to be seen as a part of every supervisor's or manager's role. It is also a service that is provided to some high potential employees or to top-level executives. When this is done, it is often an external consultant who meets regularly with the individual over a specified period to provide suggestions and to react to planned actions on the part of the individual.

Mentoring is often confused with coaching, but it serves a different purpose. Coaching is specifically focused on job performance. Although mentoring may include this, its primary purpose is for the individual's personal development and benefit, whereas the primary purpose of coaching is for the organization's benefit. Mentoring can be formal (assigned by the organization) or informal (provided by someone who simply takes an interest in the individual).

Once again, how coaching and mentoring are received by the organization and by the individual will be largely determined by the cultures of the individuals and organization involved. Anthropology can provide an understanding of what is acceptable both by the organization and by the individuals within it. This anthropological approach can suggest ways of making both coaching and mentoring acceptable, for the benefit of the employees and the organization.

Conclusions

In spite of my many references over the years to the importance of anthropology as a foundational field for HRD, I had no idea how important the connection truly is until I did the research for and wrote this chapter. Now, more than ever, I am convinced that anthropology is the root foundation for what we do in HRD—much more so than the more commonly viewed foundations of psychology, economics, and systems (Swanson, 1995). It is evident to me that anyone wishing to become competent in the field of HRD must have a deep understanding of the constructs and methods associated with anthropology. Without this grounding, it is hard to imagine anyone developing a truly successful base of HRD expertise.

References

Bass, B. M. *Bass & Stogdill's handbook of leadership* (3rd ed.). (New York: Free Press, 1990).

Deal, T. E., & Kennedy, A. A. *Corporate cultures.* (Reading, MA: Addison-Wesley, 1982).

Ember, C. R., & Ember, M. *Anthropology* (9th ed.). (Upper Saddle River, NJ: Prentice-Hall, 1999).

Hall, E. T. *The silent language.* (New York, NY: Doubleday, 1981).

Hofstede, G. *Culture's consequences: Comparing values, behaviors, institutions, and organizations across nations.* (San Francisco: Sage, 2001).

Jordan, A. T. *Business anthropology.* (Long Grove, IL: Waveland Press, 2003).

Kane, K. A. "Anthropologists go native in the corporate village." *Fast Company* (1996, October) 60–62.

Lee, M. M. "A refusal to define HRD." *Human Resource Development International,* 4(3) (2001) 327–43.

Lynham, S. A., Paprock, K. E., & Cunningham, P. W. (eds). "NHRD in transitioning societies in the developing world." *Advances in Developing Human Resources,* 8(1) (2006).

McLagan, P. *Models for HRD practice.* (Alexandria, VA: American Society for Training and Development, 1989).

McLean, G. N. "Multirater 360 feedback". In L. J. Bassi & D. Russ-Eft (eds), *What works: Assessment, development, and measurement.* (Alexandria, VA: American Society for Training and Development), (1997) 87–108.

McLean, G. N. "HRD: A three-legged stool, an octopus, or a centipede?" *Human Resource Development International,* 1(4) (1998) 375–77.

McLean, G. N. "Get the drill, glue, and more legs." *Human Resource Development International,* 2(1) (1999) 6–7.

McLean, G. N. *Organization development: Principles, processes, performance.* (San Francisco, CA: Berrett-Koehler, 2006).

McLean, G. N., & McLean, L. D. "If we can't define human resource development in one country, how can we define it in an international context?" *Human Resource Development International,* 4(3) (2001) 313–26.

McLean, G. N., Osman-Gani, A., & Cho, E. (eds). "Human resource development as national policy." *Advances in Developing Human Resources,* 6(3) (2004).

Miller, B. "Anthropology and business come together." *Puget Sound Business Journal (Seattle).* (November 11, 2005). Retrieved on July 13, 2007, from http://www.bizjournals.com/seattle/stories/2005/11/14/smallb2.html.

Orsini, J. F. "Why is cultural harmony so elusive?" *Mergers & Acquisitions: The Dealermaker's Journal,* 41(9) (2006) 59–61.

Pant, D. R., & Alberti, F. Anthropology and business: Reflections on the business applications of cultural anthropology. *Liuc papers no. 12, serie economia e Impresza* 11. (1997). Retrieved on July 13, 2007, from www.biblio.liuc.it/liucpap/pdf/42.pdf.

Saetang, D., & McLean, G. N. (2003) "Development of a measure of transformational and transactional leadership among public school principals in Thailand." In C. T. Akaraborworn, A. M. Osman-Gani, & G. N. McLean (eds), *Human resource development in Asia: National policy perspectives.* (Bangkok, Thailand, and Bowling Green, OH: National Institute of Development

Administration and Academy of Human Resource Development), 56-1-56-9.

Schein, E. *Organizational culture and leadership.* (San Francisco, CA: Jossey-Bass, 1985).

Schmidt, J. *Making mergers work: The strategic importance of people.* (Alexandria, VA: Society for Human Resource Management, 2002).

Senge, P. *The fifth discipline: The art and practice of the learning organization.* (New York: Doubleday, 1990).

Spradley, J. P. *The ethnographic interview.* (New York: Harcourt Brace Jovanovich, 1979).

Swanson, R. A. "Human resource development: Performance is the key." *Human Resource Development Quarterly,* 6(2) (1995) 207–13.

Swanson, R. A. "HRD theory, real or imagined?" *Human Resource Development International,* 2(1) (1999) 2–5.

Trompenaars, F. *Riding the waves of culture: Understanding cultural diversity in business.* (New York: McGraw-Hill, 1994).

Virakul, B., & McLean, G. N. "AIDS in the workplace: Experiences and HR practices in Thai business organizations." *Thai Journal of Development Administration,* 40(3) (2000) 27–46.

Wang, X. H., & McLean, G. N. "The dilemma of defining international human resource development." *Human Resource Development Review,* 6(1) (2007) 96–108.

Watkins, K. E., & Marsick, V. J. (eds). (1996). *In action: Creating the learning organization.* (Alexandria, VA: American Society for Training and Development).

Weber, Y., Oded, S., & Raveh, A. "National and corporate cultural fit in mergers/acquisitions: An exploratory study." *Management Science,* 42(8) (1996) 1215–27.

Weise, E. Companies learn value of grass root anthropologist help adapt products to world's cultures. *USA Today* (1999, May 26) p. 4d.

2
Go to the People: Using Emic Approaches for Cultural Understanding

Wei-Wen Chang

Rapid changes in global society have created frequent interaction across nations in the economic, social, as well as technological spheres and have increased interdependence between cultures (Kiely, 2004; Marquardt & Berger, 2003; World Bank, 2002). Friedman (2006) stated that the world has become flat; globalization after the new millennium has created a *flat-world platform* where multinational companies, small groups, and individuals can collaborate and compete globally. These contemporary opportunities and challenges have pressed the need for training and development in managing cultural diversity. Today, as the global village continues to shrink, cross-cultural interaction is no longer a fancy trend to latch on to; it is a reality that requires continuous concern.

In the field of HRD, regardless of the differing stances in the goal of HRD (Francis, 2007), many definitions suggest improving organizations through learning interventions as a major function of the field (Wang & Wang, 2004; Wilson, 2005; Yang, 2004). As learning is, implicitly or explicitly, the center of the HRD process (Yorks & Nicolaides, 2006), it needs to be better understood. In fact, "understanding the dynamics of learning is what differentiates HRD from several closely related fields of professional practice" (Yorks & Nicolaides, 2006, p. 144). With a focus on culture in HRD, this chapter will elaborate the process of cultural learning, particularly from an emic perspective.

In 1954, linguist Kenneth Pike first introduced the terms etic and emic (Headland, Pike, & Harris, 1990). More recently, these two terms have been adopted to describe two distinguished approaches for understanding human social behaviors (Franklin, 1996; Lett, 2007). The etic tends to study behavior from outside a particular system, serving as an essential initial approach to an alien system. In contrast, the emic tends to study behavior from inside the system (Pike, 1967, p. 37). These two approaches have been widely used for cultural studies in the fields of anthropology, psychology, and organizational science. Researchers interested in making universal generalizations rely on etic accounts; others who are interested in the local construction of meaning for behavior rely on emic accounts (Berry, 1990; Teagarden & Von Glinow, 1997). Although debate about the usefulness of the two approaches has continued (Von Glinow, Drost, & Teagarden, 2002), Pike (1967) explicitly suggested that both approaches are of value, which is also the assumption taken by myself.

However, this chapter discusses cultural learning in HRD particularly from an emic perspective for two reasons. First, compared with the etic, an emic perspective is less discussed in the HRD literature and practice. Second, the emic approach has the potential to enhance learning for cultural competence. In 1975, Bogdan and Taylor used "go to the people" to describe the spirit of qualitative research methods; the emic perspective shares this same spirit. To understand a culture, the emic perspective asks researchers or practitioners to touch the field, go to the people, observe, contact, and get involved. For researchers, going to the people provides an opportunity to discover what is really important in the cultural context before research questions are definitely formed; for practitioners, going to the people is a direct way to gain cultural competence, although the process may not always be pleasant and comfortable (Bogdan & Taylor, 1975; Burawoy, Burton, Ferguson, & Fox, 1991).

Therefore, this chapter begins with a clarification of etic and emic, discusses the need to include an emic perspective in HRD, explains why emic approaches can be beneficial for cultural learning, and finally suggests how to apply this approach in training and development. The purpose of this chapter is to elaborate how HRD professionals can use emic approaches to help facilitate learning about a culture, reduce confusion, and accomplish their missions internationally.

Etic and emic

Culture includes almost every aspect of human life. As Van Maanen and Laurent (1993) described:

> The way we give logic to the world begins at birth with the gestures, words, tone of voice, noises, colors, smells, and body contact we experience; with the way we are raised, washed, rewarded, punished,

held in check, toilet trained and fed; by the stories we are told, the games we play, the songs we sing or rhymes we recite; the schooling we receive, the jobs we hold, and the careers we follow; right down to the very way we sleep and dream.

(p. 278)

Culture is fundamentally involved in one's life from childhood to adulthood, and such a deep-rooted involvement makes culture complex and difficult to comprehend. Both etic and emic approaches have been used in various fields to assist scholars in accomplishing this goal.

The etic perspective is oriented to *many places* and often described as general, universal, and external. It attempts to describe behavior in numerous cultures by using external criteria developed by the researchers (Peterson & Pike, 2002). It relies on explicit analysis and extrinsic concepts and categories that have meaning for scientific observers (Lett, 2007). Typical research methods include multi-locations survey, cross-national questionnaire comparison, and measuring selected variables (Morris, Leung, Ames, & Lickel, 1999, p. 783).

On the other hand, the emic approach is oriented toward a *single place* and often described as more specific and local. It refers to nuanced understanding that retains "a substantial tacit element or the characteristics of a specific place" (Peterson & Pike, 2002, p. 6). Emic perspective focuses on the intrinsic cultural distinctions that are meaningful to the members of a given society. Focusing on the perspective of cultural insiders, researchers often rely on ethnographic fieldwork, long-standing, and wide-ranging observation of one (or a few) settings, avoiding the imposition of predetermined theoretical constructs. Through these methods, researchers gradually discern a path into indigenous thinking and local meaning.

Limitations of etic approaches

In research design

Etic methods are well recognized in the literature on organizational science, including the field of HRD (Hofstede, 1980; Hofstede, Neuijen, Ohayv, & Sanders, 1990), and survey questionnaires are widely used in research to generate universal claims (Parker & McEvoy, 1993; Searle & Ward, 1990; Ward & Kennedy, 1992). Through measurement and comparison, most organizational researchers seek to produce generalizations across cultural groups. Etic studies seem to make the "myriad cultural traditions reducible to a few simple cultural dimensions" (Morris, Leung, Ames, & Lickel, 1999, p. 792). This approach provides a broad perspective, converts abstract concepts of culture into numbers, and identifies pictures about similarities and differences among cultures. In addition, a rough and tentative etic picture can serve as a starting point for further cultural exploration (Berry, 1989; Pike, 1967).

However, for cultural studies, Pike (1996, interview with Franklin,) argued, "the etic alone is just not adequate" (paragraph 48). Three limitations of the etic approach have been identified for cultural research, namely imposed, abstract, and inequivalent problems (Berry, 1989; Ryan, Chan, Ployhart, & Slade, 1999; Von Glinow, Drost, & Teagarden, 2002). First, an imposed etic approach means that a cultural framework developed in one culture is applied directly to other cultures, overlooking possible fundamental differences between the two. For instance, a measurement structure derived in the USA for local employees is assumed to be universal and is applied to all cultures (Peng, Peterson, & Shyi, 1991; Triandis & Marin, 1983). Second, to move the measurement from one culture to another, the researchers need to handle the concepts in an abstract manner because this makes it easier to identify behavioral events with equivalent meanings across cultures. As a result, all of the concrete details that are not equivalent across cultures get pruned away in the description (Morris, Leung, Ames, & Lickel, 1999). Third, consistent doubt has been expressed as to whether instrument concepts have sufficient equivalence across cultures. Equivalence involves not only adequate translation, but also whether a concept conveys a similar meaning in different cultures (Ryan, Chan, Ployhart, & Slade, 1999). To modify problems of etic research, scholars have developed a "combined etic–emic" approach to justify cross cultural measurements (Berry, 1989; Davidson, Jaccard, Triandis, Morales, & Diaz-Guerrero, 1976).

In research application

However, applying findings from etic research still faces two challenges in practice. First, most contrasting characteristics are derived by etic research from national-level survey investigation. Using national-level findings to predict the behavior of individuals in a nation may face the pitfall of *ecological fallacy*, in that the analyst is making an inference about an individual based on the aggregate data for a group ("Ecological fallacy", 2007; Freedman, 1999). Although it is not absolutely wrong to draw the inference, directly applying the characteristics from the group to the individual could conceal the variations that are not visible at the larger aggregate level, but are critical for personal cross-cultural interaction.

In addition, these dimensions are often presented in a dichotomous way, which can barely reflect the real-life situation, for example, individualism versus collectivism, masculinity versus femininity, universalism versus particularism, and neutral versus affective orientation (Hofstede, 2003; Trompenaars, 1994). In a previous study (Chang, 2002), an interviewee looked at the two connotations of uncertainty avoidance (UAI), "Hope of success" (low UAI) and "Fear of failure" (high UAI) (Hofstede, 1980, p. 176) and said, "It is difficult to decide which one describes our culture" He continued to explain, "Maybe because I'm influenced by Buddhism, I viewed these two things (hope of success versus fear of failure) as one. The more you hope for success, the more you fear failure." Similarly, another respondent noted, "The side of *hope of success* is positive thinking; the other side is negative thinking. It depends how you look at it." In the literature, the dichotomy is used predominately to describe cultural differences. Thus, the question remains of how to apply the results to a reality where dichotomies often co-exist. Responders moved their eyes between two contrastive connotations, but could not decide which side to choose because often the situations on both sides occur in their lives.

Meaning behind etic scores

In research, etic approaches are widely used for the purpose of generalization; however, for daily cultural interaction, capturing invisible structure and complex meaning by survey questionnaires seems less possible. Bhawuk and Triandis (1996) noted, "They [surveys] can accomplish what they try to do . . . , but often do not increase greatly researchers' understanding of cultures" (p. 31). For example, in cultural literature, Taiwan's values are highly associated with the dimension of Confucianism (Hofstede & Bond, 1988; Hofstede, 2003). On the Confucian dimension (later renamed as long-term and short-term orientation), Taiwan has the much higher score of 87, in contrast with the US score of 29. These scores have been widely cited in cross-cultural training materials; however, how can these scores be used in practice? Should intercultural practitioners use them to predict that the Taiwanese follow Confucianism in their behaviors?

Chang (2004) found that the Taiwanese differed in their positions, either for or against Confucianism. For example, one interviewee mentioned that the Confucian education prevented her from expressing herself and understanding her inner emotions. She said, "Confucius advocated introspection and morals, but paid little attention to human psychology"(personal communication, 2001, October 27). On the other hand, a Taiwanese instructor defended Confucian thinking and argued that it has been misunderstood in many ways. For example, a phrase from the analects of Confucius' teachings (*Lu-yu*), "no friend worse than you" had been interpreted as "don't make friends with those who are worse than you" and, on the other hand, "there is no friend who is worse than you because you can always find someone's good points" (personal communication, 2001, October 18). According to Nan (1988), the author of *A New Approach to the Confucian Analects*, the misunderstanding of Confucianism often came from some Confucian scholars' commentaries (p. 33). As Tu, Hejtmanek, and Wachman (1992) pointed out, today's Confucian scholars still argue about the role of Confucianism in Chinese society. Therefore, the score cannot be used to predict that Taiwanese people will follow Confucianism because the Taiwanese continue to search for the values, meanings, strengths, and weakness of Confucianism in their lives. However, the variance in people's positions and interpretations may demonstrate the deep influence of Confucianism on the Chinese culture and Taiwanese society. Through emic approaches and findings, the meaning of the etic scores on cultural dimensions can be more clearly illustrated.

When people work in intercultural settings and face differences and conflicts in their very specific situations, they need cultural knowledge with more specific context. In this aspect, the emic approach has the strength to provide a path to help cultural outsiders step into the local person's structure to examine the problem closely. The emic perspective is intertwined with cultural context (Pike, 1993a) as it helps in revealing the cultural context; in turn, this context assists us further in revealing a more local emic structure.

Emic perspective and cultural learning

Learning to live in a different culture can be confusing because, as Peterson and Pike (2002) wrote, "[c]ultures, as wholes, are emically different from each other" (p. 12). The emic approach is often used to study a cultural context, helping researchers reveal the tacit knowledge, hidden hierarchy, invisible structures, and assumptions that are taken for granted in a particular culture. In practice, for the learning and development of cultural practitioners, emic approaches enhance contextual knowledge and strengthen cultural competence.

Importance of learning cultural context

Expatriate workers in various types of organization all search for feasible strategies to accomplish international missions successfully. However, lack of cultural awareness may lead newcomers to make serious mistakes. For example, a three-year study in Mozambique reported that the inrush of foreign charities and their workers during the 1990s had shredded the local healthcare system and also increased social inequality (Pfeiffer, 2003). In business settings, Cullen and Parboteeah (2005) reported that when the shoes of a US company, Thom McAn, first went on sale in Bangladesh, a riotous protest occurred which resulted in injury to more than 50 people. The reason was that the Thom McAn signature on the sole of each shoe looked similar to the Arabic script for "Allah" (God). Because the foot is considered unclean in the Muslim world, it looked as if the shoe company did not respect the name of God and asked the local people to walk on it. Absence of contextual awareness has caused conflicts and business failures.

With a lack of awareness of the local cultural context, great effort can be spent in vain. For instance, a Peace Corps volunteer reported the unsatisfied outcomes of the developmental programs run by the Peace Corps and Taiwan in Sedhiou (Culture Matters, undated, p. 122):

> We had a library with no books, a milk program with no milk, and a pre-school with no education taking place. As I looked around the region, other foreign aid programs were no better. There was an agricultural college with no students, no materials, and no instructors—of which the town officials were very proud! There was a Taiwanese agricultural mission to teach advanced farming methods, totally ignored by the farmers.

The workplace is like a stage, and context is the setting and background. Only when the actors recognize both can they act accordingly and appropriately. Through observation and participation, emic approaches provide newcomers with a growing understanding of local interpretation (Denzin, 1989) so they can adjust their work strategies. The example of ASUS below demonstrates the process of strategy adjustment.

ASUS is a quick-rising computer company in Taiwan. In 2006, it made BusinessWeek's "InfoTech 100" list for the ninth straight year. It has also been selected as the best maker of motherboards and graphics cards by the readers of Tom's Hardware Guide, the world's largest information technology website ("About ASUS", 2007). The expatriate manager in Australia, Chen, shared his mistake that occurred during the early stages of this international mission (Chen, 2007). He noted that "people management" is the most significant challenge for expatriate managers. He explained,

> Because expatriate managers have little understanding of the local market and do not have their own team, the first strategy they often use is to recruit experienced mid-mangers from other corporations. However, this is usually the beginning of the mistake.
>
> (p. 146, translated by the author of this chapter)

At that time, as ASUS was still just a small, new company in Australia. Many experienced managers were recruited through head-hunting and did not really identify with the company's vision. This proved a detriment to team performance and made employee management extremely difficult. Learning from his mistake, Chen began industriously visiting local business partners so that he could thoroughly familiarize himself with the local market. In addition, his recruitment efforts were altered to ensure that the team members had knowledge of the local culture and were committed to the company's vision.

Business strategies must take into account local context. For instance, the well-known fast-food retailer McDonald's used the happy clown, Ronald McDonald, as the major symbol in front of its stores. In the USA, the clown always extends his arm with a great joyful smile to show welcome; however, in Thailand he smiles gently with his palms pressed together to express his greetings as the Thai would do in their society. Having a sense of the cultural context helps managers make strategy adjustments and move the service closer to local people's meanings and feelings (Rigby & Vishwanath, 2006; Selmer, 2004).

In a culture, emic meaning exists in "nonverbal as well as verbal behavior of a family at breakfast, at a church service, and at a football game" (Pike, 1993b, December 4, interview with Kaye, paragraph 15). Being aware of context provides cultural foreigners with a map that allows them to walk closer to the local people's needs and hearts. Therefore, although an etic perspective offers a generalized pattern and comparative framework across cultures, an emic approach moves into a culture, usually by going to the people to gather the concrete details of a local setting. Without the cultural specifics identified through emic analysis, the abstract principles identified by etic methods are unlikely to be sufficient for practitioners to select appropriate strategies and make suitable decisions.

Cultural learning process

Understanding a cultural context relies on learning in which experience is the core. As Mezirow (1991) noted, learning, particularly adult learning, comes from re-examination and reflection on one's experience. The connection between cultural learning and experience was supported by an empirical study based on 20 expatriate humanitarian workers from Taiwan (Chang, 2007). In examining how their cross-cultural experiences influenced the development of their cultural competence, this study identified three levels in the process: peripheral, cognitive, and reflective. At the first level, international workers experience shocks and differences. They are able to describe the situation that surprised them and how they feel as it is too early for them to analyze systematically why they feel that way. At the second level, people begin to become familiar with their environment and have more sensibility about how to adjust their behaviors and work strategies. Thirdly, after a period of time, people move to deeper levels of culture and begin to reflect on their cultural assumptions and experience in the host country. Perspective transformation often occurs, changing their view about themselves, their own culture, and the host culture. From exterior to interior, expatriate workers learn the new culture from concrete experience as well as through the dialogue between their inside and outside worlds.

To comprehend the process of understanding belief systems, which moves one from cultural novice to becoming competent, intercultural scholars have tried to use *schema shift* to explain intercultural contact and how people adjust (Beamer, 1995). The term *schemata* refers to the mental structure and categories people create to make sense out of the world (Beamer & Varner, 2001). Beamer (1995) noted that as newcomers into a different culture, people use their existing schemata to project the targeted culture and to respond to their projected situations. However, the existing mental schema does not accurately reflect the reality of the new culture; as a result, cultural shocks, mistakes, and misunderstandings occur. When people work in a cultural environment different from their own, they need to learn the new emic systems. The more experience one gains through local involvement, the more one can adjust and expand one's existing mental structure, and the closer one's schema will reflect the reality of the new culture.

Applying an emic approach in cultural learning

Helping people to perform in a different culture is a demanding challenge for HRD professionals because culture has multiple levels and most of them are invisible and intangible. When HRD professionals endeavor to respond to this demand, emic approaches can provide several implications in designing training programs.

Learning through the emic cycle

The emic cycle introduced by Pike (1990, p. 45) assumes that exposure to new cultural settings helps one gain experience and cultural understanding. The cycle comprises four steps (Figure 2.1).

HRD professionals designing intercultural training can apply the emic cycle in program design. Taylor (1994) suggests three behavioral learning strategies for becoming interculturally competent: (a) as an observer—listen, watch, and read; (b) as a participant—talk, socialize, dress, eat, and shop; and (c) as a friend—commit, risk, and share. These strategies hold the same idea as the emic cycle, which is to expose the individual to the host culture as much as possible; this should take place in the earliest stage of the development of intercultural competency. In pre-departure training, materials such as videos, photographs, music, food, texts, and field trips help trainees to *see and know*. Activities such as role-play, attribution training, and behavior modeling help them to *be and do*. On-the-job training in the host nation can also follow this cycle if HRD professionals can lead expatriate workers to examine their new and real local experience. The time required for them to make

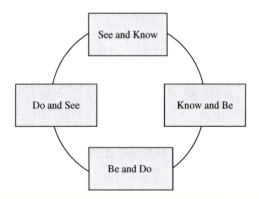

Figure 2.1 Emic cycle.
Source: Pike (1990).

adjustments may be lessened. As Morris, Leung, Ames, and Lickel (1999) pointed out, in practice, cross-cultural training has not been influenced much by the etic research found in management journals, and managers still tend to learn about cultural sensitivities in a "country-by-country fashion" (p. 792). Although the emic cycle is based on a straightforward assumption, it is practical.

Moving beyond the surface level of culture

Schein (2004) divided culture into three levels according to visibility; the levels were labeled artifacts, espoused values (conscious aspect), and basic assumptions (unconscious aspect). The deeper levels are more difficult to reveal, but usually have greater influence on why things happen in a particular way. However, many training programs focus on the surface level because of time constraints and financial pressure, and because the deeper levels can hardly be taught. Therefore, these programs provide behavioral guidelines or taboo lists in the hope of quickly getting their trainees on board. For example, do not use your left hand for food in India, do not offer a clock as a present to a Taiwanese colleague, and do not send yellow flowers in Mexico. These lists are often accurate but never complete. Beamer and Varner (2001) pointed out that, "lists never cover everything . . . Unless you understand the *why*, you will sooner or later trip up and fall on your face" [emphasis added] (p. 2). Understanding why people value certain things enables intercultural workers to make good guesses about why they behave in a certain way.

One way to communicate deep levels of culture is through storytelling (Baba, 1990). Stories contain cultural assumptions, beliefs, and myths that fundamentally affect individuals' viewpoints and perspectives (Hansen & Kahnweiler, 1993; Hansen, 2003). Stories, sometimes with symbolic or hidden meanings, convey tacit knowledge and important values of a cultural group. For example, the literature often reports that the silence of Chinese or Japanese people often confuses their more communicative business partners (Adair & Brett, 2005; Hall, 1976; Hall & Hall, 1990). Actually, many Chinese stories provided clues about how silence is viewed in Chinese value systems. For example, here is one story that shines some light on Asian silence:

One day, the Buddha was about to teach all of the pupils the meaning of life. In the session, without any words, the Buddha picked up a flower and showed it to them. While all others were still wondering, one pupil smiled apprehensively. Knowing that the pupil already

understood the meaning of life, the Buddha relinquished his position as a knowledge leader to that pupil.

Influenced by many similar stories, in which silence is often associated
with positive values, such as wisdom or insights, many Chinese people
believe that too many words could distort the truth. This becomes a
well-recognized value within the society but also causes a great amount
of confusion or even misunderstanding in intercultural contacts.

Stories are one means of moving training courses beyond the surface
level. Beamer and Varner (2001) suggested that to be effective in a foreign business setting, international workers need to understand "(the)
culture's priorities, its member's attitudes, and how they think people
should behave" (p. 11). In other words, reaching deeper levels of culture
and understanding *why* people do what they do enables expatriates to
explain *what* people are doing (their behaviors) and decide *how* to act
in their new culture.

Using cultural context in training

In a new cultural setting, successful performance usually corresponds
with the context within which the work is performed. Therefore, in a
cultural training program, instead of merely providing general descriptions about characteristics of particular nations, HRD professionals can
use contextualized information to bring trainees to the point where
they can determine what is appropriate in a given situation. The methods include case-study and scenario-based training.

Case study, based on real cultural incidents, can be used to increase
context in a training session. People learn from life incidents, case by case.
Although individual cases do not provide generalized guidelines, according to transpersonal psychology, through careful examination of individual cases the "common core consciousness" that is shared by people in
many different places can be revealed (Transpersonal Lifestreams, 2005).

Scenario-based training (Salas, Priest, Wilson, & Burke, 2006) includes
carefully designed scenarios within training exercises to which trainees
respond, and then are given feedback about their responses to these
events (Littrell & Salas, 2005). Such training design attempts to structure
practical experience and provides trainees with opportunities to apply
their skills in a contextualized situation, through which they can "create a microworld that increases the psychological fidelity, experimental
realism, and trainee experimentation" (Salas et al., 2006, p. 37). During
this process, practical scenarios and feedback are crucial for training
effectiveness.

In a nutshell, globally, a large proportion of the workforce has felt the need to manage cultural diversity and perform in different cultural settings. More expectations have been placed on HRD professionals to provide successful training and development. For cross-cultural learning, findings from previous cultural comparisons may be of more help to training participants if HRD professionals use context to facilitate the learning process.

Conclusion

Although in the literature the etic has received a high stature in organizational research (Morris, Leung, Ames, & Lickel, 1999), this chapter has argued that the emic approach can enhance cultural learning because it creates experiences for learning, provides details to consider in decision-making, helps to reach tacit knowledge, and motivates schemata adjustment to new cultural settings. In turn, these processes and experiences provide researchers with contextual information for further knowledge generation.

Traditionally, the emic or ethnographic approach has often been viewed as unfeasible for the quick-paced business environment because it includes fewer samples, focuses on specifics, and spends more time studying context. However, these derided features of the emic approach are actually its advantages for cross-cultural understanding. Learning a culture cannot rely on a fast-food style that emphasizes a simple menu, quick service, and immediate consumption. Cultural behaviors should be understood in their own terms; each aspect of behavior must be viewed in relation to its behavioral setting. Ambiguously introducing many cultures within a short period of time would inevitably scarify cultural complexity and accuracy. Compared with the etic approach, the scale of the emic approach is smaller but more concrete and very practical. This approach assists cultural learners in enhancing their cultural sensitivity and uncovering more emic structure in a given circumstance. It is characterized by learning approaches as well as learning outcomes. Today, in the field of HRD, when an alarm has been sounded over the widening gap between theory and practice (Torraco, 2005; Van de Ven & Johnson, 2006), when knowledge production relies more on the context of application (Gibbons et al., 1994; Sackmann & Phillips, 2004; Yorks, 2005), the emic approach, with its specialty of revealing cultural context, provides an alternative means of gaining cultural understanding and should, therefore, be better recognized in research and practice.

References

About ASUS. Retrieved on August 10, 2007 from Website, http://www.asus.com/aboutasus.aspx?show=1.

Adair, W. L., & Brett, J. M. "The negotiation dance: Time, culture, and behavioral sequences in negotiation." *Organization Science*, 16(1) (2005) 33–51.

Baba, M. "Decoding native paradigms: An anthropological approach to intercultural communication in industry." Paper presented in the ABC Midwest-Canada Regional Conference, luncheon program, Detroit April, 27 (1990).

Beamer, L., & Varner, I. *Intercultural communication in the global workplace* (2nd ed). (San Francisco, CA: McGraw Hill, 2001).

Beamer, L. "A schemata model for intercultural encounter and case study: The emperor and the envoy." *Journal of Business Communication*, 32(2) (1995) 141–61.

Berry, J. W. "Imposed etics-emics-derived etics: The operationalization of a compelling idea." *International Journal of Psychology*, 24 (1989) 721–35.

Berry, J. W. "Imposed etics, emics and derived emics: Their conceptual and operational status in cross-cultural psychology." In T. N. Headland, K. L. Pike, & M. Harris (eds), *Emics and etics: Insider/outsider debate* (Newbury Park, CA: Sage, 1990), 84–89.

Bhawuk, D. P. S., & Triandis, H. C. "The role of culture theory in the study of culture and intercultural training." In D. Landis & R. S. Bhagat (eds), *Handbook of Intercultural Training* (2nd ed.) (Thousand Oaks: Sage, 1996), 17–34.

Bogdan, R., & Taylor, S. J. *Introduction to qualitative research methods*. (New York: John Wiley & Sons, 1975).

Burawoy, M., Burton, A., Ferguson, A. A. & Fox, K. J. *Ethnography unbound*. (Berkeley, CA: University of California Press, 1991).

Chang, W. W. *International human resource development: A cross-cultural case study of a multinational training program in the United States and Taiwan*. Unpublished doctoral dissertation (2002). University of Wisconsin-Madison, Madison, WI.

Chang, W. W. "A cross-cultural case study of a multinational training program in the United States and Taiwan." *Adult Education Quarterly*, 54(3) (2004) 174–92.

Chang, W. W. "Cultural competence of international humanitarian workers." *Adult Education Quarterly*, 57(3) (2007) 187–204.

Chen, M. J. "ASUS workforce in Australia." *Common wealth*, 375 (2007) 145–47. [original written in Chinese].

Cullen, J. B., & Parboteeah, K. P. *Multinational management: A strategic approach* (3rd ed.). (South-Western of Thomson Learning, 2005).

Culture Matters (nd). The Peace Corps cross-cultural workbook. Retrieved June 22, 2006 from Website, http://www.peacecorps.gov/wws/publications/culture/.

Davidson, A., Jaccard, J. J., Triandis, H. C., Morales, M. L. & Diaz-Guerrero, R. "Cross-cultural model testing: Toward a solution of the etic-emic dilemma." *International Journal of Psychology*, 11(1) (1976) 1–13.

Denzin, N. K. *Interpretive interactionism*. (Newbury Park, CA: Sage, 1989).

Ecological fallacy. In *Wikipedia, The Free Encyclopedia*. Retrieved August 23, 2007 from Website, http://en.wikipedia.org/wiki/ Ecological fallacy.

Francis, H. "Discursive struggle and the ambiguous world of HRD." *Advances in Developing Human Resources*, 9(1) (2007) 83–96.

Franklin, K. J. "K. L. Pike on etic vs emic: A review and interview." (1996). Retrieved July 22, 2007 from Website, http://www.sil.org/klp/Karlintv.htm.

Freedman, D. A. "Ecological inference and the ecological fallacy." (1999). Retrieved August 10, 2007 from Website, http:// www.stanford.edu/class/ed260/freedman549.pdf.

Friedman, T. L. *The world is flat: The globalized world in the twenty-first.* (New York: Penguin Group, 2006).

Gibbons, M., Limoges, C., Nowotny, H., Schwartzman, S., Scott, P. & Trow, M. *The new production of knowledge: The dynamics of science and research in contemporary societies.* (London: Sage, 1994).

Hall, E. T. *Beyond culture.* (New York: Anchor Book, Doubleday, 1976).

Hall, E. T., & Hall, M. R. *Understanding cultural differences.* (Yarmouth, ME: Intercultural Press Inc, 1990).

Hansen, C., & Kahnweiler, W. "Storytelling: An instrument for understanding the dynamics of corporate relationships." *Human Relation*, 46(12) (1993) 1391–409.

Hansen, C. "Cultural myths in stories about human resource development: Analyzing the cross-cultural transfer of American models to Germany and the Côte d'Ivoire." *International Journal of Training and Development*, 7(1) (2003) 16–30.

Headland, T. N., Pike, K. L. & Harris, M. (eds). *Emics and Etics: The Insider/outsider debate.* (Thousand Oaks, CA: Sage, 1990).

Hofstede, G. *Culture's consequences: International differences in work-related values.* (Beverly Hills: Sage, 1980).

Hofstede, G. *Culture's consequences: Comparing values, behaviors, institutions, and organizations across nations.* (Thousand Oaks: Sage, 2003).

Hofstede, G., & Bond, M. H. "The Confucian connection: From cultural roots to economic growth." *Organizational Dynamics*, 16(4) (1988) 5–21.

Hofstede, G., Neuijen, B., Ohayv, D. D. & Sanders, G. "Measuring organizational cultures: Qualitative and quantitative study across twenty cases." *Administrative Science Quarterly*, 35 (1990) 286–316.

Kiely, R. "The World Bank and 'global poverty reduction': Good policies or bad data?" *Journal of Contemporary Asia*, 34(1) (2004) 3–20.

Lett, J. Emic/Etic distinctions. Retrieved May 29, 2007 from Website, http://faculty.ircc.edu/faculty/jlett/Article%20on%20Emics%20and%20Etics.htm.

Littrell, L. N., & Salas, E. "A review of cross-cultural training: Best practices, guidelines, and research needs." *Human Resource Development Review*, 4(3) (2005) 305–34.

Marquardt, M., & Berger, N. O. "The future: Globalization and new roles for HRD." *Advances in Developing Human Resources*, 5(3) (2003) 283–95.

Mezirow, J. *Transformative dimensions of adult learning* (San Francisco: Jossey-Bass, 1991).

Morris, M. W., Leung, K., Ames, D. & Lickel, B. "Views from inside and outside: Integrating emic and etic insights about culture and justice judgment." *The Academy of Management Review*, 24(4) (1999) 781–96.

Nan, H. C. *A new approach to the Confucian analects.* (Taipei, Taiwan: Lao Ku Cultural Foundation, 1988).

Parker, B., & McEvoy, G. M. "Initial examination of a model of intercultural adjustment." *International Journal of Intercultural Relations*, 17 (1993) 355–379.

Peng, T. K., Peterson, M. F., & Shyi, Y.-P. "Quantitative methods in cross-national management research: Trends and equivalence issues." *Journal of Organizational Behavior*, 12(2) (1991) 87–107.

Peterson M. F., & Pike, K. L. "Emics and etics for organizational studies: A lesson in contrasts from linguistics." *International Journal of Cross Cultural Management*, 2(1) (2002) 5–19.

Pfeiffer, J. "International NGOs and primary health care in Mozambique: The need for a new model of collaboration." *Social Science and Medicine*, 56(4) (2003) 725–38.

Pike, K. L. *Language in relation to a unified theory of the structure of human behavior*, part 1. (Glendale, CA: Summer Institute of Linguistics, 1954).

Pike, K. L. "On the emics and etics of Pike and Harris." In Headland, T. N., Pike, K. L. & M. Harris (eds). *Emics and Etics: The insider/outsider debate*. (Newbury Park, CA: Sage, 1990) 28–47.

Pike, K. L. *Talk, thought, and thing: The emic road toward conscious knowledge*. (1993a). Retrieved July 21, 2007 from Website, http://www.sil.org/klp/ttt/chapter2.html.

Pike, K. L. [Interview with Alan S. Kaye]. An interview with Kenneth Pike. (1993b). Retrieved July 21, 2007 from Website, http://gamma.sil.org/klp/kayeint.htm.

Pike, K. L. [Interview with Karl J. Franklin]. K. L. Pike on Etic vs. Emic: A Review and Interview. (1996). Retrieved July 22, 2007 from Website, http://www.sil.org/klp/karlintv.htm.

Pike, K. L. *Language in relation to a unified theory of the structure of human behavior*. (2nd. ed). (The Hague: Mouton, 1967). (First edition in three volumes, 1954, 1955, 1960.)

Rigby, D. K., & Vishwanath, V. "Localization: The revolution in consumer markets." *Harvard Business Review*, 84(4) (2006) 82–92.

Ryan, A. M., Chan, D., Ployhart, R. E. & Slade, L. A. "Employee attitude surveys in a multinational organization: Considering language and culture in assessing measurement equivalence." *Personnel Psychology*, 52(1) (1999) 37–58.

Sackmann, S. A., & Phillips, M. E. "Contextual influences on culture research: Shifting assumptions for new workplace realities." *International Journal of Cross Cultural Management*, 4(3) (2004) 370–90.

Salas, E., Priest, H. A., Wilson, K. A. & Burke, C. S. "Scenario-based training: Improving military mission performance and adaptability." In: Adler, A. B., Castro, C. A. & Britt, T. W. (eds). *Military life: The psychology of serving in peace and combat*. vol. 2, *Operational Stress*. (Westport, CT: Praeger Press, 2006), 32–53.

Schein, E. H. *Organizational Culture and Leadership* (3rd ed.). (New York: Wiley Publishers, 2004).

Searle, W., & Ward, C. "The prediction of psychological and socio-cultural adjustment during cross-cultural transitions." *Intercultural Journal of Intercultural Relations*, 14 (1990) 449–64.

Selmer, J. "Expatriates' hesitation and the localization of Western business operations in China." *The International Journal of Human Resource Management*, 15(6) (2004) 1094–107.

Taylor, E. "Intercultural competency: A transformative learning process." *Adult Education Quarterly*, 44(3) (1994) 154–74.

Teagarden, M. B., & Von Glinow, M. A. "Human resource management in cross-cultural contexts: Emic practices versus etic philosophies." *Management International Review*, 37(1) (1997) 7–20.

Torraco, R. J. "Ratings, rankings, results, and what really matters." *Human Resource Development Review*, 4(1) (2005) 3–7.

Transpersonal Lifestreams. Transpersonal psychology theory and definitions. (2005). Retrieved July 20, 2007 from Website: http://www.transpersonal.com. au/transpersonal-theory.htm.

Triandis, H. C., & Marin, G. "Etic plus emic versus pseudoetic: A test of a basic assumption of contemporary cross-cultural psychology." *Journal of Cross-Cultural Psychology*, 14 (1983) 489–500.

Trompenaars, F. *Riding the waves of culture: Understanding diversity in global business.* (New York: Irwin, 1994).

Tu, W., Hejtmanek, M. & Wachman, A. (eds). *The Confucian world observed: A contemporary discussion of Confucian humanism in East Asian.* (Honolulu: Institute of Culture and Communication, The East-West Center, 1992).

Van de Ven, A. H., & Johnson, P. E. "Knowledge for theory and practice." *Academy of Management Review*, 31 (4), (2006) 802–21.

Van Maanen, J., & Laurent, A. The flow of culture: Some notes on globalization and the multinational corporation. In S. Ghoshal & E. Westney (eds), *Organization theory and the multinational corporation.* (New York: St. Martin's, 1993), 276–98.

Von Glinow, M. A., Drost E. & Teagarden, M. B. "Converging on IHRM best practices: Lessons learned from a globally distributed consortium on theory and practice." *Human Resource Management*, 41(2) (2002) 123–40.

Wang, G. G., & Wang, J. "Toward a theory of human resource development learning participation." *Human Resource Development Review*, 3(4) (2004) 326–53.

Ward, C., & Kennedy, A. "Locus of control, mood disturbance, and social difficulty during cross-cultural transitions." *International Journal of Intercultural Relations*, 16 (1992) 175–94.

Wilson, J. (eds). *Human resource development— Learning and training for individuals and organizations* (2nd ed.) (London: Kogan Page, 2005).

World Bank. "Globalization, growth, and poverty: Building an inclusive world economy." A World Bank Policy Research Report. (Oxford: Oxford University Press, 2002).

Yang, B. "Can adult learning theory provide a foundation for human resource development?" *Advances in Developing Human Resources*, 6(2) (2004) 129–45.

Yorks, L., & Nicolaides, A. "Complexity and emergent communicative learning: An opportunity for HRD scholarship." *Human Resource Development Review*, 5(2) (2006) 143–47.

Yorks, L. "Nothing so practical as a good theory." *Human Resource Development Review*, 4(2) (2005) 111–13.

Part II

3

The Cross-Cultural Transfer of American Models and Myths to Germany and the Côte d'Ivoire

Carol D. Hansen

Although myths may often exceed reality, they, nonetheless, consciously and unconsciously influence the work paradigms that frame decision-making, values, perceptions, situational evaluation, and communication styles (Campbell, 1964; Otte, 1991). Occupational groups are culturally influenced by such assumptions (Hansen & Kahnweiler, 1997; Mapstone, 1993; Van Maanen & Barley, 1984). Like all belief systems, work myths are additionally influenced by societal cultures (d'Iribarne, 1989; Hofstede, 1984; Laurent, 1986) and so the archetypes that shape occupational beliefs are vulnerable to misunderstanding and rejection when working with foreign colleagues (Hofstede et al., 1990). This reasoning led me to examine the cross-cultural transferability of HRD models where the belief systems embedded in the human side of work play a major role.

As HRD first became a distinct occupational specialty in the USA (Desimone & Harris, 1998; Pace et al., 1991), this chapter focuses on the cross-cultural transferability of American practitioner myths. An examination by Hansen and Brooks (1994) of over 100 studies related to cross-cultural transfer, which was updated by Petersen (1997), found that the local culture is a key variable that causes HRD professionals to define their roles and spheres of influence differently. Meanwhile, research (Ardichvili et al., 1998) consistently identifies culture as an important predictor of national variance; however, little attempt has been made to identify ethnographically the content and evolution of these cultural constructs. This chapter will address this theoretical gap with data from an ethnographic study of how three national cultures (the United States, Germany, and the Côte d'Ivoire) influence the role and function of HRD. In the study discussed, the cultural assumptions contained in stories about the need for and implementation of HRD interventions were analyzed. These stories reflect the myths of their cultural membership and thus act as a kind of composite cultural code (Hansen and Kahnweiler, 1993).

Background

Myths and work cultures

Drawing on Campbell's (1964) theory of mythology in the workplace, I view the concept of myth as a belief that is neither true nor false. Myths may be functional in nature (Campbell, 1959) and, as theorized by Otte and Kahnweiler (1997), they guide the work, energy, and spirit of HRD. Thus, whether their origins are grounded in fact or fiction, over time, myths evolve into overstated realities that influence expectations for appropriate and inappropriate behavior (Otte, 1991). Moreover, as myths are sensational and "bigger than life" versions of what people believe to be true, they can greatly shape the ideals that frame policy and strategy.

Myths, like all belief systems, are culturally bound. In the workplace they reflect national, organizational, and occupational differences. In this environment, when myths are shared by members of the same culture or subculture, they become a kind of code for organizational "meaning-making" which can influence, for example, ways to resolve conflict, the information needed for sound decision-making, the criteria for promotion, and the appropriate level of assertiveness. Culture can create a sense of solidarity in both territorial and spiritual senses. Members of a given culture tend to see themselves as separate and unique. Cultures lend themselves to ethnocentricity and therefore members tend to see themselves as superior to others. When individuals from one culture encounter those of another culture, solidarity is emphasized and increased. What occurs is a tendency to protect and defend one's cultural identity as a way of maintaining the integrity and relative importance of its beliefs and values. This form of behavior is the source of much tension and misunderstanding in cross-cultural work situations.

HRD as an occupational culture

Organizational researchers increasingly view occupational groups as a distinct cultural entity (Hansen & Kahnweiler, 1997; Mapstone, 1993; Van Maanen & Barley, 1984). As a culture, groups form their own professional norms and expectations for workplace behavior. Occupational cultures are shaped through similar organizational experiences, training, and personality characteristics. Overall, studies indicate that members develop a similar worldview and act as reference groups through self-definitions, common and unusual emotional demands, a failure to socially distinguish work from non-work, and a belief that that their self-image is enhanced by their work (Trice & Beyer, 1993). Research by Hansen et al. (1994) suggested that American HR practitioners involved in developmental interventions constitute an occupational culture. The following myths for American HRD functions are supported by Hansen et al.'s study and are reflected in research where HRD practitioners described their role and functional scope in American corporations (McLagan, 1983/1989, 1997). The results were used by the American Society for Training and Development to develop a set of professional HRD competencies.

- *Training* should allow learners to grow and develop beyond the present needs of their job. In addition to task-related material, trainees should learn about communication, team building, strategic planning, and participative management.
- *Career development* should include committed, systematic, professional advice, career planning, career paths, developmental appraisal systems, and results tracking. Career planning should reflect an integration of personal and business goals.
- *Organizational development* should allow organizations to move toward more collaborative, developmental, flexible, de-layered, and customer-focused cultures. It should enhance communication, work structures, and processes.

Overall, these competency assumptions suggested that American HRD practitioners strive to participate in the strategic management process (Torraco & Swanson, 1995).

National cultures

Business cultures are additionally influenced by the societies in which they reside (Hofstede, 1984; Laurent, 1986). In fact, societal culture may be where the largest differences in the causes and beliefs of cross-cultural organizations reside. In a landmark study, Hofstede found that work behavior was more a factor of the local national culture than of the culture of parent organization. These data indicate that work beliefs are shaped during childhood and are determined at a very young age. The depth of this early orientation remains relatively constant and more powerful than the temporal effect of organizational affiliation.

The comparative weight of occupational beliefs tends to fall in the middle as they are mostly shaped by educational experience and relatively influenced by the investment made in prior training (Hofstede et al., 1990).

Data are available that describe national differences in work beliefs. For example, Americans, as seen in Handy's (1988) work, place high value on corporate training as an investment in one's future. Along with Stewart and Bennet (1991), he linked this educational orientation to a "still flourishing frontier mentality"—one where almost anything is possible, and above all, where every individual has the chance to influence his or her destiny (p. 53). D'Iribarne, in his (1989) ethnography of the American workplace, also found that individual self-reliance was critical to the cultural make-up of the United States.

Scholars of cross-cultural organizational and work behavior have developed typologies of national differences. Perhaps the best known are those by Hofstede (1984) and Trompenaars (1993). Of the dimensions contained in these classification sets, individualism and collectivism tend to best clarify cross-cultural differences in HRD. Both the United States and Germany ranked high on individualism in Hofstede's 1984 study. Conversely, the Côte d'Ivoire (Hofstede, 1984; Triandis, 1995) is classified as collective. Countries that rank high on collectivism are more group oriented and tend to de-emphasize issues of personal control. They are also associated with lower levels of national modernity. This premise suggests that societies with a collective orientation are less advanced because they discourage innovation, risk-taking, competition, and personal recognition and achievement (Bradshaw & Wallace, 1996; Hofstede, 1984; Triandis, 1995). The issue of modernity may additionally impact the cross-cultural transferability of HRD. Hansen and Brooks (1994) found that industrial development and its associated urbanity and intellectual tolerance tended to increase HRD adoption rates when approaches were compatible with local belief systems. These theoretical issues shaped the focus questions of the study that serves at the central focus of this chapter:

- How will American HRD professional myths and practice models transfer to a foreign culture of similar economic progress but with a dissimilar cultural history of industrial and management development? German reaction to American myths and practice models was examined.
- How will American HRD professional myths and practice models transfer to a foreign culture of dissimilar economic progress and with a dissimilar cultural history of industrial and management

development? Ivorian reaction to American myths and practice models was compared with German reaction on the same measures.

The study

Setting and procedures

German and Ivorian response to American HRD models offered very different research settings. This allowed the exploration of the effect of distinct cultural orientations as well as the impact of different levels of modernity. In addition, in both countries there was a growing sentiment that new ways of developing human resources might better address current business problems. Meanwhile, difficulties in implementing American-based approaches were consistently reported by American practitioners who worked in these countries, their foreign HRD counterparts, and their foreign manager clients.

In Germany, the study's key informants reported that companies were ill-prepared for the recession of the 1990s. As a result, HR personnel were encouraged to support needed change by adopting new models of employee and organizational development, which were mostly American in origin. Meanwhile, as European labor pools shrank and costs increased, German companies increasingly exported work and relied more on local employees in expanded overseas operations. There was an especially strong German presence, for example, in the southeast United States, which brought German managers in contact with American HRD models. Likewise, Ivorian exposure to American strategies grew in the 1990s as much of their state capital came from abroad. Until the government coup in December 1999, the United States was the Côte d'Ivoire's most important non-European foreign investor. American business partnerships ranked second in imports and third in exports (CIA, 2000). A full description of procedures, sampling, raw findings, and data analysis is contained in Hansen (2003).

The analysis of organizational perceptions and commonalities in the informants' stories was used to develop four composite non-national and non-organizationally specific story stems, one of which is presented below. Each story stem presented an organizational problem that could conceivably be solved by an HRD intervention as defined by American practitioners. Story problems reflected perceptions about: (a) the role and scope of training, career, and organizational interventions in organizations; (b) appropriate roles and interactions for employees and managers; (c) the importance of organizational culture; and (d) the perceived need for HRD interventions.

Story stem and endings

An organization plans to introduce a new technology, which will affect the entire company. Implementation will require additional personnel, some job modification for some existing employees, and new coordination of employees' time and skills. There is concern about whether employees and managers have the necessary skills to use and manage the new technology. The concern is voiced to the Human Resource (Personnel) Director, who works with the Training Manager. Table 3.1 contains a cross-country comparison of informant-generated endings.

Myths

These endings reflected likely disagreement about the function, role, and scope of HRD. American HRD practitioners are schooled ideally to view training requests as probable performance deficiencies that are driven by larger, more pervasive organizational problems. Thus, trainers analyzed the organizational roots of performance problems that may not be immediately evident. Their studies often identified systemic issues such

Table 3.1   Cross-country comparison of the endings

American ending	German ending	Ivorian ending
Ideally, the Human Resource Director and Training Manager will conduct a large-scale organizational analysis to identify required jobs, skills, personnel, and technical and management development training, as well as any organizational barriers that might hinder the implementation of new technology. A more conservative ending calls for the Training Manager to conduct a training needs assessment study to determine what content should be taught about the new technology, and to identify learning objectives and evaluation criteria that will guide the design and development of a series of new technical training courses.	The HR Director will ask the Training Manager to respond to a given manager's training request by meeting with external training vendors to identify existing technical training courses that can teach the manager's employees about the new technology. Another possibility is to re-evaluate hiring and promotional criteria to ensure that personnel allowed to work with the new technology will already have the necessary technical training.	The Human Resource Manager will respond to a given manager's training request by meeting with external training vendors to identify existing training courses that can teach the manager's employees how to apply the new technology practically. It is decided that trainees will receive a bonus for their participation. Plans are also made to hire relevant experts from Europe and North America during the initial phase of the technology's implementation.

as management styles, or reporting, reward, and feedback procedures as the cause of poor performance instead of a perceived deficiency in required skills and knowledge. Furthermore, front-end organizational analyses were linked to cultural or other organizational issues that can affect training retention and transfer to the job. This approach to HRD, which may be triggered by the need for new training design and development, is conceptually linked to strategic planning and change management, and has been practiced in large American companies for well over two decades (McLagan, 1997; Torraco & Swanson, 1995).

Overall, the informants reported that training, as the only clearly practiced HRD function in German and Ivorian corporations, is seldom performed according to American HRD ideals. Few small- and medium-sized companies in Germany and none in the Côte d'Ivoire have the internal resources to conduct large-scale front-end analysis, nor are they able to develop their own training programs. Informants indicated that even in large companies, German and Ivorian trainers primarily administer management training requests for training pre-developed by external vendors.

In Germany, instruction was most clearly linked to mastery of specific tasks. Training resources were typically spent on refining current and anticipated skills as new employees are already trained through technical institutes and government-sponsored apprenticeships. Training constitutes up to 4 percent of labor costs and is generally longer than similar education in American companies as it is designed to teach both theoretical and task-specific aspects of work. Virtually all the informants indicated that the theoretical expertise to creative problem solving is more highly valued by Germans at all organizational levels than in American companies. Thus, content experts were ultimately seen as responsible for both training development and delivery. The highly in-depth nature of tutelage is often viewed as too technical for training professionals, who are primarily schooled in personnel psychology, education, and organizational theory, to identify training needs and direct course development.

Although all Germans have access to technical instruction at any point in their job history, management development training was available for a limited few. German HRD informants spoke of management development as grooming programs for "high potentials." One informant said: "We do not have management development training in this company. We only have assessment centers for high potentials."

Many large German companies have identified certain characteristics that they believe are essential attributes of good managers. Using these criteria, management employees are recruited and selected for the "high potential" pool. Once selected, they experience a very structured program of management development that is designed to develop skills ratio of approximately 80 percent technical skills. HR personnel suggested that about one-third of these executive hopefuls would eventually be offered key management positions. This counters the American myth that anyone can be a manager if given the right management development training and mentoring (Handy, 1988).

The Ivorian informants tended to discuss training practices as a desired means, rather than a current means, of helping organizations improve their output, processes, and competitive status. In the Côte d'Ivoire, training programs occurred regularly because all companies were mandated to spend about 2 percent of their labor costs on employee instruction. However, the expenditure of training funds did not necessarily reflect a need for new or improved skills, knowledge, or attitudes. Additionally, such programs were not strategically tied to the business objectives of the organization. The informants explained that training was typically seen as a reward, as a travel benefit, or as time away from work. One informant made this comment: "Since we [managers] must pay, we send people. Few are really motivated to learn, so they are just 'tourists'."

Contrary to the Americans and Germans, the Ivorians described their work environment as one in which favoritism based on seniority and nepotism often replaced performance competency as the catalyst for hiring and promotional decisions. One informant said: "Everyone is related in Ivorian organizations, at least in all of the sensitive positions." This statement implied that there was little real motivation to ensure technically proficient employees because there was no guarantee that their new skills would be used or translated into new responsibilities and promotions. Meanwhile, managers often feared enhanced competency in their employees. An informant gave this explanation: "A manager does not want his employee to know more than him nor does he want him to know how incompetent he [the manager] already is." Improved employee performance was thus viewed with caution. Similarly, organizations were hesitant to use systematic needs assessments that might identify the need for organizational change and upset the status quo. The use of foreign experts was often preferred, not because their expertise was considered superior to that of local counterparts, but because their work would not be biased by kinship obligations. Additionally, the experts would not remain long enough to encourage significant change in the organizational structure.

The myths that comparatively shape these assumptions are in Table 3.2.

Table 3.2 Cross-country comparison of the myths

American myths	German myths	Ivorian myths
• HRD should be a key player in the development of strategic business plans.	• Managers and supervisors should determine training needs. In some companies these decisions include input from the employee.	• Managers and supervisors should determine training needs. In some companies these decisions include input from the employee.
• HRD should conduct organizational analyses to identify HRD and non-HRD solutions for organizations.	• Training should teach both the theoretical and the applied aspects of the work.	• Training should teach the applied aspects of the work, as pre-work training is too theoretical.
• When needed, HRD should recommend organizational changes in reporting structures, job design, hiring, and promotion criteria.	• Management development is more a function of one's innate personality and traits.	• Management development is a function of one's innate personality and traits, one's social and family network, and one's credentials. A diploma from an elite university is important.
• HRD should act as change agents and change managers.	• Training development and delivery should ultimately be viewed as the responsibility of the content expert, that is, someone who is functionally trained and experienced in doing the work.	• Training is taken seriously only when linked to a perk or a promotion.
• HRD should diagnose and facilitate organizational cultural change as needed.	• Training designers should be first trained in the instructional content followed by knowledge of learning theory and instructional design principles.	• Training development and delivery should ultimately be viewed as the responsibility of the content expert, that is, someone who is functionally trained and experienced in doing the work.
• HRD should manage training need assessments and development.	• New employees should already have acquired most required skills through university or vocational institute training and through post-educational apprenticeships.	• Training designers should be first trained in the instructional content followed by knowledge of learning theory and instructional design principles.
• HRD should develop career-planning systems and work with managers to improve their counseling skills.		
• HRD should manage the evaluation of HRD interventions.		

Other HRD functions

Contrary to the American ideal, which describes HRD practitioners as working with top management as change agents to bring about broad organizational changes in culture, communication, management, and employee work style, German corporations often resisted such interventions. The organizational structure was fairly compartmentalized and work styles were deliberate and methodical. Organizational hierarchy and formal reporting structures were perceived as positive. German informants indicated that organizations were less political, less competitive, and, in turn, less stressful when everyone was clear on expectations and positioning. Stability and formality implied, as suggested by the informants, that conformity is valued. Conformity drove the observation that workplace cultural homogeneity was preferred over workplace diversity. Informants reported, for example, that cultural assimilation was fairly successful despite the large number of foreign "guest workers" who filled many German semi- and non-skilled positions.

The need for empowerment was discussed differently by American and German informants. Americans defined empowerment in terms of respect, responsibility, and decision-making, and saw themselves as champions and change agents in addressing this ongoing challenge to American companies. German informants indicated that workers' strong emphasis on technical expertise coupled with high levels of technical preparation encouraged professional respect and independence among both blue- and white-collar workers. The Germans agreed with American HRD professionals that managers and supervisors should delegate, facilitate, develop, and coach rather than act as enforcers of work behavior. Furthermore, like the American philosophy of self-managed work teams, German employees were expected to take initiative and manage their own task and work behavior with little direct control. Germans also reported that communication channels were open and new ideas were encouraged from all workers. For example, German informants' story-lines included cases of management and non-management after-hours socializing where ideas were generated and problems were informally identified.

Compared with the Americans, German requirements for effective working relationships differed in precise feedback, rapport, and formality in reporting systems. Germans perceived Americans as too vague and unfocused. In characterizing job feedback as often accusatory and highlighting employee fear in approaching sensitive issues, the German informant data were again contradictory. The HRD informants' indicated that internal trainers were often afraid to promote problem-centered front-end analysis because the findings might jeopardize their positions. Finally, Germans did not equally share the American HRD practitioners' belief that most companies require major organizational reform that in turn required professional guidance.

In Ivorian companies, empowerment in the form of shared decision-making and participative management was desirable, but impracticable. Managers micro-managed to ensure the quality and timeliness of their employees' work. They were reluctant to delegate because if a worker made a mistake or used poor judgment, it was the manager who was blamed. Key informants surmised that managers felt very much out of control and somewhat impotent in their ability to achieve their productivity objectives.

The informants indicated that managers were averse to the conflict that often accompanied the acknowledgment of organizational problems and their resolution. Like the Germans, they talked about the need for harmony. Unlike the Germans, whose need for harmony was tied to smooth performance, the importance of unruffled family ties shaped this concern. First, family ties complicated sanctioning of employee performance, as a manager might find himself punishing a relative. Change was also feared because of its downsizing potential in previously state-owned companies where full employment was often more important than productivity. If a worker lost his income, then his entire extended family and village would be affected. Family ties were also linked to difficulties in implementing change interventions as planning efficiency was constrained by the interference of one's kin. Family obligations, such as funerals or the needs of a village member in distress, were not taken lightly, and typically came before one's job and business. Finally, change, as an alien concept, was viewed as highly traumatic.

Discussion

Scholars note that industrialization occurred at a faster pace in North America than it did in Europe or Africa (Handy, 1988; Stewart & Bennett, 1991). Given this trend, a system was quickly needed to produce and refine the skills required to lead flowering business ventures. As industry grew, the study of management evolved into a respected science. On the other hand, industry came to Europe as early as the mid-1700s, when management skills were considered inborn, elite, and to be refined through experience. European cultures are, for the most part, older, more formal, and homogeneous. In this regard, it appears that conformity, stability, formal hierarchy, and rapport building were instrumental in shaping human resource ideologies and structure among German organizations, as well as Ivorian organizations that were influenced by the colonial French.

Yet, among Europeans, there are differences (Reed, 1998). The division between German management and workers appears to be less finite, for example, than with the French and their colonial legacies. The German concept of the master craftsmen goes back to the Middle Ages and the guild system. Most managers respect the technical expertise of their blue-collar workers, which may allow greater autonomy. In the Côte d'Ivoire, a sense of managerial elitism prevailed thanks to the French, whose concept of management long remained the property of the aristocracy. French and Ivorian business schools continue to perpetuate the importance of credentials over performance and knowhow by catering to future heads and not to the managerial mass (Gordon, 1988; Henry, 1995; Reed, 1998).

Henry observed that management in the Côte d'Ivoire, as with its neighbor Ghana (Gardiner, 1996) whose people share many of the same ethnic bonds, is a hybrid of European and African traditions. The African side of management reflects the paternalistic and consultancy aspects of traditional tribal governance. It is customary, for example, for the chief and his council of elders to discuss options with clan members as decisions are based on the collective welfare of the clan (Lessem, 1998). However, in making decisions, the ultimate authority and responsibility rest with the chief. Gardner noted that the centrality of *chieftaincy* frames the fundamental philosophy of the seniority system, which is based on age and family networks.

Meanwhile, the Côte d'Ivoire is a highly diverse country, with over 60 ethnic groups, each with its own dialect, that are primarily associated with four major cultural regions: the Akan (east Atlantic), Kru (west Atlantic), Mandè, and Voltaic (north). Collectivism, in such societies, presents a formidable challenge to American-based HRD models that are culturally grounded in individualism. In addition to different concepts of self and group behavior, an understanding of collectives is made more difficult because of the underestimated and potentially destructive power of group alliances. That is, the solidarity found in collectives can cause not only fierce loyalty within groups, but can also lead to territoriality and rivalry between groups in the workplace. In culturally heterogeneous societies, these trends can dominate organizational life and fragment an organization's attempts to advance economically and technologically in general, and jeopardize HRD efforts to advance needed change management in particular.

Clearly, a collective orientation in a highly heterogeneous society with poor resources can retard the adoption of HRD models. However, it is also important to note that an individualist orientation alone does not assure that American HRD myths will transfer across cultures. Triandis (1995) offers more insight into the cultural context of individualism. He suggested that although the United States and Germany are both individualistic, Americans are more hierarchical in their work relationships, which he calls vertical individualism, and that post-World War II Germans, based on research by Scwartz (1994), have become less so. Younger Germans may thus appear somewhat more horizontal and egalitarian in their orientation toward individualism. This difference in verticality may explain, for example, American HRD practitioners' tendency to see empowerment as an ongoing struggle, whereas German managers, in particular those who are 45 or younger, see this as less of an issue.

Triandis suggests that the vertical aspect of American culture may stem from the early European settlers, among whom were many members of the Anglo-Saxon gentry who set the tone for class distinctions. As no clear American aristocracy developed based on blood ties, the notion of a class system manifested itself in work status, money, and property. However, the twenty-first century may see change in the verticality of dominant American social patterns as recent immigrations and existing minorities increasingly constitute more of a majority position. Triandis also notes that crisis and trauma can affect the individualism–collectivism (I–C) dimension. An individualist society can become more collective when faced with external threats. He noted a period in German history, for example, when economic crisis fueled by a historical respect for authority gave rise to the vertical collectivism associated with Nazism. He also noted that aspects of collectivism have always been present in small portions of the German population and that they periodically surface, as was evidenced in the recent conflict between neo-Nazi groups and racially different immigrants. Vestiges of vertical collectivism may in part explain a German preference for formality and conformity. Organizational theorists who link the I–C dimension to modernity suggest that nations whose orientation is vertical collectivism, like the Côte d'Ivoire, will evolve into more individualistic societies as they become more technologically and economically advanced (Bradshaw & Wallace, 1996; Triandis, 1995). Ivorian informants, in this study, reported that it would require the time equivalent of at least one and possibly two generations before the Côte d'Ivoire rejects its clan orientation and obligations.

Conclusion

Although generational differences may have limited the findings to some extent, the data presented in this chapter may be more representative of traditional corporate thinking than newer approaches adopted by younger and more technologically oriented German companies and by successfully privatized companies in the Côte d'Ivoire. However, the findings of the study discussed in this chapter may assist in explaining and anticipating confusion and uncertainty faced by younger organizations in transition. Moreover, such changes may be utilitarian and not constitute a fundamental change in sociocultural referents. Myths are not necessarily rational, nor do they change quickly.

Early grounding in values may explain the relatively small impact of two additional limitations. These were differences in line/staff perspectives among story informants and national differences in HRD staff training. First, to first address the concern that the American informants were HRD staff whereas the German and Ivorian informants and were non-HRD line managers, German and Ivorian HRD counterparts were asked to review the data. German staff confirmed the assumptions and concerns of their line compatriots. In the Côte d'Ivoire, HRD informants expressed a strong desire to implement American ideology, but continually pointed out cultural differences as a key constraint. Likewise, non-HR manager informants, trained in Europe or the USA, equally referred to the sabotaging effect of the local culture as a barrier to implementing more modern performance-based management models designed to reduce the impact of clan loyalty and nepotism. Second, in both Germany and the Côte d'Ivoire HRD is not yet viewed as a separate professional field, therefore little or no university training is available. In Germany, certified psychologists typically perform HRD, whereas in the Côte d'Ivoire HRM specialists with business degrees take certification workshops in HRD. Nevertheless, all foreign HRD staff were familiar with American models through professional journals and American-based associations such as the American Society for Training and Development and the Society for Human Resource Management.

Clearly, this exploratory study validates the need for anyone in any occupation to be cognizant of the ethnocentrism of their own work values. Studies of expatriate adjustment indicate that between 10 and 40 percent of expatriates fail in their foreign assignments (Black et al., 1991). A variable that is continually cited is not the lack of technical expertise, but rather the inability to understand and adjust to different ways of working. What is known is that national context affects work behavior in general. What is little known, however, is how behavior is affected at the occupational level. This benefit is crucial to HRD as the human element in its myths and its cultural roots affect what individuals view as culturally appropriate forms of learning, career counseling, and organizational development. It is important for the field to know that its practices may not transfer across national borders without adjustment.

References

Ardichvili, A., Cardozo R. N., & Gasparishvili, A. "Leadership Styles Management Practice of Russian Entrepreneurs: Implications for Transferability of Western HRD Interventions." *Human Resource Development Quarterly*, 9(2) (1998) 145–55.

Black, S., Mendenhall, M., & Oddou, G. "Toward a Comprehensive Model of International Adjustment: An Interaction of Multiple Theoretical Perspectives." *Academy of Management Review*, 16(2) (1991) 291–317.

Bradshaw, Y. W. & Wallace, M. *Global Inequalities* (Thousand Oaks, CA: Pine Forge Press, 1996).

Campbell, J. *The Masks of God: Primitive Mythology* (New York: Viking, 1959).

Campbell, J. *The Masks of God: Occidental Mythology* (New York: Viking, 1964).

CIA (Central Intelligence Agency of the United States) "Country Economic Profile for the Côte d'Ivoire" (1 January), in *The 2000 World Fact Book* (Langley, VA: CIA, 2000).

Desimone, R. & Harris, D. *Human Resource Development* (2nd ed.) (Fort Worth, TX: Dryden Press, 1998).

d'Iribarne, P. *La Logique de l'Honneur: Gestion des Enterprises et Traditions Nationales* (Paris: Editions du Seuil, 1989).

Gardiner, K. "Managing in Different Cultures: The Case of Ghana." In Towers, B. (ed.), *The Handbook of Human Resource Management* (London: Blackwell, 1996).

Gordon, C. "France," In C., Handy, C., Gordon, I., Gow, & C., Randlesome (eds) *Making Managers* (New York: Pitman, 1988).

Handy, C. (1988), "The United States." In C., Handy, C., Gordon, I., Gow, & C., Randlesome (eds), *Making Managers* (New York: Pitman).

Hansen, C. "Cultural Myths in Stories about Human Resource Development: Analyzing the Cross-Cultural Transfer of American Models to Germany and the Côte d'Ivoire." *International Journal of Training and Development*. 6(1) (2003) 16–30.

Hansen, C. & Brooks, A. "A Review of Cross-cultural Research for the International Practice of Human Resource Development." *Human Resource Development Quarterly*, 5(1) (1994) 55–74.

Hansen, C. & Kahnweiler, W. "Storytelling: An Instrument for Understanding the Dynamics of Corporate Relationships." *Human Relations*, 46(12) (1993) 1391–409.

Hansen, C. & Kahnweiler, W. "Executive Managers: Cultural Expectations through Stories about Work." *Journal of Applied Management Studies*, 6(2) (1997) 117–38.

Hansen, C., Kahnweiler, W., & Wilensky, A. "Human Resource Development: A Study of Occupational Culture through Organizational Stories." *Human Resource Development Quarterly*, 5(3) (1994) 253–68.

Henry, A. "Quand donc les experts patiront-ils?" *Gérer et Comprendre*, 39(27) (1995) 71–81.

Hofstede, G. *Culture's Consequences: International Differences in Work-Related Values*. (Sage Publications Inc., 1984).

Hofstede, G., Neuijen, B., Ohayv, D. D., & Sanders, G. "Measuring Organizational Cultures: A Qualitative and Quantitative Study across Twenty Cases." *Administrative Science Quarterly*, 35(2) (1990) 286–316.

Laurent, A. "The Cross-cultural Puzzle of International Human Resource Management." *Human Resource Management*, 25(1) (1986) 91–102.

Lessem, R. *Management Development Through Cultural Diversity* (London: Routledge, 1998).

Mapstone, R. "The Military in a Divided Society: The Occupational Culture of Soldiers in Northern Ireland." *International Journal of Sociology and Social Policy*, 12(1/2) (1993) 3–17.

McLagan, P. A. *Models for Exellence: The Conclusion and Recommendations of the ASTD Training and Development Study* (Alexandria, VA: ASTD, 1983/1989).

McLagan, P. A. "Competencies: The Next Generation." *Training and Development*, 51(5) (1997) 40–47.

Otte, F. L. "Myth, Spirituality and Career Development." Paper presented at the 47th National Conference and Exposition and of the American Society for Training and Development, 20 May 1991, San Francisco.

Otte, F. L. & Kahnweiler, W. "In Search of the Soul of HRD." *Human Resource Development Quarterly*, 8(2) (1997) 171–81.

Pace, R. W., Smith, P. C., & Mills, G. E. *Human Resource Development: The Field* (Englewood Cliffs, NJ: Prentice-Hall, 1991).

Peterson, L. A. "International HRD: What We Know and Don't Know." *Human Resource Development Quarterly*, 8(1) (1997) 63–80.

Reed, M. I. "Industry and Society in Europe, Stability and Change in Britain, Germany, and France." *Organization Studies*, 19(4) (1998) 729–31.

Schwartz, S. H. "Beyond Individualism and Collectivism: New Cultural Directions of Values." In U., Kim, H. C., Triandis, C., Kagitcibasi, S. C. Choi, & G., Yoon (eds) *Individualism and Collectivism: Theory, Method, and Applications* (Newbury Park, CA: Sage, 1994).

Stewart, E. C. & Bennett, M. J. *American Cultural Patterns: A Cross-cultural Perspective* (Yarmouth, ME: Intercultural Press, 1991).

Torraco, R. J. & Swanson, R. A. "The Strategic Roles of Human Resources Development." *Human Resource Planning*, 18(4) (1995) 10–20.

Triandis, H. *Individualism and Collectivism* (Boulder, CO: Westview Press, 1995).

Trice, H. & Beyer, J. *The Cultures of Work Organizations* (Englewood Cliffs, NJ: Prentice-Hall, 1993).

Trompenaars, F. *Riding the Waves of Culture* (London: Nicholas Brealey, 1993).

Van Maanen, J. & Barley, S. R. "Occupational Communities: Culture and Control in Organizations." *Research in Organizational Behavior*, 6 (1984) 287–365.

4

The Cultural Context of Human Resource Development Paradigms and Practices in South Africa

Susan A. Lynham, Fredrick M. Nafukho, and Peter W. Cunningham

The Republic of South Africa was called a *Rainbow Nation* by the Nobel Laureate Desmond Tutu, to highlight the diversity of its past, and the myriad of challenges and opportunities embodied in celebrating and leveraging this diversity toward a prosperous future for all.

> We are regarded with awe and admiration for showing the world that it is possible for those who had been involved in bloody conflict to evolve into comrades; to undergo the metamorphosis of the repulsive caterpillar into the gorgeous butterfly by opting for the path of forgiveness and reconciliation instead of retaliation, retribution and revenge. Let us become what we are, the rainbow people of the God, proud of our diversity, celebrating our differences that make not for separation and alienation but for a gloriously rich unity.
>
> Tutu, 2007

One of the richest nations on the continent, South Africa is midway through its second, and arguably most delicate, decade of political independence from a history of colonial rule and social, political, and economic inequality (Taylor, 2004a; Terreblanche, 2002). Among its most important challenges is the purposeful development and upliftment of its people, particularly that majority disadvantaged by its past. Concomitantly, it must fight to hold on to much-needed existing expertise for its social, economic, and political wellbeing, and it must do so within increasing global competition for this expertise. As a result, the development of its human resources on multiple fronts has become a national imperative. It is the purpose of this chapter to consider the rainbow context of South Africa, and how this shapes HRD thought and practice.

Narrowing the notion of culture to an expression of a society's norms and values, we begin this exploration by offering an overview of the country's social, economic, and political past and present. Next, we describe the principles core to the dominant cultural worldview of *ubuntu*. This description dovetails into a comparison between this (social) philosophy and the dominant political and economic philosophies of liberal democracy and capitalism, and highlights the dissonance among these three systems (Huntington, 1994). Thereafter we provide an overview of the current construction of HRD in the country. A consideration of how this cultural context affects HRD practices in South Africa follows with a description of related challenges in two particular areas of application—teambuilding and empowerment. Finally, we offer concluding thoughts on implications of our discoveries for HRD practice in the future.

From past to present: A rainbow nation in the making

South Africa's present-day cultural mix is the result of a long multi-period history. These periods include 200,000 more years of pre-colonial past, almost 500 years of colonial rule, and its pre- and post-apartheid-dominated eras. Each period saw the influx of new peoples, with new customs, values, and beliefs—all foundational to the forging of a new social, economic, and political milieu.

Rich in fossil evidence of the origins of humankind, South Africa's early inhabitants date back several millions of years. Although its human ancestors predate its modern human inhabitants by more than 100,000 years, the Khiosan (the collective European term for the Hottentots and Bushmen) resided in the South African region some 2,000 years ago, primarily living a pastoral lifestyle near the coast, "between modern-day Namibia and the Eastern Cape" (CIA, 2007, p. 1). At more or less the same time "Bantu [Black]-speaking agro-pastoralists began arriving in southern-Africa, bringing with them an Iron Age culture and domesticated crops" (p. 1). The Bantu became established cattle farmers and had chiefdoms and a hierarchy of communities. Colonial presence began with the arrival of Portuguese explorers at the Cape of Good Hope in the late fifteenth century. In 1652, the Dutch East India Company established the first European trading station in Table Bay (Cape Town). So commenced a long period of European domination and the importation of slaves to the region (Editors Inc, 2004).

The next 200 years saw the arrival of the French Huguenots, in 1688, annexation of the Cape by the British in 1795, a brief return to Dutch occupation in 1803, and a British reoccupation in 1806 and subsequent influx of British settlers in the early 1820s. During this period the "trekboers" (Afrikaners) began their migration north, increasingly conflicting with the numerous Black tribes that had been moving south since the 1400s. The abolition of slavery in 1834, discovery of diamonds in 1867 and gold in 1886, and the arrival of Indian workers in 1860, followed, the latter mostly brought in to work on the fast-expanding sugar plantations in the northeast of the country (now KwaZulu-Natal). British occupation and rule continued until the formation of the Union of South Africa in 1910. The next 40 years were marked by successively declining rights to the "non-European" sectors of the population, a trend that culminated in a Nationalist apartheid government in 1948 and only ended with the election of the first democratic government led by the African National Congress (ANC) in 1994.

The subsequent 15 years has seen a persistent influx of ethnicities. This trend continues to feed the rainbow texture of the nation and has ushered in a new era of diversity and concomitant strains on the economic, political, and social environs, as shown in Table 4.1.

South Africa's estimated population of 48 million is differentiated into four main ethnic–racial groups: Black African (79 percent), White (9.6 percent), Colored (8.9 percent), and Indian/Asian (2.5 percent). After 2004, the country entered its second decade of liberal democracy.

Table 4.1 The Influential sociocultural, economic, and political contexts of South Africa

| | Changing Contexts: During and After Apartheid | | |
	Sociocultural	Economic	Political
Apartheid	• Superiority of white cultural values • Destruction of many material cultural artifacts of the non-White groups by Whites	• An espoused form of Thatcherism • Elite White domination and ownership	• Minority nationalism, with White elite domination • Elitist, minority vote
Post-Apartheid	• Tolerance of cultural diversity • Building of a common identity • Promotion of all indigenous cultures • Need for an African Renaissance	• Liberal capitalism; free market driven • Elite White and emerging elite Black domination	• Majority nationalism • One person, one vote • Democracy

South Africa enjoys a modern infrastructure that enables the distribution of goods and services throughout the region, continent, and world.

Then-President Thabo Mbeki spearheaded the vision of an *African Renaissance* in September 1998 (Makgoba, 1999). Aimed at renewal of the African continent, this strategy explores and develops issues such as what constitutes Africanness, African culture and language, and pursues "the provision of a better life" for the "masses of the people, . . . the right to determine their future," and through "sustainable development" to affect positively their "standard of living . . . and quality of life" (Mbeki, 1999, p. xvi). This vision is driven by such factors as:

> minority rights and fears; the shifts in power relationships within Africa and in the world at large; the emerging new world order where the equality of difference, nonracism and human rights are becoming core values; the demise of white supremacy with its racial, colonial and apartheid consequences; the ascendancy and assertion by Africans on their and Africa's proper and equitable role or place in the globalising world; and, finally, the emerging historically conscious and Africa-focused leadership within the continent.
>
> (p. ix)

An ambitious vision, Mbeki described the related tasks:

> Our first task . . . is to transform our society . . . Our second . . . to join hands with like-minded forces on our continent, convinced that the peoples of Africa share a common destiny, . . . which must result in the new century going down in history as the African century. Yesterday is a foreign country—tomorrow belongs to us!
>
> (p. xxi)

He continued:

> We can reel off the list of things that have to be done . . . including human resource development, the emancipation of women, the building of a modern economic, social and communication infrastructure, the cancellation of Africa's foreign debt, an improvement in terms of trade, an increase in domestic and foreign investment, the expansion of development assistance, and better access for our products into the markets of the developed world . . . [To do so] we must . . . insert ourselves into the international debate (p. xvii) . . . [and thereby] confront the challenge of the reconstruction and development of our continent anew.
>
> (pp. xvi–xvii, xix)

In part, this vision set the stage for the 2002 launch of the New Partnership for Africa's Development (NEPAD), a project essentially "for supporting development in Africa" (Taylor, 2004a, p. 1). Both initiatives are focused on national, regional, and international cooperation in the form of social, economic, and political development; they include attention to the "role of African social values in a globalising world" (Makgoba, 1999, p. iii). It is to this system of African social values, embodied in the philosophy of *ubuntu*, that we turn next. For it is within this communal social context, and its relationship to the operating political and economic systems, that HRD in South Africa is located.

Ubuntu: A special kind of worldview

Ubuntu is a worldview grounded in a way of being, a code of unwritten ethics, deeply embedded in the African culture. *Ubuntu* acknowledges that as human beings, we are interdependent and interconnected. We are people through other people, and we cannot be fully human as individuals alone (Bangura, 2005; Nafukho, 2007). Mbigi and Maree (1995) noted that the core values of *ubuntu* included group solidarity, uniformity, compassion, respect, dignity, and collective unity. Desmond Tutu, as cited by Mbigi (2004, p. 20), noted:

> Africans have a thing . . . ubuntu; it is about the essence of being human. It is part of the gift that Africa is going to give to the world. It embraces hospitality, caring about others, being willing to go that extra mile for the sake of another. We believe that a person is a person through other persons; that my humanity is caught up and bound up in yours. When I dehumanize you, I inexorably dehumanize myself. The solitary human being is a contradiction in terms, and therefore you seek work for the common good because your humanity comes into its own in community, in belonging.

Ubuntu is an undeniably important cultural dimension that scholars must endeavor to address in their effort to define and practice HRD. Modern business organizations need to emphasize profit maximization efforts undergirded by humanity toward its employees, customers and other competitors—an emphasis rather atypical of business today.

Core principles of *ubuntu*

Ubuntu emphasizes the need for a *humane* society. It provides the rules of conduct for all in society, recognizes the human being as a social being who prefers others, and comprises three core principles: spiritual-ity, consensus building, and dialogue (Bangura, 2005; Nafukho, 2006, 2007). In this context, HRD seeks to promote collective advancement and *humane* learning and work environments.

The spirituality principle

According to Bangura (2005), like all other human beings, Africans are decidedly "spiritual." Spirituality plays a key role in many African societies and unites people to live in harmony as a com-munity. It promotes the African extended family (Mbiti, 1991), focuses on the meaning and purpose of life, and seeks answers to critical questions like: Who am I? Why do I exist? Where am I going? (Nafukho, 2007).

Spirituality aims at promoting societal moral values such as honesty, respect, trustworthiness, fairness, truth, compassion, and caring for each other. It also emphasizes the value of positive work and com-munity spirit, both necessary for the survival of the individual, family, community, an organization, and society at large. "Africans have a profound understanding between the connections of past and present, between human beings and nature, of our common humanity, and of a shared spirituality" (Nussbaum, 2003, p. 8).

The consensus building principle

Ubuntu requires that humans endeavor to cultivate an infinite capac-ity for the pursuit of consensus and reconciliation. African-style democracy operates in the form of, often perceived as lengthy, discus-sions (Bangura, 2005). Although discussion acknowledges and values the hierarchy of importance among the contributors, the speakers are normally provided with an equal chance to speak until consensus is reached. The desire to agree within the context of *ubuntu* safeguards the rights and opinions of individuals and minorities to enforce group solidarity. "The hallmark of ubuntu is about listening to and affirming others with the help of processes that create trust, fairness, shared understanding and dignity and harmony in relationships" (Nussbaum, 2003, p. 3).

The dialogue principle

Bangura (2005, p. 23) noted, "ubuntu inspires us to expose ourselves to others, to encounter differences of their humaneness in order to inform and enrich our own." Dialogue enables learning from others and builds an individual's knowledge base and wisdom, thereby allowing for collective living and understanding. It promulgates that to be human, one needs to recognize the otherness of one's fellow humans. The guiding assumption is that the *others* we meet and interact with have good human intentions, as, for example, demonstrated by Nelson Mandela.

Dialogue consequently emphasizes the importance of the individual in society—that an individual is defined in terms of his or her relationship with others. Individuals in organizations and society therefore exist in their relationship with others. The word *individual* signifies a plurality of personalities corresponding to the multiplicity of relationships in which the individual in question stands. It does not refer to individualistic aspects of human existence to the detriment of group, team, communal, or society at large. This construction of individuality involves moving from solitary to solidarity, from independence to interdependence, from individuality vis-à-vis community to individuality à la community (Bangura, 2005):

> [b]ecause of its emphasis on our common humanity and the ethical call to embody our communal responsiveness in the world, *ubuntu* offers an alternative way to create a world that works for all. Simply put, people, businesses and countries would re-learn how to live together with respect, compassion and dignity and to re-organize resources accordingly.
>
> (Nussbaum, 2003, p. 3)

Striking a balance among inherently dissonant systems

To understand the influence of the sociocultural context, particularly that of *ubuntu*, on HRD in South Africa, it is helpful to ponder its interaction with the prevailing economic, social, and political contexts. These last three interacting components (see Figure 4.1) are necessary for a democratic free-market system (Huntington, 1994) and represent the source of multiple struggles faced by "new democracies"—"those democratic regimes that have emerged since the 1970s" and which are still "in the making" (Weffort, 1994, p. 27), South Africa being a case in point. Each of these systems represents a dominant philosophical (ontology, epistemology, methodology, axiology, and teleology) (Denzin & Lincoln, 2005) perspective, which, when misaligned, can be the source of significant dissonance, dissatisfaction, and tension.

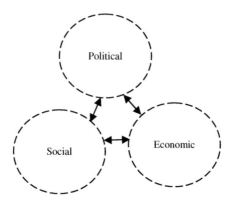

Figure 4.1   Three necessary components for a sustainable democratic, free-market system.

Huntington (1994) explicated the move away from authoritarian to democratic political systems as a global phenomenon with widespread implications accompanied by a "parallel and simultaneous movement towards . . . economic liberalization" (p. 16). The strong relationship and tension between political democratization and economic liberalization have significant implications for a country's ability to attend to concomitant needs of social reform and upliftment. There is therefore an economic and social basis necessary for the successful introduction and sustainability of democratic systems, and one, according to Huntington, closely linked to individualism as well as the development of a substantial middle class.

As part of its independence, South Africa adopted the policies of a liberal democracy and economy, both epistemologies of individualism—political and economic—which typify the current global era of democracy and market-driven economies (Chaibong, 2000; Turner, 1988). The adoption of a liberal economic policy, although currently necessary for successful participation in what Mbeki (1999) described as "the context and framework of the world economy" (p. xvii), has made it difficult, if not impossible, for the government to intervene sufficiently to redirect much-needed economic resources to the upliftment of the predominantly poor section of the population (Huntington, 1994; Taylor, 2004a, b; Weffort, 1994). Put another way, and underscored by Tocqueville, a notable sociologist and critic of democracy (Turner, 1988), such individualism—democratic and economic—threatens civil society (Chaibong, 2000), an outcome that in turn threatens the sustainability of these same liberal systems.

Taylor (2004b, pp. 10–11) illustrated this tendency in his description of the contemporary economic order in South Africa:

> the economic solutions which have been chosen for South Africa's future advance the single idea of redistribution through growth in an economy which continues to display the symptoms of white wealth and black poverty.

The above highlights that one way this dilemma has been dealt with is to promote "a new black middle class" (p. 11) predicated on the believed link between a burgeoning middle class and sustainable economic wellbeing (Huntington, 1994; Weffort, 1994). This approach, which is described as tantamount to the adoption of an "American-style affirmative action" policy, "has included the direct economic empowerment of blacks by racial distribution of stock-market wealth" (p. 11) leading, in turn, to what has often been described as "a tiny clique of top-level ANC contacts" who "have become millionaires" while at the same time creating "almost no new jobs" (*Sunday Independent*, 1997 as cited in Taylor, 2004b, p. 11). He continued:

> "empowering" a middle class simply because it is black runs the risk of diverting attention and resources away from the real task at hand: the upliftment of the majority of Black South Africans from intense poverty.
>
> (p. 11)

Within the interacting context of these two liberal and predominantly individualistic systems, the social system that most characterizes South Africa, and indeed Africa, is a communal one "which defines the peoples' perception of self-interest, their freedom, and their location in the social whole" (Ake, 1993, p. 243). "Liberal democracy," said Ake, "assumes individualism, but there is little individualism in Africa." Encapsulated in the philosophy of *ubuntu* "participation"—economic, political, social—"is linked to communality" and "consciousness is directed towards belonging to an organic whole."

> People participate . . . because they are part of an interconnected whole . . . [and] . . . rests . . . on the assumption of . . . the social nature of human beings. . . . Participation is as much a matter of taking part as of sharing the rewards and burdens of community membership.
>
> (p. 243)

Essential Essences of the Communal Socio-cultural Philosophy	Essential Essences of the Liberal Eco-Political Philosophies
Typical of a pre-capitalist and pre-industrial society	A creation of industrial civilization and a "socially atomized society" (Ake, 1993, p. 242)
Designed to safeguard and reward the individual within a social whole	Designed to safeguard, celebrate, and reward the individual
Is built on a tradition of extended family ties, sharing, and "being part of an interconnected whole" (Ake, 1993, p. 243)	Threatens traditional family ties and civil society
Citizens tend to have a spiritual view one another, as part of an integrated, interconnected social whole	Citizens tend to have an instrumental view of one another
Interest of man is in those in the community and whom he considers part of himself	Interest of man is in those in close proximity to himself
Participation rests on "the social nature of human beings" (Ake, 1993, p. 243)	Participation rests on the self in a potentially conflicting and competitive relation to others
Emphasis tends to be on process, or 'means'	Emphasis tends to be on outcome, or "ends"

Figure 4.2   The dissonant tension among the communal sociocultural and liberal economic and political philosophies operating in South Africa.

Although liberal capitalism and democracy are often referred to as cultures in and of themselves (Chaibong, 2000; Diamond, 1994; Huntington, 1994; Taylor, 2004b; Turner, 1998; Weffort, 1994), they are value systems typically at odds with that of the predominant social culture of South Africa (Jeppe, 1994). Figure 4.2 illustrates this juxtaposition among these three systems—an "at oddness" that leads to a clear dissonance among the indigenous sociocultural system (community with an "Us/I" focus) and those of capitalism and democracy (individualistic with an "I" focus) (Jeppe, 1994). As will be shown later, this dissonance directly impacts the practical world of HRD.

The above evidences a "dissonance" in South African culture—between being materialistically driven and economically active (as essential features of globalization and its concomitant systems of liberal capitalism and democracy) and adhering to a belief system of community, which is essentially ancestral. The result is the country shows signs of a disintegration of beliefs and norms, and a struggle to reach a state of connectivity of values. This state of dissonance means that most Blacks are confronted with the need to operate in two typically disparate spheres: for example, as a manager in a highly individualistic and materialistic capitalist world, and as a member of an ethnic group still operating off ancestral notions of community and oneness.

This historical legacy and sociopolitical–economic milieu inform a very specific context in which HRD is constructed and practiced in South Africa. We look next at this contextual construction of HRD.

Ubuntu management approach and its relevance to HRD

Ubuntu can form a strong cultural foundation of HRD. This worldview is an important one, quite different from its Western counterpart, and emphasizes the importance of people to an organization. It is also well aligned with the field of HRD, which argues that people are the real assets that organizations have and should be nurtured through learning. HRD professionals must demonstrate how the discipline can be advanced by the various worldviews such as *ubuntu*.

To illustrate the relevance of an *ubuntu* management approach in South Africa, we draw upon the work of Mbigi and Maree (1995, p. 10). They observed that such an approach leads to the development of cooperative and competitive

- people
- paradigms and perspective
- practices
- processes
- policies and procedures
- values as well as institutions

The points identified above emphasize the importance of cooperation in all human endeavors. This approach can be compared with that of teamwork and team learning as discussed by Senge (1990) in his book *The Fifth Discipline of the Learning Organization Paradigm*. On the value of the *ubuntu* philosophy to modern organizations and HRD practices, it is observed:

> Ubuntu may mark the departure from the current confrontational approach in our industrial relations to a more cooperative and competitive approach . . . a new way of forming a creative and competitive dialogue aimed at finding joint solutions. There is no suggestion that conflict will disappear. The collective solidarity of the various groups in the company should be respected and enhanced.
>
> (Mbigi & Maree, 1995, p. 15)

Management practices are confounded by increasing physiological and worldview tensions as cultural differences permeate the economy.

The current situation can at best be described as collaborative capitalism— a capitalism driven by individual advancement but underscored by a belief in the need to share individual gains specifically among extended family members and significant others in the community. The latter gives credence to the philosophical principles of *ubuntu*. Consequently, HRD policies and practices are a combination of self-responsibility for advancement within the framework of communal gain and empowerment. Individual freedom, which is juxtaposed with collective advancement means that democracy and capitalism are not negated. Rather, there is a manifestation of an *ubuntu*-entrenched democracy, and an *ubuntu*-embedded capitalism. The result is a feeling of entitlement or redress, specifically in terms of wealth redistribution, within the context of a willingness to work for the self. South Africa's HRD philosophical underpinnings parallel in many respects Chiabong's (2000) notion of "Confusion democracy and Confusion capitalism" (p. 134). In this regard he argued that it is necessary to "maintain one's cultural identity in a rapidly globalizing and democratizing world" (p. 129), and enable countries "of non-western civilizations . . . to be brought into the debate" (p. 127) of whether "it is possible to have liberal democracy and a free-market economy without individualism." How this worldview is manifested in HRD in South Africa is outlined next.

Human resource development in South Africa: Paradigms

A direct result of its past, the South African government launched, in April 2001, as part of then-President Mbeki's vision of "a nation at work for a better life for all," a national HRD strategy (Asmal, 2001, p. 1). The mission of this strategy and subsequent national policy framework underscored the essential national nature of HRD in the country as:

> to maximize the potential of the people of South Africa, through the acquisition of knowledge, skills, and values, to work productively and competitively in order to achieve a rising quality of life for all.
>
> (Asmal, 2001, p. 2)

From this policy a national qualifications framework (NQF) emerged, with a plethora of HRD-related Acts. The NQF specifies and monitors the registration and delivery, by relevant stakeholders, of necessary standards- and qualifications-based education and training for all learners. It is hoped that the resulting accreditations are thereby made more meaningful, transferable, and comparable; and most importantly, linked to the perceived national expertise (skills and knowledge) needs. Together with the ensuing legislation, in the form of national Acts, this policy spells out a clear framework of national HRD (NHRD) in South Africa (Lynham & Cunningham, 2004), and informs its possible definition as:

> A process or processes of organized capability and competence-based learning experiences undertaken within a specified period of time to bring about individual and organizational growth and performance improvement, and to enhance national economic, cultural, and social development.
>
> (p. 319)

Another area of note is in the construction and location of HRD. In the USA, HRD is typically conceptualized as a summative model of: human resources = human resource management + human resource development. On the other hand, and typical of Europe and South Africa, is what we like to term the embedded/nested model of HRD (Lynham & Cunningham, 2006). This model locates HRM within HR, and HRD within HRM. While the former tends to fragment HR and place HRD in competition with HRM, the latter makes for a more aligned and cooperative relationship between HRD and HRM. This second conceptualization of HRD provides a better *fit* with the sociocultural character of South Africa.

HRD as an emerging field of study and practice has borrowed heavily from other disciplines such as economics, psychology, and the social sciences; or, specified another way, disciplines concerned with people, processes/systems, and performance (Lynham & Cunningham, 2006). In addition, HRD has incorporated concepts from fields such as politics, anthropology, business management, and even engineering. HRD, particularly the typical Western USA models, has also been defined in many ways by several scholars. For instance, McLagan (1989) defined HRD in terms of its main foci, namely, organization development, training and development, and career development. Mclean and Mclean (2001) defined HRD as:

> any process or activity that, either initially or over the long term, has the potential to develop adult's work-based knowledge, expertise, productivity and satisfaction, whether for personal or group, team gain, or for the benefit of an organization, community, nation, or ultimately, the whole of humanity.
>
> (p. 10)

Swanson and Holton (2001, p. 4; Swanson, 1999) defined HRD as "a process for developing and unleashing human expertise through organization development and personnel training and development for the purpose of improving performance." From the definitions provided, HRD has mainly been viewed from an economic, psychology, and systems perspective.

Given the significance of the field of HRD, not just in South Africa but the world over, it is important that we examine it from the cultural perspective, too. In the next subsection we advance the importance of using this African perspective of looking at HRD from the human philosophy of *ubuntu*. An African worldview, "characterized by a deliberate emphasis on people and their dignity–the emphasis on the collective brotherhood of mankind called *ubuntu*" (Mbigi, 2004, p. 20), ought therefore to inform and direct HRD practice in the country.

Human resource development in South Africa: Practices

Areas of HRD practice in which the philosophy of *ubuntu* needs to be considered and advanced include, but are certainly not limited to, teambuilding and empowerment. Considerations of how this sociocultural philosophy impacts these areas of practice are discussed next.

Teambuilding

Western teambuilding literature, particularly that from the USA, has largely grown out of one of the stems of organization development, namely laboratory training—more specifically T-group training (Cummings & Worley, 2005). As such, it is rooted in Western philosophy. Considered an important area of practice within HRD (McLean, 2006), teambuilding is vital for skill development in South Africa.

In terms of dimensions of culture, teambuilding in the Western context can be described along a continuum of individualism–collectivism (Hofstede, 1991). As practiced from the Western model, this approach means that teambuilding efforts move individuals along the continuum, from a focus on the individual to one on the collective. Effectively this refocus requires the individual to give up "self" for the collective, to become "We." In the USA, the highest scoring individualistic culture in the world (Hofstede, 1980), it is therefore little wonder that organizations enjoy limited success with teambuilding practices. They create, by their very design, dissonance for such individualistically oriented participants. As a result, team participation typically becomes a competition and decision-making is reduced to that of the majority vote/voice.

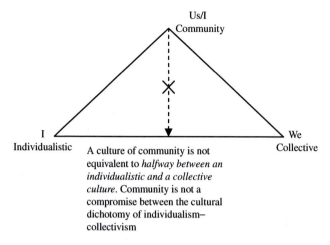

Figure 4.3 A culture of community—integration of the whole and the individual.

This cultural continuum of individualism–collectivism is not sufficient to accommodate the African culture of *ubuntu*, of community. For in this context community is not just a collective—it is not about "We," but about "I within Us" neither is it the midpoint along this continuum, a compromise of the "I" and "We." Rather, it must be understood as a necessary third dimension of culture, as illustrated in Figure 4.3, where "I am because we are, and none of us is greater than all of us," and where the individual and the collective co-exist in a shared humanity, as I *and* Us.

Within this cultural context, teambuilding in South Africa needs to accommodate a community orientation. This means that the inputs, processes, and outputs typically associated with teams and teambuilding need to be adapted to this end.

Empowerment

After 1994, "empowerment" became a pivotal value in the new South Africa—to deepen democracy and to entrench a culture of equality through broad-based participation in the society's transformation. Gaining ground through popular and government acceptance, empowerment has become part of the anti-poverty and economic growth strategy, and the transformation agenda. Then-President Mbeki (2007), a strong supporter of women's upliftment, linked empowerment to economic and social leveling in his address to a Women's Day celebration under the theme, *Emancipation, Empowerment, Equality and*

Eradication of Poverty NOW. Fourteen years on, as a young democracy, South Africa still shows evidence of extensive race, class, and gender divides, as well as "a culture of rampant materialism and consumerism" (Gqola, 2006). Consequently, empowerment is needed to underpin state policy and inform the institutional mechanism to eradicate the legacy of apartheid.

Underpinning all policy, empowerment as a value is congruent with South Africa's deeply rooted *ubuntu* tradition of mutual help and the vision of equal justice enshrined in its Constitution. Smith (2006) pointed out that *ubuntu* is combined with an extensive web of religious affiliations and sophisticated systems for financial and non-financial mutual community help. Empowerment, as expressed in sharing, reciprocation, mutual advancement, and collective dependence, is therefore an intrinsic part of life for most South Africans. These values are juxtaposed with commitment to a society based on the principles of non-racialism, non-sexism, democracy, freedom, and equality. Over the past decade, empowerment has progressively been institutionalized in law and practice. Its embodiment in law is seen as a mechanism to deal with a historically male-dominated society and address the systematic exclusion of Black people from the economy before 1994. However, rather than seeing it as affirmative action or a moral program to address the injustices of the past, the South African government defines Black economic empowerment within the context of a broader national empowerment strategy. This strategy is expressed in initiatives such as the Expanded Public Works Program, the Accelerated and Shared Growth Initiative for South Africa (ASGISA), the Integrated Human Resource Development Strategy, the Urban Renewal Program, the National Small Business Development Promotion Program, and various anti-poverty programs. In addition, in 1998, the government created the National Empowerment Fund. There is also a plethora of HRD-related legislation, such as The Promotion of Equality and Prevention of Unfair Discrimination Act, the Employment Equity Act, and the Competition Act, to support this strategy. Underpinning all is an ethos of increasing the stake of economic ownership among historically disadvantaged groups. The South African government therefore views Black economic empowerment (BEE) as an aspect of HRD to bring about a significant increase of Black ownership and control of the economy.

In line with the society's collective conscience, to achieve the goals of BEE and to give credence to one of its tenets, namely inclusivity, partnerships between public–private enterprises, the unions, and community-based organizations have been initiated. BEE therefore represents a realignment of South Africa's value system to meet the demands of global competition while simultaneously seeking to address the country's most vulnerable point: inequality.

Empowerment strategies and policies are not without their critics. Over a decade after the demise of apartheid, income inequality remains one of the highest in the world, and gender inequality is growing. As Maharaj (1999) commented, on average the income of the richest 20 percent of South African households, which are largely White, is 45 times more than the average income of the poorest 20 percent of households, which are largely Black. Furthermore, with the feminization of poverty and exceptionally high levels of gender-based violence, only a small segment of women have benefited from the empowerment strategies. In this regard, Gqola (2006) remarked that women are trapped in a "culture of femininity" and that "women's empowerment" only applies to women while they are in the official "public space," such as the workplace. Consequently, empowerment still needs to extend beyond policy and law to a "psychological liberation from patriarchy."

Conversely, South Africa's philosophical transformation has resulted in gains for many previously disadvantaged people. For example, 40 percent of national government ministers and deputy ministers are women (Mbeki, 2007), and the percentage of women in senior management in South Africa is 29 percent—compared with a global average of 22 percent. This places South Africa eighth out of the 32 countries reported in the Grant Thornton International Business Report (South Africa Business, 2007).

As an HRD strategy and philosophy, empowerment of previously disadvantaged groups will continue to be seen as an important policy consideration to address potential social conflict. For "Societies characterized by entrenched gender inequalities or racially entrenched defined wealth disparities are not likely to be socially and politically stable, particularly as economic growth can easily exacerbate these inequalities" (Alexander, undated, no page).

Conclusion

South Africa's patchwork of cultural values is rooted in the practices and beliefs of a diverse racial and ethnic mix. Although there are signs of an emerging nation with a loose web of commonly held beliefs and practices, significant cultural differences are still evident. The process of value alignment has been fostered by the post-1994 Constitution and Bill of Rights.

Despite the development of a national identity since 1994, the HRD challenges are likely to continue well into the second decade of democracy. Given the current political tensions and a slowdown in the global economy, these challenges are likely to exacerbate. Current HRD laws and policies will likely have a marginal impact on the current and future skills shortage, the increasing influx of foreign peoples from South Africa's northern borders, and the consequent increase in xenophobia and dilution of a common value system. More importantly, unless HRD addresses the current lack of capital redistribution, rising inequality, and an increase of elite formations, future social and political volatility is probable.

The combined Afrocentric and Eurocentric mix (Jeppe, 1994) implies the need for boldness in the construction and practices of HRD. In addition, South Africa needs to take a national focus. This does not have to mean that HRD is taken out of organizations. Rather, those South African organizations, or foreign organizations operating in the country, have an obligation beyond the proverbial "bottom line" to include one of sociopolitical engagement and responsibility. Furthermore, HRD practices need to be directly aligned, not just to their own HR needs, but also to those of the nation—both current and future. HRD thus becomes a matter of individual, state, and corporate responsibility in South Africa. How *ubuntu* relates to management practices and HRD in particular in Africa will only be satisfactorily addressed once the current dearth of credible research into this field has been addressed.

References

Alexander, M. *Black economic empowerment.* Retrieved on December 4, 2007 from http://www.southafrica.info/doing_business/trends/empowerment/bee. htm.

Ake, C. "The unique case of African democracy." *International Affairs,* 69(2) (1993), 239–44.

Asmal, K. *A nation at work for a better life for all.* Opening of Parliament media address by the minister of education, Cape Town, South Africa. Retrieved August 15, 2003, from http://www.gov.za/speeches/hrd.pdf.

Bangura, K. "Ubuntogogy: An African educational paradigm that transcends pedagogy, andragogy, ergonagy and heutagogy." *Journal of Third World Studies,* 22(2), (2005), 13–53.

Chaibong, H. "The cultural challenge to individualism." *Journal of Democracy,* 11(1), (2000), 127–34.

CIA. *The World Factbook: South Africa.* Retrieved on November 18, 2007 from http://www.cia.gov/library/publications/the-world-factbook/geos.

Cummings, T. G., & Worley, C. G. *Organization development and change* (8th ed). (Mason, OH: Western, 2005).

Denzin, N. K., & Lincoln, Y. S., (eds) *Handbook of qualitative research* (3rd ed.). (Thousand Oaks, CA: Sage, 2005).

Diamond, L. "Civil society and democratic consolidation: Building a culture of democracy in a new South Africa." In H. Giliomee, L. Schlemmer & S. Hauptfleisch (eds), *The Bold Experiment: South Africa's New Democracy* (Halfway House, Gauteng: Southern Book Publishers, 1994), 48–80.

Editors Inc. *SA2004–2005: South Africa at a glance.* (Greenside: Paarl Print, 2004).

Gqola, P. D. The hype of women's empowerment. November 27, 2006. Mail and Guardian Online. Retrieved on December 5, 2007 from http://mg.co.za/print-Page.aspx?area=insight/insight_comment_and_analysis/.

Hofstede, G. *Cultures and organizations: Software of the mind.* (San Francisco: McGraw Hill, 1991).

Hofstede, G. *Culture's consequences: International differences in work-related values.* (Beverly Hills, CA: Sage, 1980).

Huntington, S. "Democracy and/or economic reform?," In H. Giliomee, L. Schlemmer & S. Hauptfleisch (eds), *The Bold Experiment: South Africa's New Democracy* (Halfway House, Gauteng: Southern Book Publishers, 1994), 16–26.

Jeppe, J. "Cultural dimensions of development policy management in the new South Africa." *DPM Bulletin*, 2(2), (1994), 8–10.

Lynham, S. A., & Cunningham, P. W. "National human resource development in transitioning societies in the developing world." In S. A. Lynham, K. E. Paprock & P. W. Cunningham (eds), *National human resource development in transitioning societies in the developing world*, 116–35. *Advances in Developing Human Resources*, 8(1), (2006).

Lynham, S. A., & Cunningham, P. W. "Human resource development: The South African case." In G. N. McLean, A. M. Osman-Gani & E. Cho (eds), "Human resource development as national policy." *Advances in Developing Human Resources*, 6(3), (2004), 315–25.

Maharaj, Z. *Gender inequality and the economy: Empowering women in the new South Africa.* Keynote speech at Professional Women's league of KwaZulu Natal, August 9, 1999. Retrieved on December 5, 2007 from http://www.africa.upenn.edu/Urgent_Action/apic_82299.html.

Makgoba, M. W. *African Renaissance.* (Sandton, Gauteng: Mafube and Tafelberg publishers, 1999).

Mbeki, T. Address by the President of South Africa, Thabo Mbeki, at the Galeshewe Stadium, Kimberly, during the Women's Day Celebrations. Retrieved on December 5, 2007 from http://www.anc.org/ancdocs/history/mbeki/2007/tm0809.html.

Mbeki, T. Prologue. In M. W. Makgoba (ed.), *African renaissance.* (Sandton, Gauteng: Mafube and Tafelberg publishers, 1999), xiii–xxi.

Mbigi, L., & Maree, J. *Ubuntu: The spirit of African transformation management.* (Johannesburg, South Africa: Knowledge Resources, 1995).

Mbigi, L. "Spirit of African leadership: A comparative African perspective." *Convergence*, 3(4), (2004), 18–23.

Mbiti, J. S. *Introduction to African religion.* (Portsmouth, NH: Heinemann Educational Books, 1991).

McLagan, P. *Models for HRD practice.* (Alexandria, VA: American Society for Training and Development, 1989).

McLean, G. N., & McLean, L. "If we can't define HRD in one country, how can we define it in an international context?" *Human Resource Development International*, 4(3), (2001), 313–26.

McLean, G. N. *Organization development: Principles, processes, performance.* (San Francisco: Berrett-Koehler, 2006).

Nafukho, F. M. "Ubuntu worldview: A traditional African view of adult learning in the workplace." *Advances in Developing Human Resources*, 8(3), (2006), 408–15.

Nafukho, F. M. "Ubuntuism: An African social philosophy relevant to adult learning and workplace learning." In K. P. King & V. C. X. Wang (eds), *Comparative Adult Education around the Globe.* (Hangzhou: Zhejiang University Press, 2007), 59–83.

Nussbaum, B. "African culture and ubuntu: Reflections of a South African in America." *World Business Academy*, 17(1), (2003), 1–12.

Senge, P. *The fifth discipline: The art and practice of the learning organization.* (New York: Doubleday, 1990).

Smith, B. Building a culture of giving and "social justice philanthropy" in South Africa. Retrieved on December 5, 2007 from http://www.synergos.org/knowledge/06/cultureofgivinginsouthafrica.htm.

South Africa Business. SA above average in businesswomen's empowerment. March 09, 2007. Retrieved on December 04, 2007 from http://www.sagoodnews.co.za/benchmarking_progress/sa_above_average_in business.

Sunday Independent. Ex-activists contemplate what it means to become filthy rich. Johannesburg (3 August 1997).

Swanson, R. A. "The foundations of performance improvement and implications for practice." In Torraco, R. J. (ed.). *Advances in Developing Human Resources*, 1, (1999), 1–25.

Swanson, R. A., & Holton, E. F. *Foundations of Human Resource Development.* (San Francisco: Berrett-Koehler Publishers, 2001).

Taylor, I. *Why NEPAD and African politics don't mix.* Retrieved on December 16, 2005 from www.fpif.org.

Taylor, I. The globalization myth and the discourse of South Africa's democratic transition. Retrieved on November 18 2007 from hhtp://www2.univ-reunion.fr/~ageof/text/74c21e88-607.html.

Terreblanche, S. *A history of inequality in South Africa: 1652–2002.* (Scottsville, KwaZulu-Natal: University of Natal Press, 2002).

Turner, B. *Status.* (Milton Keynes: Open University Press, 1988).

Tutu, D. Interview report. Retrieved on October 23, 2007 from http://www.belifnet.com.story/143/story_14326_2.html.

Weffort, F. C. New democracies: Which democracies? In H. Giliomee, L. Schlemmer & S. Hauptfleisch (eds), *The Bold Experiment: South Africa's New Democracy.* (Halfway House, Gauteng: Southern Book Publishers, 1994), 27–47.

5

Empowerment: A Practice Embedded in Cultural Contexts. A Comparison between the United States and France

Sylvie Chevrier

In the most recent French encyclopedia of human resources (Allouche, 2006), which includes over 200 entries, the phrase "Human Resource Development" does not appear. HRD has not formed into a well-established and clear concept or set of practices in France. This does not mean that French companies are not concerned with training, career development, and organizational development; they simply do not actively separate these activities from human resource management at large. Human resource developers are present in organizations, but their job includes a broad scope of tasks; generally, they are responsible for managing human resources in conjunction with organizational change. Beyond some differences in the scope of practices that may be included in the function, variations across countries are mainly concerned with meaning. Cultural contexts frame the interpretations and thus the implementations of organizational practices. To illustrate this diversity, this chapter focuses on empowerment and compares its meaning and implementation in the United States and France. Empowerment inherently involves HRD practitioners because it cannot be implemented without enabling people through training, and adjusting the organization through organizational development.

In the late 1980s, empowerment rose to the fore as a popular technique for managing people in changing and competitive environments (Bowen and Lawler, 1992; Kanter, 1983; Thomas & Velthouse, 1990). This development signaled a break with the bureaucratic management techniques, inherited from Taylor, which did not appropriately fit the requirements of the new economic era. Issues such as cutthroat competition, rapid change in consumer demands as well as in production technology could not be addressed through the compliance of employees and management with command and control mechanisms predicated upon traditional management structures. The rise of unpredictability in organizations prevented a reliance on more prescriptive, traditional approaches to work. Empowerment became popular in the human resources literature as it offered a new alternative that divested information and authority to employees and allowed them to make decisions on their own within a structured set of organizational goals and values (Blanchard et al., 2000). Indeed, empowerment offers several advantages. First, it enables the use of additional employee abilities (Ripley & Ripley, 1992). Promoting employee involvement empowers workers to perform as whole, thinking human beings. It turns passive executants into an active and creative workforce. Second, empowerment makes people accountable for their choices; they assume responsibility for their decisions and associated consequences. Third, commitment and the ability to express one's creativity tend to lead to higher satisfaction for employees as self-actualization replaces alienation. However, empowerment experiences in organizations in the United States as well as abroad have shown some limits (Bernstein, 1992; Hardy & Leiba-O'Sullivan, 1998; Argyris, 1998). A central conclusion of human resource research is that empowerment should not be considered absent of its appropriate context, meaning that it should be viewed in tandem with organizational or national culture (Robert et al., 2000; Wilkinson, 1998). As with most HRD practices, empowerment is not universally effective: success depends on an acceptable fit between the cultural environment and its characteristics. This chapter seeks to explore how the meaning and the implementations of empowerment are embedded in national political cultures. Specifically, the first part details the American concept of empowerment; the second part provides an analysis of the French equivalent.

The American concept of empowerment

Before the concept of empowerment was imported into the field of management it was used extensively in social work (Adams, 2003; Simon, 1994). Empowerment is seen as an effective way to achieve social change both at micro- and macro-levels. For instance, in healthcare, it is believed that patients get better results if health educators help them to develop the knowledge, skills, and attitude to manage their own health-related decisions effectively (Feste & Anderson, 1995). Empowerment has also been used by sociologists to deal with the issues of the powerlessness of minority groups within the USA (Bobo & Gilliam, 1990). To empower citizens, especially those who have historically been excluded from positions of power, is a requirement of participatory democracy.

The American cultural roots of empowerment

The concept of empowerment fits well with the American political culture. As Kotter (1992) states, Americans have always been suspicious of power. The country itself was born out of a rebellion against central power, a fact that has been especially formative as many political processes such as checks and balances were designed to guard against the abuse of power.

D'Iribarne (2008) asserts that each society can be associated with a major peril and has developed its own way of organizing social life in such a way that seeks to avoid this most dangerous threat. In the case of the USA, this threat is the possibility of being brought under any power without the consent of the people. It is believed that any uncontrolled authority will necessarily turn into tyranny and expose people to encroachments and abuses. Control mechanisms have to be set up to protect everyone against unlimited and arbitrary power. These cultural representations concerning the ultimate threat foster the development of empowerment. Through giving power back to basic workers, empowerment thrives upon the mistrust toward strong central power; more importantly, it allows everyone to be more in control of their own destiny.

To ensure protection against abuses of power, American society developed contracts as the basis of social relationships. The social contract theory upon which the Declaration of Independence is based means that consent is necessary to establish any form of government. The business world itself has been heavily influenced by this contractual regulation. Just like customers and providers, managers and employees precisely define the expected work through definite contracts (D'Iribarne, 1989).

However, the contractual form of regulation is not exclusive. The USA was founded by religious communities, a factor that has imbued the country with a strong attachment to the community. These communities are no longer religious only; they have pervaded most social spheres. They still derive some basic characteristics from the very first communities: that is the moral role of the leader showing the right path to the members, who are expected to espouse the values and strictly observe the rules of the community (D'Iribarne, 2002). Among the communities in contemporary America are the companies. For instance, the literature about corporate culture develops, more or less explicitly, this analogy between communities and companies (Peters & Waterman, 1982). Like the former, the latter are supposed to be led by charismatic leaders who have a vision and instill values throughout the organizations. Employees are expected to adhere to the values and to work hard to turn the vision into reality. All these cultural features (mistrust toward central power, contract as the basis of social ties, and the prevalence of communities bounded by shared values) contribute toward a specific national environment within which the implementation of empowerment must take place.

Empowerment in practice

American organizations implement empowerment through different methods and tools, but empowerment of employees requires several prerequisites, which are detailed below (Blanchard et al., 2000).

Setting clear, challenging but fair and attainable goals

The department head defines jointly with each employee the expected results and the performance target. This joint goal-setting process differentiates management by objectives from empowerment because goals are created as milestones toward continuous improvement rather than end results. In addition, managers should commit to helping employees achieve goals, a process that shifts relationships more toward partnership. Furthermore, employees must be aware that their individual goals are aligned with more global organizational goals. In other words, they should feel that their work has some impact on overall organizational results.

Setting an enabling work environment

Empowerment cannot be decreed; it relies on the fulfillment of several favorable conditions. For Randolph (1995), the first and most important step in implementing empowerment is sharing information. Opening the books to employees and sharing sensitive information with them have two major positive effects. First, this raises the level of trust in the organization. Second, sharing strategic information about the company allows people to understand the challenges that the company faces and creates a sense of ownership. Employees feel part of the organization and increase their commitment. Training is another key to empowerment because it provides people with tools such as problem-solving methods or collaborative work, which are required to foster and develop autonomy. Empowerment requires knowledge and skills, which allow employees to evaluate situations and to make appropriate choices. Training may also contribute to change behaviors and attitudes. Indeed Quinn and Spreitzer (1997) assert that empowerment is a mindset, a belief about one's role in the organization; and Conger (1988) consider empowerment as a "motivational construct" (p. 473) that is an intrinsic need for self-determination and a belief in self-efficacy. Therefore, empowerment requires conditions, and specifically a psychological state that supports risk taking. Employees need social support to be held accountable and to accept the consequences of their decisions. Thus, supervisors must act like coaches and team leaders rather than traditional chiefs. As Randolph (1995) states: "team must become the hierarchy" (p. 28). In brief, an enabling environment provides employees with the necessary information, training, and support to take proper action. The role of HRD practitioners is to help managers and employees in establishing this favorable environment.

Giving authority to make decisions within a structured set of organizational values

The exercise of personal discretion takes place within the framework of the defined goals and the values of the organization (Blanchard et al., 2000). By defining what is right or wrong, the dos and dont's, values channel behaviors. Thus, the power granted to employees does not allow them to do whatever they want; rather, the decisions they should make are shaped by corporate values and the direction provided by leaders. HRD practitioners should contribute to the diffusion of this organizational culture through training and promoting employees who embody the company values.

Holding employees accountable and rewarding performance

The freedom to make choices goes with accepting responsibility for their consequences. Practically, this means employees should have regular appraisal interviews, during which the supervisor compares performance to the expectations. Accountability means that employees are held responsible for their performance, whether it be poor or outstanding. For Bowen and Lawler (1992), empowered employees should be compensated for their increased responsibility through an appropriate reward system. HRD practitioners participate in acknowledging employees' performance through career management using mechanisms such as fast-track career ladders for the highest potentials credited with exceptional performance.

Empowerment in the workplace is a matter of debate in the United States. Some say that it increases motivation and fosters both performance and wellbeing (Kanter, 1989), whereas others argue that it has failed. Some authors evoke practical limits such as the reluctance of managers to disclose information because they fear the loss of control (Quinn & Spreitzer, 1997). Others criticize empowerment's internal inconsistency. For instance, Argyris (1998) reproaches empowerment in the workplace, noting that it may act as pseudo-empowerment and a kind of double bind. According to him, empowerment turns into the motto: "do your own thing—the way we tell you"! Wilkinson (1998) adds that, in many cases, empowerment aims to secure an enhanced contribution from the employee to the organization through attitudinal shaping although there is no actual change in work or organizational structure. This highlights a need to increase organizational development and to align structures and processes with the new distribution of power, which is a critical function of human resource developers.

Beyond its strengths and weaknesses, empowerment practices make sense within American culture. First, the setting of goals, which constitutes the first step of empowerment, and the accountability of the empowered worker fit with the contractual approach of supervisor–employee relationships. When signing a performance contract, the supervisor acts as an internal customer and specifies the expectations. The employee acts like a provider, is committed to the contract, and is responsible for the delivered work. Second, corporate culture frames individual behavior and orients decisions, which is consistent with the view of organizations as communities. From such a standpoint, the leader of a company may shape corporate values and expect employees to adhere to them. The socialization process legitimately helps orient actions. Third, the emphasis on training people and giving them appropriate resources falls in line with the strong national focus on personal development and initiatives as a means to better chart one's own destiny.

In sum, empowerment draws upon explicit delegation through contracts, the representation of the organization as a community, and the belief that each individual should have the ability to take control of their life, all of which are part of the American cultural environment.

The French vision of empowerment

The cultural dimension of social practices remains invisible until these practices are implemented in another context. The specificity of the French version of empowerment is best evidenced through cross-cultural interactions.

French managers in trouble

Several studies report that French managers have difficulty when they begin to work in international environments. Franck (2000), who has studied several acquisitions of American companies by French corporations, concluded that until the 1990s most managers suffered from several shortcomings:

- they failed to communicate a clear vision of the future for the acquired company;
- they avoided making quick decisions about the personnel that they would keep or dismiss and thus usually lost the most competent;
- they did not engage in participative management to identify potential synergies clearly;
- they failed to create clear objectives and detailed procedures of control to monitor the new subsidiary;
- they failed in developing common cultures and values.

These difficulties are illustrated in a case study presented by Dupriez & Simons (2000), which highlights the misunderstandings between a French top manager and the American manager whom he recruited to develop the business of the newly created subsidiary of a French company. In this case, the American manager reproached the French supervisor for setting unclear objectives, betraying an initial commitment to organize a business trip to France, letting him work alone without help, and so on.

Grégoire (2007) draws upon several testimonies to report that Chinese, Russian, and Indian employees feel confounded by their French managers. Some of these employees find their managers give them too much autonomy, and many even report feeling stressed when they are asked about their opinion. As an example, an Indian who worked in Paris declared that superiors let him take many initiatives, they delegated a lot. They just entrusted a task without saying how to do it. At the same time, other workers who experienced a French chief said their managers were authoritarian and readily imposed their views.

Reciprocally, empirical studies show that French workers in American companies do not feel comfortable. They acknowledge that they loosely apply organizational procedures and they often complain about the time lost in fastidious reporting, the irrelevance of rough figures taken out of their context, or the inadequacy of procedures as they relate to the local environment (Louy-Moise, 1998).

This characterization may lead some to the hasty, incorrect conclusion that French managers and employees lack professionalism and hold in contempt the most basic rules of effective management and HRD. However, a closer look at these cross-cultural incidents reveals the specificity of French practices. At its core, French management and HRD relies on a different interpretation of empowerment, which is rooted in French culture.

Empowerment revisited through French culture

Research on French business culture has shown that management practices, as well as broader social interactions, are underlain by the so-called logics of honor (D'Iribarne, 1989). The fundamental threat, at the heart of French culture, is the loss of one's honor by subjecting oneself to brutal force or financial incentives. The ultimate weakness is to give up when faced with overwhelming power or to act to secure personal benefits against the broader public interest. Therefore, French myths glorify brave actions of resistance and stigmatize those who give up the fight to gain personal advantages. French culture places a strong focus on adhering to the responsibilities of one's place in society, whatever that rank may be. If ever someone does not fulfill what their rank commands, they demean themselves and often suffer a loss of honor.

As far as organizations are concerned, doing one's job correctly means to be up to one's status and profession. The image of the profession rules behavior, and each worker personally judges what is required to be equal to their own perceived professional duty. By tradition, a profession confers rights and obligations that each professional internalizes through socialization processes. Referring to the requirements of the profession avoids having to obey the orders of superiors. Employees claim to do what the work situation commands rather than to execute slavishly what the chief asks for. Thus, whereas American workers feel committed by the details of their job description and performance contracts, French workers are committed through a more subjective conscientiousness that involves a sense of duty associated with their profession and status. What should be done in a work situation is interpreted through these two strong references in French organizations.

In such a cultural context, empowerment of employees involves the following practices, which differ significantly from those that prevail in the United States.

Setting a broad mission

Instead of definite goals, French managers give general directions for actions: in other words, a mission. They suppose that workers, as good professionals, will know what to do. They will be free to define appropriate actions according to changing circumstances. A broad mission is seen as more effective than precise goals and procedures, which may become inadequate when the situation evolves, as is often the case in the business world. It allows more initiatives and flexibility. Expectations remain implicit; they are supposedly known and shared by both parts, while respect for professional workers prevents a more "taking them by the hand" approach in which the provision of detailed instruction may be construed as humiliating.

Developing competences

To ensure that empowered people will be able to make appropriate decisions, the manager should develop their competences. The abundant French literature about managing competences precisely defines competences as the ability to make adequate choices when faced with always new and unpredictable situations (Dejoux, 2001; Le Boterf, 1994; Zarifian, 1999). For Zarifian (2005), competences refer both to professional skills and strategic skills; it means that the initiatives are taken because employees have developed their own view of the strategy of the company and are able to take relevant action. The authors also insist on the fact that competences can only be assessed at work, far from assessment centers that rely on in-basket tests and artificial work situations. Competences correspond to the ability to mobilize whatever information or expertise is needed to react to particular situations such as customer complaints or technical breakdowns. Developing competences can be seen as the French version of training, fitting the French cultural context. Indeed training is focused on providing the employee with whatever is needed to adjust to the job and on socializing into the firm's way of acting and doing things. Developing competence requires the adoption of the necessary strategy and skills to allow each employee to devise adequate solutions, no matter what the work situation. It means that employees should exert their discretion to find out appropriate actions; it sets them free from slavishly implementing rigid procedures and gives them room to decide what should be done based on their own professional conscientiousness. In such a perspective, coaching may be welcome if it provides an avenue to enlighten one's judgment in difficult professional situations, but it often raises mistrust as it may also present a pressure toward behavior conformity. Thus human resource developers may focus on competence development, which in turn is focused on professional skills.

Controlling loosely

Too close a control may appear as meddling in the subordinate's business and would be perceived as a lack of trust. If the mission is appropriated and if workers are skilled enough, the sense of duty is supposed to be sufficient to get the job done correctly. Thus a significant degree of autonomy should be granted and control should not be too insistent (D'Iribarne, 1989). The appropriate distance between manager and employees cannot be prescribed: each manager has to find it out for each employee.

However, if the French concept of empowerment, inspired by the "logics of honor," leads to giving subordinates a broad frame and vast margins of action, the very same "logics of honor" may also result in deep interferences with the work of others. When, for any reason, a manager does not trust an employee and does not consider the subordinate to be a good professional, he may do the job in the place of that employee. Indeed the manager's sense of duty makes him feel responsible for delivering what is expected from the department. If he feels that a subordinate is not able to make an appropriate contribution, he may stand for the defaulting worker and take on his own responsibility. Such common reactions prove that culture frames meanings and influences practices, but it does not determine them unilaterally. One given culture is compatible with a variety of behaviors, but all behaviors do not take a positive meaning in this culture. Thus French culture gives a special flavor to empowerment and induces specific empowerment practices (personal responsibility is not delegated through clear-cut contracts but appropriated through increased professionalism), but at the same time it also fosters extreme centralism when trust is bankrupt.

The French version of empowerment has both advantages and drawbacks. One of its strengths is that, when one deals with "professionals" (*gens de métier*), a strict control is not necessary, a sense of duty ensures results. As D'Iribarne (1989) stated, French managers need not necessarily motivate their team; they just should not de-motivate it. This implies that human resource developers provide each worker with opportunities to develop the professional skills that are required for both doing their job and having a clear status in the organization. Another central consideration involves intricate and unpredicted situations where workers feel they have to find a way, even if they cannot rely on procedures or clear directions. This fosters creativity and innovation. The other side of the coin is that vast delegation may create coordination problems. When each employee does what they think is best according to their own professional view of the problem, all the personal actions may not be consistent, which can lead to long negotiations and conflicts. Problems are supposed to be solved through personal arrangements; however, these arrangements rely on the quality of the relationship between the people involved, which is not necessarily good. Eventually, as said before, the French version of empowerment cannot be exported easily. When faced with employees from other countries, French managers may not be positively perceived, with workers often blaming them for not giving detailed enough directions, leaving ambiguity, and others blaming them for being too assertive and authoritarian.

To further our comparison about empowerment and to extend it to the main issues of HRD, we propose Table 5.1 as a summation of the two cultural systems.

Table 5.1   American and French cultures and HRD practices

	United States	**France**
Fundamental threat	• Abusive authority, which prevents employees from controlling their destiny	• Submission to brutal force or mean personal benefit
Social regulation patterns	• Contractual regulations • Willingly joining communities federated by values that a leader embodies	• Behaviors are guided by rights and obligations associated with status • Eventual conflicts are solved by interpersonal arrangements
Main objectives of HRD	• To ensure that employees have the required skills and information to fulfill their objectives • To support sharing and adherence to organizational values	• To contribute to define a meaningful mission for each employee • To increase professionalism
Training	• Giving employees knowledge and skills they need to perform their job • Socialization into the corporate culture	• Developing competences to enable employees to exert their own judgment on relevant actions • Fostering the appropriation processes of organizational strategic issues
Career management	• Career paths are closely related to work performance	• Careers are related to status (granted by a degree) and professional skills
Organizational development	• Functional alignment of organizational structures and processes to the strategy	• Organizational change is interpreted in terms of power relationships and its impacts on the profession's status

Conclusion

Empowerment, like most HRD buzzwords, is not a universal concept. The first difficulty in transferring it across cultures starts with translation. For instance, the French language has no exact semantic equivalent for empowerment. *Délégation de responsabilité* is the translation for empowerment as delegation of authority (that is, a juridical transfer of responsibility), but there is no literal translation for empowerment as enabling people.[1] No word conveys the meaning of sharing power, resources, and putting people in conditions to take action.

HRD and, more generally, management practices were born in definite cultural contexts and make sense in these contexts (D'Iribarne, 2000). If they are to be exported, they should be adapted. For example, as shown in this chapter, we may assert that making personnel take responsibility for individual actions is part of effective HRD all over the world, but the appropriate way to empower people varies across cultures. In each place, HRD practitioners should ask what being responsible means locally. Every interpretation offers potential advantages and limitations and human resource developers should be aware of these nuances to adapt their practices in cross-cultural contexts better.

Notes

1. The *Oxford English Dictionary* defines the verb "empower" as "to enable."

References

Adams, R. *Social work and empowerment*. (New York: Palgrave Macmillan, 2003).

Allouche, J. *Encyclopédie des ressources humaines*. (2nd ed.) (Paris: Vuibert, 2006).

Argyris, C. "Empowerment: The emperor's new clothes." *Harvard Business Review*, 76 (3) (1998) 98–105.

Bernstein, A. J. "Why empowerment programs often fail." *Executive excellence*, 15 (2) (1992) 161–84.

Blanchard, K. Carlos, J. P., & Randolph, A. *Empowerment takes more than a minute*. (Benett Koehler Publishers, 2000).

Bobo, L., & Gilliam, F. D. "Race, sociopolitical participation and black empowerment." *The American Political Science Review*, 84 (2) (1990) 377–93.

Bowen, D. E., & Lawler, E. "The empowerment of service workers: What, why, how and when." *Sloan management review*, 33 (3) (1992) 31–39.

Conger, J. A. "The empowerment process: Integrating theory and practice." *Academy of management review*, 13 (3) (1988) 471-82.

Dejoux, C. *Les compétences au coeur de l'entreprise*. (Paris: Editions d'Organisation, 2001).

D'Iribarne, Ph. *La logique de l'honneur*. (Paris: Seuil, 1989).

D'Iribarne, Ph. "Management et cultures politiques." *Revue Française de Gestion,* n 128. Mar–Apr–May (2000) 70–75.

D'Iribarne, Ph. "La légitimité de l'entreprise comme acteur éthique aux Etats-Unis et en France." *Revue Française de Gestion,* n 140, Sept–Oct. (2002) 23–39.

D'Iribarne, Ph. *Cultures. Penser la diversité du monde.* (Paris: Editions du Seuil, 2008).

Dupriez, P., & Simons, S. *La résistance culturelle.* (Bruxelles: de Boeck, 2000).

Feste, C., & Anderson, R. M. "Empowerment: From philosophy to practice." *Patient Education Counseling,* 26 (1–3) (1995) 139–44.

Franck, G. "Acquisitions américaines: le management français en question." *Revue Française de Gestion,* Nov–Dec. (2000) 136–44.

Grégoire, B. "Petit manuel de management interculturel." *Newzy,* June 2007.

Hardy, C., & Leiba-O'Sullivan, S. "The power behind empowerment: Implications for research and practice." *Human relations,* 51 (4) (1998) 451–83.

Kanter, R. M. *The change masters.* (New York: Simon & Schuster, 1983).

Kanter, R. M. "The new managerial work." *Harvard Business Review,* 84 (5) (1989) 85–92.

Kotter, J. P. "Power, dependence and effective management." In J. J. Gabarro, *Managing People and Organizations* (Boston: Harvard Business School Publications) (1992) 33–49.

Le Boterf, G. *De la compétence: essai sur un attracteur étrange.* (Paris, Editions d'Organisation, 1994).

Louy-Moise, A. C. *Management interculturel: Gestion des différences de cultures et aspects franco-américains contemporains,* Ph.D. thesis, Université de Metz, 1998.

Peters, T., & Waterman, R. *In search of Excellence: Lessons from America's best run Companies.* (Warner Books, 1982).

Quinn, R. E., & Spreitzer, G. M. "The road to empowerment: Seven questions every leader should consider." *Organizational Dynamics,* Autumn (1997), 37–49.

Randolph, A. "Navigating the journey to empowerment." *Organizational Dynamics* (1995) 19–32.

Ripley, R. E., & Ripley, M. J. "Empowerment, the Cornerstone of Quality: Empowering Management in Innovative Organizations in the 1990s." *Management Decision,* 30 (4) (1992).

Robert, C., Probst, T. M., Martochio, J. J., Drasgow, F., & Lawler, J. J. "Empowerment and continuous improvement in the United States, Mexico, Poland and India: Predicting fit on the basis of the dimensions of power distance and individualism." *Journal of Applied Psychology,* 85 (5) (2000) 643–58.

Simon, B. L. *The empowerment tradition in American social work: A history.* (Columbia University Press, 1994).

Thomas, K., & Velthouse, B. "Cognitive elements of empowerment." *Academy of Management Review,* 15 (4) (1990) 666–81.

Wilkinson, A. "Empowerment: Theory and practice." *Personnel Review,* 27 (1998) 40–56.

Zarifian, P. *Objectif competence.* (Paris: Editions Liaisons, 1999).

Zarifian, P. *Compétences et stratégies d'entreprise.* (Paris: Editions Liaisons, 2005).

6

Human Resource Development in Austria: A Cultural Perspective of Management Development

Astrid Reichel, Wolfgang Mayrhofer, and Katharina Chudzikowski

Cultural sensitivity is of central importance when dealing with human resource practices such as recruitment, selection, or development. There is voluminous literature devoted to cultural values at a general level. These studies are based on surveying attitudes or values of respondents in large samples from different countries, and they provide general frameworks for understanding cultures as a whole. Not surprisingly, these models lack specificity when it comes to predicting and understanding specific HRD practices (Klarsfeld et al., 2004). Only a few writers (Budhwar et al., 1998; Segalla et al., 2001a, b; Sparrow, 1996) apply a more cultural lens to work-related issues. Thus, the application of this cultural perspective to the development of human resource practices is limited. Especially scarce is empirical research that addresses different cultural approaches to the training and development of managers in organizations. In these very few studies (Derr, 1987; Klarsfeld et al., 2004; Ramirez et al., 2005a) that actually deal with management development (MD) from a cultural perspective, Austria is never considered. This chapter describes MD in Austria and offers explanations derived from its cultural values and institutional environment.

From a global perspective, one might ask why it is important to analyze a country as small as Austria in detail. For centuries Austria has been one of the ruling powers and biggest countries in Europe. After a very rough start to the twentieth century, with defeats in World Wars I and II, it emerged as a prosperous country. Today, owing to shared borders and a common history with many former communist countries, it has a strategically important role acting as a mediator between East and West. Immediately after the fall of the Iron Curtain, Austria and many other European companies began their investment from bases in Vienna. Austria became a door to the East, as it provided an extremely stable political and economic environment and expertise for expansions. Austria, despite its small size, plays an important role internationally.

MD is an important topic to focus on because training and development in general (Gmür et al., 2005) and management development in particular (Mabey et al., 2005a, b) have an impact on organizational performance. Investment in the development of an organization's managers, especially, pays off because of their exposed position within the company. On the one hand, they make strategic decisions for the company like expansion; on the other, they manage employees. Their behavior toward their subordinates heavily influences employees' work performance. However, following a contextual approach, the development of human resources is culture-sensitive. Depending on the cultural and institutional context, different measures of MD are effective.

Stressing the relevance of contextual factors for training and development in general, and management development in particular, is one central tenet of this chapter, which focuses on one country that, despite its small size, is in an important position within Europe. Although not explicitly dealing with multinational enterprises, it still gives international companies expanding to Austria or expanding to Eastern Europe through Austria, valuable information about cultural, institutional environment, and preferred ways of MD. From the explanations given one might also be able to derive rules for other countries that are similar to Austria.

This chapter starts with some basic information on Austria, focusing on its history. We then provide a description of the political environment and industrial relations that are directly relevant for HRD. The next part focuses on Austrian culture, differentiating between societal and leadership culture. In this section, literature on cultural values on a general level is used to describe the cultural setting in which MD in Austria takes place. Then MD in Austria is described based on empirical results. Lastly we use the information on Austria's history, institutional environment, and culture to explain the mechanisms that lead to our empirical illustration.

Austria—country information

Basic information about Austria and its history

Austria is located in central Europe, has an area of about 84,000 km, and shares borders with eight countries. In 2008 the population was estimated to be 8.21 million (CIA Factbook, 2008a), with more than

1.6 million people living in Austria's capital, Vienna. Almost 13 percent of people living in Austria are foreign born (in the US: 11 percent) (Statistik Austria, 2008b).

Austria has a very long history. Settlement dates back 200,000 years, the first record showing the name Austria to 996 AD. From the thirteenth century until World War I, Austria's history was tied to its ruling dynasty, the Habsburgs. They created a huge empire in which at times "the sun never set." In 1918, the Habsburg empire and the monarchy were dissolved, and Austria was proclaimed a republic of about today's size (Johnson, 1989; Szabo et al., 2007). This so-called first republic was affected by unstable economic and political conditions, which in 1933 lead to a short civil war between Socialists and Christian Democrats. In 1934 National Socialists assassinated Austria's dictator and Hitler marched into Austria, incorporating its territory into the German Reich (Szabo et al., 2007). After the victory of the Allied Powers in 1945, Austria was revived as the Second Republic. In 1955, the Austrian State Treaty was signed, re-establishing Austria as a sovereign nation (Putzger, 1969). In 1995 Austria joined the European Union (EU), later signed the Schengen Agreement, and in 2002 introduced the Euro as the official currency (Szabo et al., 2007).

Austria is a federal democratic republic embracing nine provinces. The national government consists of a president, a cabinet headed by a chancellor and a bicameral legislature, the National Council with 183 representatives, and the Federal Council, representing the provinces (Szabo et al., 2007).

Austria is a well-developed market economy closely tied to other EU economies (especially Germany and Eastern Europe) and is characterized by a large service, sound industrial and small, but highly productive, agricultural sector. The standard of living is very high. Gross domestic product per capita (purchasing power parity) ranks fourth in the EU (CIA Factbook, 2008b). The comprehensive social-welfare system produces the fifth highest social spending in the EU (Sozialausgaben in Europa, 2008).

Political environment and industrial relations

Since World War II, domestic politics in Austria have been largely dominated by coalition governments between the two largest parties, the Social Democrats (SPÖ) and the conservative People's Party (ÖVP) (Johnson, 1989). Currently, both parties again form a so-called grand coalition government, with the Liberal Party (FPÖ), the Greens, and the Alliance for the Future of Austria (BZÖ) in opposition.

Through the so-called system of *Proporz*, the dominance of the two large parties was, and to a certain extent still is, transferred to the Austria's institutional and economic environment. *Proporz* was established in the aftermath of the experience of the civil war. It refers to a system in which the Social Democrats and the People's Party create equal proportions of power when staffing positions in the public sector and nationalized industry. Thus, many of the economic leaders in Austria are still directly or indirectly linked to and dependent on the political system.

Consensus politics has been one of the hallmarks of Austrian working life since World War II. One of its most important manifestations is the social partnership model. This model is a system of economic and social cooperation at the national level between top representatives of employers (Chamber of Commerce), employees (Chamber of Labour), farmers (Chamber of Agriculture), the government, and unions. The *Österreichischer Gewerkschaftsbund* (ÖGB) is the largest Austrian trade union and holds the monopoly for collective bargaining. Membership is voluntary and has been declining over the years, but it still reached about 35 percent of the working population in 2005 (Statistik Austria, 2008a). The general idea of the social partnership system is that the basic aims of economic and social policy can be better realized through cooperation between key actors than by confrontation (Arbeiterkammer, 1996). Accordingly, between 1993 and 2002, the average number of working days lost due to strikes in Austria was one day per year (EU average: 64; Statistics UK, 2008).

Compared with most European countries, the Austrian system of employee relations and labor law is highly regulated. For example, co-determination in large organizations is legally mandated and employee representatives are part of the supervisory board (Hammer, 1996). Also, membership of employers and employees to their respective collective bodies, the Chambers of Commerce, Labor, and Agriculture, is obligatory, which is crucial for the functioning of the social partnership. The social partnership model, seemingly in contrast to the highly regulated environment, is informal and based on voluntary participation of the respective groups. So, the social partnership system also manifests the importance of informal arrangements in Austria. Because Austrians have lived in a well-organized bureaucracy that has regulated all aspects of life since the time of the Habsburgs, they have typically sought informal arrangements that although not against the law, offer a way around these considerable regulations.

Austrian culture

When mentioning the word culture in the context of Austria, music, literature, and fine arts are usually associated. To get an impression of Austrian culture in the sense of shared values, we mainly draw on the results from the Globe study as arguably the most recent, comprehensive, and management-relevant cultural study of major countries in the world (for detailed information see Chhokar et al. (2007) and House et al. (2004)). In Austria the sample consisted of 169 middle managers from the food processing and service sectors. In the questionnaire the managers were asked "about their perceptions of 'as is' practices and on 'should be' values pertaining to nine societal and organizational dimensions defined within the Globe project" (Szabo et al., 2002, p. 62). Scales ranged from one (high agreement) to seven (high disagreement). Apart from these questions on societal culture, the same managers were also asked to evaluate characteristics and behaviors contributing to or inhibiting outstanding leadership in order to gather information on leadership culture. The scale ranged from one (indicating that a certain characteristic or behavior greatly inhibits outstanding leadership) to seven (behavior or characteristic greatly attributes to outstanding leadership). In line with the number of countries included in the study, rankings ranged from 1 for the country with the highest to 61 for the country with the lowest score in the respective dimension (Szabo et al., 2002).

Societal culture

The Globe study uses nine dimensions to describe a society's culture: future orientation, uncertainty avoidance, assertiveness, performance orientation, institutional collectivism, In-group collectivism, power distance, gender egalitarianism, and human orientation. Each dimension is further differentiated into perceptions ("as is") and values ("should be"). In both cases scores range from one to seven and the highest possible rank is 61. Below the nine dimensions are employed to portray Austrian culture. The respective scores (Szabo et al., 2007) are specified in brackets.

Austria is very future-oriented compared with other countries. It ranks number six with an even higher score for "should be" (5.11) than for "as is" (4.46). However, compared with other countries the value of future orientation is rather low (rank 50).

Uncertainty avoidance reflects the desire to control one's environment, to have high levels of standardization, regulations, laws, and bureaucracy. Ranking sixth, Austria shows a very high degree of perceived uncertainty avoidance (5.16). Manifestations are the many bureaucratic hurdles that entrepreneurs face during the start-up of their company, the highly regulated employer–employee relationship, and the high saving rate. The current perceptions, however, are in sharp contrast to what is ideal (3.66). Austrian managers think that uncertainty avoidance should be low (rank 57) and opt for less regulation.

Assertiveness as "should be" has a low value (2.81) and only ranks 60, in line with the consensus orientation found in the systems of *Proporz* and Social Partnership. Given the prevailing value of not being too assertive, managers perceive the situation "as is" (4.62) as very assertive already. Here, Austria ranks number six.

Austria is rather performance oriented (4.44). It ranks number 14 with an even higher "should be" value (6.10). This is reflected in the fact that incentive systems and performance-based pay are popular in Austrian organizations, especially for managers. However, performance orientation also includes the extent to which a society rewards innovation. If one takes entrepreneurship as an indicator, for performance orientation Austria's high value is somewhat surprising (House et al., 2004). Although Austria has a history of major inventions in the past, such as Josef Ressl's marine propeller, current bureaucracy is a major barrier for entrepreneurs. Entrepreneurship is not as highly valued in Austria as in other countries.

Austria is seen as more collectivist than individualistic country. In particular, institutional collectivism, or the degree to which societal, organizational, and institutional practices encourage and reward collective distribution of resources and collective action, scores relatively high "as is" (4.30) and as "should be" (4.73). In-group collectivism ranks about average. One manifestation of collectivism in Austria is the traditionally long-lasting organizational affiliation to the same organization. Although younger people change workplaces more often than their parents, a CV with too many changes in employers is still looked on with a certain degree of suspicion.

Power distance results are divergent and somewhat puzzling in different studies. Although the Globe data suggest a lower medium score in both perception (4.95) and values (2.44) ranking number 44 and 48 respectively, Trompenaars as well as Hofstede report very low power distance (Hofstede, 1980; Trompenaars, 1993). One can find examples supporting both results easily. On the one hand, participation in decision-making through co-determination in organizations and the social partnership model is deeply rooted in Austrian culture (Trompenaars, 1993). On the other hand, status symbols such as the use of academic and profession-related titles (*"Frau Doktor"* or *"Herr Hofrat"*) when addressing people are still important. In civil service, titles in recognition of seniority are still awarded (Szabo et al., 2007).

Gender egalitarianism is highly valued (4.83) and rank number 18 compared to other countries. Following a long-standing political agenda as well as EU law, equal opportunities for women are a hot political topic. However, the relation between men and women "as is" (3.09) still is characterized by inequality: Austria ranks number 45 in gender egalitarianism, which is in line with the high level of masculinity found by Hofstede (1993). These results find their reflection in small proportions of women in top management, full professorship positions, or in parliament, as well as few fathers taking advantage of paternity leave (Szabo et al., 2007).

Humane orientation, the degree to which being fair, caring, and kind is rewarded, is an important value for Austrians. The "should be" score (5.76) ranks number four. Humane orientation "as is" (3.72) is not seen as living up to these values (rank 46). The example of the treatment of migrants reflects this. Austria is one of the European countries with the highest percentages of immigrants, especially from former Yugoslavia. Yet, the large numbers of migrants evoke increasing uneasiness and political tensions.

Leadership culture

Respondents to the Globe study ranked 112 leadership items on a scale ranging from one ("attribute greatly inhibits a person from being an outstanding leader") to 7 ("attribute contributes greatly to a person being an outstanding leader"). These items are combined into 21 first-order subscales. Related to these subscales, the most favorable leadership characteristics for Austrian managers are integrity, being non-autocratic, inspirational, participative, performance oriented, a team integrator, visionary, and decisive. Some of these characteristics, such as team integration or decisiveness, can be taught to a certain extent, whereas others such as integrity, vision, and being inspirational have trait-like character. Combining the first-order subscales into second-order leadership scales, being charismatic (subscales: visionary, inspirational self-sacrificial, integrity, decisive, performance oriented), participative, and team oriented are found to be most characteristic for outstanding leaders, whereas self-protective leadership (subscales: self-centred, status-conscious, conflict inducer, face-saver, procedural) is frowned upon. This holds true compared with other styles as well as with other countries (rank 49) (Szabo et al., 2007). Most outstanding is the participative leadership style. Although charismatic leadership is favored more universally (Austria ranks number 12), the high scores on participative leadership set Austria (together with Germany and Switzerland) apart (Szabo et al., 2002). This finding is in line with the low power distance scores and is consistent among several studies (Maczynski et al., 1994; Reber et al., 2000).

Management development in Austria—empirical illustrations

Samples

The empirical view of MD in Austria is based on a project funded by the European Commission, which led to the foundation of the European Management Development Partnership (EMDP) aimed at researching management training and development systems in Europe. Coming equally from three sectors, manufacturing/production, logistics/transportation, and service, 100 companies in each of eight European countries (Austria, Denmark, France, Germany, Ireland, Norway, Romania, Spain, and the UK) were surveyed between 2002 and 2004 (Ramirez et al., 2005b). Multinational enterprises were explicitly excluded. The Austrian EMDP sample is compared with Denmark, France, Germany, Norway, Spain, and the UK. In addition, findings from 270 Austrian companies from the 2004 survey round of Cranet, an international HRD research network, were used (Brewster et al., 2004).

Results

Who?

Asking who takes responsibility for training and development reveals that the degree to which companies feel responsible for MD is quite homogenous in Europe. Yet, Austria ranks last in organizational responsibility for MD. To the extent to which training and development are provided, the Cranet study reveals that HRD in cooperation with line management is responsible for training and development. In most companies, line management takes the lead, particularly in defining the training needs.

To whom?

In Austria, internal recruitment is highly preferred to external recruitment, and most managers come from inside the organization. Cranet data reveal that the amount of training and development heavily depends on the respective hierarchical position: the higher the hierarchical position, the more training (Erten-Buch et al., 2006).

When?

The question of "when" addresses the time perspective of managers and their development. Austria's managers can expect to stay in their company for a long time because organizations very strongly expect to retain their managers for more than five years. Compared with the other European countries, Austria by far ranks first. The focus on long-term development of their managers, however, is not that strong. Austria is only located in the middle of the countries used for comparison.

How?

"How" deals with the general approach to MD: systematic or ad hoc. MD systems (Mabey et al., 2005a) suggest a deliberate and often consultative rather than an ad hoc approach to the way managers are developed. Mabey and Gooderham (2005) name the following systems as effective: (1) the appraisal of development needs (Mabey et al., 1993); (2) career planning and development (Baruch et al., 1997); (3) intensive development for high-potential managers (Thomson et al., 2001); and (4) mechanisms for monitoring and evaluating these activities (Hillage et al., 1996). In Austria, managers' career steps are well planned. With a value significantly higher than all the other countries evaluated, Austria ranks first in career planning. Also, a clear written MD policy is widespread in Austrian companies. It shows by far the highest value of all the countries used for comparison. Almost a third of all Austrian companies have a written MD policy. Having a system discussing the development needs of managers during appraisal interviews is very common in Austrian companies. Again, Austria reaches a much higher value than the other six European countries. For over 80 percent of the firms, development needs are a fixed part of appraisal talks. The extent to which MD is evaluated systematically and to which succession planning for managers is used both reach values slightly above the average of the seven countries. Intensive development for high-potential employees, in contrast, is not very common in Austrian firms, which rank second to last in comparison with the other countries. Altogether, however, the variables of the construct MD systems suggest a very systematic approach to MD.

How important?

This question informs the significance given to MD by HR managers and by line managers, a perspective that is often neglected (Legge, 1995; Truss, 2001). Austria's HR managers ascribe medium priority to MD. Line managers as recipients of MD regard MD as even less important than HR managers. Both values are about average compared with the other six countries. The degree to which MD is linked to the business strategy provides another indication for the importance of MD. Austria ranks second behind Norway, indicating that it is quite important for Austrian companies. However, using the mean number of days in training per year as another proxy for importance, we find that on average an Austrian manager only spends 5.80 days (standard deviation 4.13) a year on training. This is the smallest number compared with the other six countries. Combining all these indicators, MD only seems to be of medium importance to Austrian HR and line managers.

What?

The question of "what" relates to the specific training methods used for MD. Internal programs are used very frequently for MD in Austrian companies, whereas external courses are used to a lesser extent. With job rotation, movement within a company is more popular than external job rotation. Compared with other countries, Austria is about average in all four training methods. Mentoring and gaining academic qualifications, such as an MBA, are training methods used only to a small extent. Austria ranks second to last and last, respectively, for these compared with the other European countries in the study.

Why?

"Why" addresses the intended outcome of training. The answers build on basic assumptions about whether effective managers are born or made; are abilities or training more important. In Austria, natural abilities are considered most important for managers. The Austrian (and Norwegian) values are significantly higher than in the other five countries. The importance of formal job training is similar across countries, with Austria ranking in the middle. "Other formal training," not immediately relevant for the job, is considered unimportant and Austria ranks last. In contrast, company training and experience are seen as very important, outranking five of the other six countries. Management education is only considered as moderately important. Training targeted to specific tasks is seen as being equally important to the development of manager's personal potential. In both cases Austria ranks first compared with the other European countries. The extent to which current MD is able to develop managers that meet the needs of the organization reaches a medium value. Line managers evaluate the effectiveness of MD a little lower than HR managers.

Austrian management development in context

In section three we made use of large-scale cultural-value-based studies (particularly Hofstede, 1980, 1993; House et al., 2004; Trompenaars, 1993) to describe Austrian culture. As we already explained in the introduction, studies of this type, although very valuable for providing general frameworks for understanding cultures, lack specificity when it comes to predicting and understanding specific HRD practices (Klarsfeld et al., 2004). Consequently, some writers apply a more cultural lens to work-related issues. Examples include d'Iribarne (1989) and Hofstede (2001), who show that perceptions of management practice and management practices themselves differ widely between countries. Others argue that there are differences between countries in relation to HR practices such as selection and development (Laurent, 1986), perceptions of career management (Derr et al., 1989), hiring strategies (Segalla et al., 2001b), and layoffs (Segalla et al., 2001a). Sparrow (1996) found that national values such as individualism–collectivism influence the social cues that managers use to decode information in their psychological contract. Budhwar et al. (1998) note the influence of culture on socialization of managers into British and Indian organizations and the role of social relationships and political connections on selection, promotion, and transfer decisions.

However, with a few notable exceptions, very little research on management development from a cultural perspective has been done. Derr (1987) analyzes potential identification and development in major European corporations including subsidiaries of Japanese multinational enterprises. He finds four types of management development model: the Anglo-Dutch or Managed development approach, the Germanic or functional approach, the Latin or elite political approach, and the Japanese or elite cohort approach (Derr, 1987). Klarsfeld et al. (2004) build hypotheses differentiating between these approaches and find most of them supported in their empirical study. Ramirez et al. (2005a) identify clusters of management training and development among six European countries. The remainder of this chapter focuses on core characteristics of MD in Austria, hitherto neglected in these studies, and cultural influences.

Internal orientation

The most significant feature of MD in Austria is its internal perspective. Austrian companies prefer to recruit their managers internally and plan to retain managers for a long time. Organizational decision-makers are convinced that management training should be provided by the organization. The preferred methods of MD are internal ones. Experience and development within the company are seen as very beneficial for effective management. In contrast, extensive, external programs such as MBAs are only rarely used. On the one hand, this is the result of a strong tendency in Austria to take control of MD activities and tightly link them to organizational tasks. On the other hand, this is due to a lack of tradition in lifelong learning. Only within the past decade has continuing professional training like MBAs became popular. It is likely that the number of MBAs will increase in forthcoming years.

Austria is a rather collectivist country. Collectivist societies are traditionally associated with long-lasting employer–employee relationships (Szabo et al., 2007). In-group collectivism, especially, stresses loyalty and commitment to organizations. Thus, many Austrians are very loyal toward their employers. The general intention to stay with the current company for a long time is further increased by the prevalent high degree of uncertainty avoidance. New jobs normally are connected to a much higher level of uncertainty. Owing to the preference for internal recruitment, employees have a very good chance of actually climbing the organizational ladder. Thus, the perspective of a future management position further enhances the probability of staying in the same company.

Organizational authorities also value loyal employees who contribute to an internal orientation. Traditionally, loyalty was rewarded by the emperor and, until today, is recognized in civil service with titles according to seniority. Status and signs of power, despite low power distance, still remain important in Austria (Trixier, 1994) and often come with internal progress more or less irrespective of actual performance, particularly in the public sector. In a similar vein, labor law makes it difficult to make employees redundant and until recently heavily favored company loyalty through special regulations for severance payment.

Being part of an in-group is important in Austria, too. The importance of tight-knit, elite groups dealing with politics, the economy, and the arts, with joint roots in student's councils or youth organizations of the political parties, has already been described. Being an insider and of "the same breed" is important at all levels of society. Internal training activities support internal networking, the forming of such in-groups and loyalty.

Medium priority

In contrast to the very high importance of development within organizations, MD is only assigned medium priority. This is reflected in the level of importance line managers assign to development and the average responsibility taken by the company for their managers' development. Also, the time frame of MD is short compared with the amount of time companies want managers to stay with them. Again, these numbers are not extremely low per se, but low given the long-term, inward orientation of Austrian MD. Another sign of medium importance is the small number of days a manager spends in training. In addition, a strong belief in natural abilities and formal job training for effective management, and a few special measures for high-potential employees, reflect the basic conviction that people can only develop to a limited extent anyway. This scepticism toward change and the flexibility of people in general is a main reason for the medium priority of development and training. Largely because of Austria's high degree of uncertainty avoidance, change is not welcomed without critical consideration. One example is the hypercritical stance regarding innovations.

The very rare use of "fast track" programs is in line with the high relational orientation in Austria. Austrian culture is low in power distance, high in collectivism, and values as "should be" for gender egalitarianism and humane orientation are high as well. Participative leadership is highly preferred. The institutional environment is dominated by attempts to find consensus and compromise. In such a culture of balance and equality, special treatment of some managers does not fit easily. Some managers would even try not to stand out of the crowd because they feel uncomfortable in exposed roles. On the other hand, there are clear differences between the amount of training and development for managers as opposed to non-managers. Within the group of managers, an egalitarian culture exists; however, there are marked hierarchical differences compared with workers or administrative staff.

Most managers are satisfied with the medium level of initiative companies take in terms of their employees' training. Because organizations accept some responsibility for MD and training is offered to a certain extent, organizational goodwill is shown and signals "we are taking care of you." Austrians expect authorities to look after them because there is a strong belief in only limited possibilities of the individual. This is reflected in the high collectivism. Thus, Austria is a *Schicksalsgesellschaft* (society of fate) as opposed to a *Willensgesellschaft* (society of will). This is deeply rooted in history because Austrians are used to a strong, organized elite (for a long time this was the aristocracy) creating an environment allowing a good life for most of the population; however, this was often at the cost of individual freedom and initiative. Today the welfare state takes care of its citizens when they are old, sick, disabled, or unemployed. It also provides education for everyone, almost for free.

Systematic

Austrian MD is systematic. The typical career steps of managers are very well planned and so is succession. Most companies have a development policy that is usually derived from the business strategy. Although most heads of HR are heavily involved in strategy formulation, actual training needs are usually defined by line managers using information gained from periodical appraisal interviews. Then line management turn to the HR department which, in cooperation with line management, provide the employees with the training they need.

Most organizations systematically evaluate MD. Most commonly, participants' immediate reactions after training are used for MD evaluation. This is often accompanied by the assessment of behavior modification. In addition, measuring change in organizational performance and learning effects is used for MD evaluation in two-thirds and one-half of the companies, respectively.

The high future orientation of Austria is reflected in the long-term planning of future career steps and in succession planning. Collectives with a high desire for uncertainty avoidance tend to have high levels of standardization, regulation, law, and bureaucracy. The highly regulated employer–employee relationship supports this desire at the national level, but also within organizations systematic approaches are preferred. However, the "should be" rank for uncertainty avoidance suggests that many people would actually value fewer regulations. Austrians confronted with a lot of bureaucracy usually try to find a way around these regulations, applying considerable creativity. Often with the help of one's social network or by authorities turning a blind eye, so-called *österreichische Lösungen* (Austrian solutions), are developed. They are compromises that offer ways around the regulations and match actual needs without invalidating the general rule. Employees with and without management responsibilities might perceive policies developed by the board of management as regulations imposed on them. Discussing training needs primarily with their line managers with merely secondary involvement of the HR department could be a seen as a way around these regulations.

Conclusion

Overall, quite a clear picture emerges about the cultural role of HRD in Austria. Core cultural factors, shaped by the unique history of Austria, provide the backdrop for HRD systems and activities used in Austrian organizations. They include uncertainty avoidance, a strong consensus orientation in line with low assertiveness and participative leadership, a collectivistic stance, and a markedly humane orientation. Together, they contribute to shaping HRD in Austria. To be sure, "hard" institutional elements such as legal regulations, especially in labor law, demographics, and economic developments, do play a significant role. However, the importance of the respective cultural factors as an underlying current can hardly be overestimated. In particular, cultural factors contribute to the internal orientation of organizations when establishing HRD systems and processes, the importance given to HRD within organizations, and the systematic and sometimes even bureaucratic approach toward HRD.

Beyond the current picture, the importance of cultural factors for HRD raises several issues for HRD practice as well as research. For HRD practice, culture-boundedness becomes an issue because of the culturally diverse workforce in many parts of Austria. For example, nearly one-third of the population in Vienna is of non-Austrian heritage. Many of these individuals have a cultural socialization not restricted to the "Austrian way of life." This has consequences for the adequacy of HRD systems and processes, regarding the distribution of responsibility for HRD measures between individuals and the organization, the type of training or gender issues in HRD, as well as for general concepts of career and personal development used in HRD. Cultural influences also become relevant in the light of the changing economic situation in Europe. Austria, at the interface of the long-time and the new members of the EU, is one of the largest foreign investors, often not only in relative but also in absolute terms, in many of the new and potential member countries. Many small- and medium-sized Austrian companies start or enlarge their cross-border business activities, thus becoming "multi-national." Inevitably, this leads to culture-related management issues. HRD in these Austrian organizations is heavily affected by these developments as it has to take into account multicultural environments when setting up systems and processes.

Theoretically, there is an increasing need to conceptualize cultural aspects and link them to HRD issues. Beyond that, the link between the cultural and institutional context, conceptually often kept apart, but particular relevant for HRD, should be strengthened. Likewise, country- and culture-comparative HRD research is of essence. The increasing importance of a multicultural and multinational context within which HRD takes place requires a better understanding of different models of HRD in a variety of contextual settings.

References

Arbeiterkammer (Bundeskammer für Arbeiter und Angestellte). The Chamber of Labour—an Austrian Solution. http://www.ak-salzburg.at/pictures/d55/Mandarin.pdf. (1996, accessed May 20, 2008).

Baruch, Y., & Peiperl, M. A. "High Flyers: Glorious Past, Gloomy Present, Any Future?" *Career Development International*, 2 (7) (1997) 354–58.

Brewster, C., Mayrhofer, W., & Morley, M. (eds) *Human Resource Management in Europe. Evidence of Convergence?* (Oxford: Elsevier/Butterworth-Heinemann, 2004).

Budhwar, P., & Sparrow, P. R. "National Factors Determining Indian and British HRM Practices: An Empirical Study." *Management International Review*, 38 (2) (1998) 105–21.

Chhokar, J. S., Brodbeck F. C., & House R. J. (eds) *Culture and Leadership across the World*. Edited by Brief, A. P., Walsh, J. P., & Rynes, S. L. *Lea's Organization And Management Series*. (New Jersey: Lawrence Erlbaum Associates, Inc., 2007).

CIA Factbook (Central Intelligency Agency, The World Factbook). Austria. https://www.cia.gov/library/publications/the-world-factbook/geos/au.html. (2008a, accessed May 3, 2008).

CIA Factbook (Central Intelligency Agency, The World Factbook). Country Rank order 2004. https://www.cia.gov/library/publications/the-world-factbook/rankorder/2004rank.html. (2008b, accessed May 3, 2008).

d'Iribarne, P. *La Logique De L'honneur*. (Paris: Le Seuil, 1989).

Derr, C. B. "Managing High Potentials in Europe: Some Cross Cultural Findings." *European Management Journal*, 5 (2) (1987) 72–79.

Derr, C. B., & Laurent, A. "The Internal and External Career: A Theoretical and Cross-Cultural Perspective." In Arthur, M. B., Lawrence, B. S., & Hall D. T. T., *The Handbook of Career Theory*. (New York: Cambridge University Press, 1989) 454–71.

Erten-Buch, C., Mayrhofer, W., Seebacher, U., & Strunk, G. *Personalmanagement Und Führungskräfteentwicklung*. (Wien: Linde Verlag, 2006).

Gmür, M., & Schwerdt, B. "Der Beitrag Des Personalmanagements Zum Unternehmenserfolg. Eine Metaanalyse Nach 20 Jahren Erfolgsfaktorenforsch ung." *Zeitschrift für Personalforschung*, 19 (3) (2005) 221–51.

Hammer, T. H. "Industrial Democracy." In Warner, M. *International Encyclopedia of Business and Management*. (London: Routledge, 1996).

Hillage, J., & Moralee, J. *The Return on Investors*. (Brighton: Institute of Manpower Studies 1996).

Hofstede, G. *Culture's Consequences: International Differences in Work-Related Values*. (Beverly Hills: Sage, 1980).

Hofstede, G. (1993) "International Conflict and Synergy in Europe." In Hickson, D. *Management in Western Europe: Society, Culture and Organizations in Twelve European Countries*. (New York: De Gruyter) 1–8.

Hofstede, G. *Culture's Consequences. Comparing Values, Behaviours, Institutions, and Organizations across Nations*. 2nd ed. (London: Sage, 2001).

House, R. J., Hanges, P. J., Javidan, M., Dorfman, P. W., & Gupta, V. (eds) *Culture, Leadership, and Organizations: The Globe Study of 62 Societies*. (Thousand Oaks, CA: Sage, 2004).

Johnson, L. *Introducing Austria: A Short History*. (Riverside: Ariadne Press, 1989).

Klarsfeld, A., & Mabey, C. "Management Development in Europe: Do National Models Persist?" *European Management Journal*, 22 (6) (2004) 649–58.

Laurent, A. "The Cross-Cultural Puzzle of International Human Resource Management." *Human Resource Management*, 25 (1) (1986) 91–102.

Legge, K. *Human Resource Management: Rhetorics and Realities*. (Basingstoke: Macmillan Press Ltd., 1995).

Mabey, C., & Gooderham, P. N. "The Impact of Management Development on Perceptions of Organizational Performance in European Firms." *European Management Review*, 2, (2005a) 131–42.

Mabey, C., & Iles, P. "The Strategic Integration of Assessment and Development Practices: Succession Planning and New Manager Development." *Human Resource Management Journal*, 3 (4) (1993) 16–34.

Mabey, C., & Ramirez, M. "Does Management Development Improve Organizational Productivity? A Six-Country Analysis of European Firms." *International Journal of Human Resources*, 16 (7) (2005b) 1067–82.

Maczynski, J., Jago, A. G., Reber, G., & Böhmisch, W. "Culture and Leadership Styles: A Comparison of Polish, Austrian and U.S. Managers." *Polish psychological Bulletin*, 25 (4) (1994) 303–15.

Putzger, F. W. *Historischer Weltatlas*. (Bielefeld: Velhagen & Klasing, 1969).

Ramirez, M., & Mabey, C. "A Labour Market Perspective on Management Training and Development in Europe." *International Journal of Human Resource Management*, 16 (3) (2005a) 291–310.

Ramirez, M., & Mabey, C. "Management Training and Development in Europe." *International Journal of Human Resource Management*, 16 (3) (2005b) 291–310.

Reber, G., Jago, A. G., Auer-Rizzi, W., & Szabo, E. "Führungsstile in Sieben Ländern Europas—Ein Interkultureller Vergleich." In Regnet, E. & Hofmann, L. M. *Personalmanagement in Europa*. (Göttingen: Verlag für angewandte Psychologie, 2000) 154–73.

Segalla, M., Jacobs-Belschak, G., & Muller, C. "Cultural Influences on Employee Termination Decisions: Firing the Good, Average or the Old." *European Management Journal*, 19 (1) (2001a) 58–71.

Segalla, M., Sauquet, A., & Turati, C. "Symbolic Vs Functional Recruitment: Cultural Influences on Employee Recruitment Policy." *European Management Journal*, 19 (1) (2001b) 32–41.

Sparrow, P. R. "Transitions in the Psychological Contract: Some Evidence from the Banking Sector." *Human Resource Management Journal*, 6 (4) (1996) 75–92.

Statistics UK. Labor Disputes 2003. http://www.statistics.gov.uk/articles/labour_market_trends/labour_disputes_2003.pdf. (accessed May 20 2008).

Statistik Austria. 2008a. Arbeitsmarktstatistik Schnellbericht 2005. http://www.statistik.at/web_de/static/arbeitsmarktstatistik_jahresergebnisse_2005_schnellbericht_023574.pdf. (accessed May 20 2008).

Statistik Austria. 2008b. Bevölkerung. http://www.statistik.at/web_de/statistiken/bevoelkerung/index.html. (accessed May 20 2008).

Szabo, E., Brodbeck, F. C., Den Hartog, D. N., Reber, G., Weibler, J., & Wunderer, R. "The Germanic Europe Cluster: Where Employees Have a Voice." *Journal of World Business*, 37 (1) (2002) 55–68.

Szabo, E., & Reber, G. "Culture and Leadership in Austria." In Chhokar, J. S., Brodbeck, F. C., & House, R. J. *Culture And Leadership across the World.* (New Jersey: Lawrence Erlbaum Associates, Inc., 2007) 109–46.

Thomson, A., Mabey, C., Storey, J., Gray, C., & Iles, P. *Changing Patterns of Management Development.* (Oxford: Blackwell, 2001).

Trixier, M. "Management and Communication Styles in Europe: Can They Be Compared and Matched?" *Employee Relations*, 16 (1) (1994) 8–26.

Trompenaars, F. *Riding the Waves of Culture: Understanding Cultural Diversity in Business.* (San Francisco: Jossey-Bass, 1993).

Truss, C. "Complexities and Controversies in Linking HRM with Organizational Outcomes." *Journal of Management Studies*, 38 (8) (2001) 1121–49.

WKO (Wirtschaftskammer Österreich). Sozialausgaben in Europa. http://www.wko.at/statistik/eu/europa-sozialausgaben.pdf. (accessed May 3 2008).

7

Malleability in Spain: The Influence of US Human Resource Development Models

Javier Quintanilla, Mª Jesús Belizón, Lourdes Susaeta, and Rocío Sánchez-Mangas

This chapter describes the evolution of HR practices in Spain, particularly the strategic management of HR. Prompted by recent political, economic, and social change, we have seen considerable and growing interest in a more holistic and systematic view of developing individuals and their organizations. In this chapter, note that we refer to HR or HRM, which are terms used in the Spanish business community. However, our focus is on the developmental side of the HR function. Key to understanding Spain's recent transformation is the cultural malleability of its business system (Dickman, 1999; Ferner et al., 2001; Muller-Camen et al., 2001; Quintanilla, 1998). The concept of malleability is synonymous with the notion of flexibility; that is, Spanish managers are very open to new and sophisticated "best practices" from afar.

Why are the Spanish malleable? Perhaps it is because there is a historical void in the development of large business traditions and systems. The notion of "big business" is new to Spain, where commerce has until recent times been in the hands of small entrepreneurs and highly regulated by the government. Management styles in Spain have traditionally not generated a well-defined business model, as is the case of other countries, such as Germany, France, and the USA. A weak business tradition and the fundamental asymmetry of the relationship between Spain and its foreign investors have motivated Spanish companies to follow a model of HRD used by foreign multinationals operating in Spain; primarily in large firms who are headquartered in the USA. Spanish multinational corporations (MNCs) and large firms have now developed HR departments and have incorporated HR managers into their boards. The HR function, previously limited to technical aspects such as payroll or recruitment, is now changing to more of a strategic and developmental function which incorporates activities such as succession planning, managerial coaching, and performance management (Quintanilla et al., 2004). In general, HR practices in Spain continue to exist in a stage of infancy, especially in medium- and small-sized companies. However, in larger Spanish companies, "American" policies have been well accepted by Spanish managers, especially those that work in a multinational context.

In this chapter, we begin with a brief history of the economic and business development that explains the influence of foreign operations on Spanish companies. Next, we illustrate how the influence of American investment has contributed to a developmental approach to HR in Spanish companies. In this section, we include data from a case study of Spanish subsidiaries of US MNCs. The final section links the culture of Spanish "malleability" to implications for the developmental side of HR.

Historical evolution of economic development in Spain

Institutional arrangements typically reflect key formative events in the evolution of the nation state, such as the manner and timing of industrialization, the process of class formation, the development of political representation, and the role of government (Crouch, 1993). Such is the case in Spain (Quintanilla, 1998). The Spanish economy and the industrial infrastructure remained underdeveloped until the late 1950s, when contacts with the International Monetary Fund and the goodwill of the USA transformed and modernized the country. Since the late 1950s, foreign investment has played an increasingly crucial role in Spain's economic modernization. The "economic miracle" of the 1960s was based on tourism, the export of surplus labor to other countries, and high foreign direct investment. The latter was promoted by the complete removal of barriers on trade coupled with government incentives to attract multinational companies in capital-intensive industries (Campa & Guillen, 1999). The democratic reforms of the late 1970s consolidated the country's modernization of its economic structures, which led to a rapid change in the profile of firms (García Delgado, 1995).

Since 1980, Spain's industrial fabric has experienced dramatic change due to increased liberalization and privatization. The suppression of the restrictions on foreign capital persuaded many MNCs to set up in Spain between 1970 and 1980. Spain became attractive to foreign investors not merely because it offered opportunities for participating in a rapidly expanding domestic market, but also because it served as a base for further export and trade with EU countries. By the 1990s, the state's main role was to create a favorable climate for private-sector investment. Spain became a member of the EU in 1986, and in 1999 it was integrated into NATO. As in most European countries, the Spanish service sector grew steadily from the middle of the twentieth century. It now accounts for two-thirds of the country's GDP, of which tourism accounts for approximately 10 percent. Trade with EU Member States accounts for 70 percent of Spanish foreign trade. Spanish investment in Latin America is significant, and for many of these countries Spain is the largest foreign investor.

The development of large, privately owned corporations has thus historically been constrained by late industrialization, difficulty in obtaining financial support, and the lack of real competition caused by decades of isolation and the small size of the business market (Banco de España, 2002; Guillen, 2006). Given these circumstances, three trends in Spanish ownership are noteworthy. First, despite the spectacular growth of the private sector in recent decades, the presence of public enterprise remained significant until the state's privatization program began in 1996. Since then, there has been a steady increase in domestic ownership which has strengthened the holdings of former state-owned firms and industrial banks (Aguilera, 2005). Secondly, firms quoted on the Spanish stock market possess a different owner-ship structure thanks to an increase in market consolidation during the 1990s. Third, the deregulation of the banking system in the 1960s led to fewer restrictions on foreign capital and persuaded many MNCs to set up in Spain between 1970 and 1990. After 1986, this pattern was enhanced by a more open financial system yielding a current economy that is now internationalized.

According to a recent United Nations Conference on Trade and Development (UNCTAD) report, *World Investment Report 2007*, Spain is one of the main recipients of foreign direct investment, rank-ing fourteenth in the world (out of around 220) and seventh in the European Union (out of 27 member states, 2007), with foreign capital as one of its most important driving forces for economic development. MNCs dominate major sectors of production, and the proportion of industrial output in the hands of foreign enterprises is exceptionally high at around 42 percent. The United States is Spain's sixth largest trading partner, and since the mid-1990s trade with the USA has been approximately 5 percent of Spain's total trade. However, despite Spain's recent entry into and outlay from other EU member nations, investment from the USA continued to grow and now represents 20 percent of foreign direct investment (Ministerio de Economía y Hacienda, 2006[1]).

Given this high level of exposure, in particular, to American investment, and the malleability of the Spanish business system, we argue that Spanish companies are uniquely vulnerable and perhaps overly encouraged, to follow (or even copycat) US developmental approaches to HR.

Spanish labor market features

In the 32 years since Franco's death, Spain has gone from being one of Europe's most centralized countries to one of its most decentralized. However, the decentralization process led to more interventionism in business matters.[2] The Spanish case is an excellent example of a country and a business system that, despite undergoing radical modernization in a very short span of time is still highly influenced by its institutional past. With the arrival of democracy in 1975, a new highly legalistic (Martinez, 1998) Industrial Relations (IR) system based on modern and democratic work ethics was born (Hamann, 1998) which left the labor market highly regulated. Stringent rules govern areas such as redundancy and employment contracts. As a result, redundancy payments, indemnities paid to employees who have been made redundant or laid off, have traditionally been the highest in Europe. We now have a dual market structure with a protected core workforce of strong and stable permanent employees, which operates alongside a secondary and precarious sector of employees on temporary contracts with far fewer rights and little job security (Pérez Díaz & Rodríguez, 1995). Spanish employers rely heavily on numerical flexibility as a means of job creation and job maintenance, by using temporary contracts as the main form of hiring blue-collar workers. A study by Amuedo-Dorantes (2000) shows that temporary employment is non-transitional and involuntary, which means that such employees can be hired and fired at will. This kind of policy is attractive to employers when profits are low, but can backfire because of its lack of employee commitment.

According to the Organisation for Economic Co-operation and Development (OECD), Spain has the highest percentage of temporary employees in the EU. In recent years, however, temporary contracts have been restricted to temporary work, or to ease workload peaks, and the dual structure of the labor market is very slowly disappearing. MNCs also have a high proportion of permanent contracts and use these temporary contracts very infrequently. This characteristic is particularly true of American MNCs, whose developmental philosophy of HR is seen as a kind of "welfare capitalism" designed to encourage employee loyalty through greater permanency and worker security.

Two more constraints placed on the Spanish labor market are the failure of vocational training systems and the legally regulated nature of job and skill classifications (Köhler & Woodard, 1997; Pérez Díaz & Rodríguez, 1995). Given the emphasis on traditional university education, the training infrastructure, as well as a culture of training, is underdeveloped in Spain compared with America and European countries, such as the UK (Martin Artiles, 1999). However, recent changes due to more relaxed labor legislation, the influence of multinational company practices, and the spread of collective bargaining at firm and industry levels, are leading to new, more fluid models of work organization.

In recent years, many managers in Spanish subsidiaries of US MNCs have had an American-style business education, either in Spanish business schools or in the USA itself (Quintanilla, 2001). The American style strongly favors a high degree of suppleness in new labor policies and ease in adaptation to the general business praxis of US headquarters. The malleability and openness of the Spanish system complements and brings it in some ways closer to the deregulated Anglo-Saxon model. Given the strong influx of foreign capital, Spain thus functions as a sort of crossroads on the international "trade routes" for management styles and practices, where Spanish subsidiaries of multinational companies are potentially in a position to be innovative because they often fulfill a strategic function for the corporation as a whole (Ferner et al., 2001). That is, certain subsidiaries play a key role and are very profitable, allowing them a certain leverage and power in allocating critical resources.

The approach of Spanish companies toward our labor market is a critical issue. The intensity of legally sanctioned workforce councils or unions has paralleled other European countries. This tendency in Spain reflects high government regulation, as found in other parts of Europe. Severe regulation has shaped the nature of redundancy and the way in which employment contracts are created. Despite the dual market structure, the use of temporary and other precarious contracts have been decreased by more relaxed labor legislation and the influence of multinational firms, which has impacted both the configuration of HR practices in Spain, and the training of managers in Spanish business schools.

Evolution of the HR function in Spain

As in other European countries, the introduction of modern HR
developmental practices began slowly during the 1980s and is acquir-
ing more importance in larger firms. However, the scope of HRD
practice, implementation, and subsequent results has been patchy
and even contradictory (Baruel, 1996; Pérez Díaz & Rodríguez, 1995).
Sophisticated personnel management and work organization designs
are still scarce and, in many cases, only permanent workers tend to
benefit from them. However, smaller employers have also been looking
to HR practices "as a way of pre-empting strong and independent labor
representation" (Martinez Lucio, 1999, p. 447).

As the chairman of a carmaker declared:

> I think that there is a great transformation in human resources
> because of our desire to manage with better results and with the
> collaboration of employees. In the last years, several sociological
> ingredients have appeared, such as the fact that people feel that they
> are part of the company . . . These issues were of little concern fifteen
> years ago. However, there increasing importance has been revealed
> through the HR function.
>
> (Quintanilla et al., 2004)

At the same time, social and psychological needs begin to be considered
relevant factors in Spain as organizations strive to become more flexible
and adaptive,

> that is, the management of people is based on concepts such as
> culturally responsive leadership, communication, and employee
> involvement.
>
> (Valle, 1995: 8)

These concepts allude to critical processes, which enhance people's
professional development as well as a firm's performance.

A general manager of an important Spanish firm stated a few years ago:

> yes, there is no doubt that I have seen an evolution in the HR func-
> tion in recent years. HR is now more strategic and more professional.
> It is perceived as a change agent with the expectation that HR will
> help create new and more dynamic organizational cultures through
> training designed to motivate and enhance employee satisfaction
> and commitment.

Although the HR function in Spain moved beyond a tool to deal with personnel administration, it was not initially integrated into the activities to which businesses are dedicated. Thus, the work and inter-departmental relationships of Spanish HR managers are changing as a result of emerging demands derived from their new roles in Spanish companies. HR managers are slowly becoming strategic partners who play a critical role in development, cultural transmission, and corporative strategy configuration and implementation within organizations. In short, the Spanish HR function has begun to evolve with the aim of aligning its competences with organizational strategy.

Empirical study of US MNCs in Spain

In this section, we highlight the principal results of a case study conducted in Spain that examined the transfer of HR policies of US MNCs operating within the country. The following is based on detailed case studies of the Spanish subsidiaries of nine US MNCs. We interviewed 58 managers from several sectors, over a period of two and a half years. The interviews were semi-structured and all were recorded and transcribed. These data were supplemented with information from corporate web pages, company and subsidiary annual reports, other internal documents from the firms, and secondary data sources such as press articles.

The case-study results confirm a portrait of centralization and standardization of international HR practices. This aspect has been reinforced in recent years by the use of IT systems such as People Soft or SAP HR, which compile HR information worldwide. Nevertheless, the way in which US MNCs exert control over their subsidiaries depends on a wide array of variables including: the way the company has been established, the subsidiary's profitability, the weight and prestige of a subsidiary's managers internationally, their ability to contribute in key areas such as R&D, and their ability to bargain politically.

This situation was strongly manifested in an IT Spanish affiliate, which was one of the pillars of the group. It had the greatest market share of any of the company's subsidiaries, was the most profitable subsidiary, and was ranked third in terms of number of employees and partners. The senior manager of the Spanish subsidiary stated that:

> Although the multinational operates under certain directives until 2012, the Spanish subsidiary has come up with its own plan until 2010 compatible with the world strategy but adapted to how things are done in Spain.

In this case the perfect adaptation to the idiosyncrasies of the Spanish context was possible thanks largely to the "resource power" of the subsidiary and its strategic role in the company as a whole. Changes in the degree of centralization or decentralization could provoke tensions as they hold the potential to restructure power relations among different corporate interest groups and distort the resources available to them (Ferner et al., 2004).

We argue that the findings are in accordance with the wider body of literature, which shows that US companies tend to standardize their HR policies internationally. Our research also highlights how, and to what extent, some of the American HR practices transferred by corporate headquarters are shaped by the influence of Spanish business systems. Some of the main policies pertinent to this chapter that we analyzed in this study were recruitment and development, mechanisms to transmit culture, and workforce diversity.

Recruitment and Development

The US labor market is characterized by its reliance on the external labor market, with high mobility of managers and non-managerial staff between companies (Dore, 1989; Evans et al., 1989). Nevertheless, large US companies have traditionally hired employees in "internal labor markets" (ILMs), preferring to hire and train their own employees rather than those taken from the external labor market (Handy et al., 1988). This largely reflects the preference of firms for the strategy of "making" rather than buying managers. This is evident in our case study of MNCs, as illustrated by strong policies promoting the early recruitment of the managerial cohort, extensive succession planning, the systematic development of "high potential" managers, and ample opportunity for both functional and international rotation (Almond et al., 2003). US MNCs have commonly adopted a hybrid approach based on a mix of internal and external labor market strategies. These MNCs try to acculturate foreign employees into the work values of the parent organizational culture (Selmer & de Leon, 2002). This mode of operation reflects anti-unionism in the US business system (Marginson & Guglielmo, 2006).

The practice of "hire and fire," common among some US MNCs, accompanied by high employee turnover, is difficult to implement in Spain as a result of the restrictions imposed by labor legislation and, in some occupations, labor scarcity and mainly the frontal opposition of unions. Hence most of the US MNCs studied took particular care to attract good candidates and to offer them professional careers within the company.

In most of the case-study subsidiaries, the HR department pre-ferred to recruit university graduates directly, to avoid influences from employees working in other companies and to better preserve and transmit the corporate culture. Subsidiaries deployed an array of tools focusing on the graduate entry-level positions and on train-ing programs and development paths within the company for high-potential employees. Practically all of these systems were developed at a corporate headquarters and adapted at local level. Other MNCs often employed the parent company's international development programs as a retention tool for their best candidates. The HR manager of busi-ness services explained:

> [W]e hire candidates directly from the universities. Afterwards, we have a pre-established development process that includes mostly professional experiences in different departments within the firm. In some ways this is helping us to identify and retain the best ones by offering them an attractive international career.

Several companies emphasized geographical mobility in career devel-opment and succession planning. For instance, in an engineering com-pany the HR manager said:

> In the USA mobility and international experience is highly valued, but the situation is more complex for the Spanish. Here the culture is different and geographical mobility is difficult. If you have ten people identified as high potentials probably only two will reply that they are willing to accept international assignments, but no more. And those two will demand greater perks and rewards [laughs].

This problem of mobility in Spain occurs because there is no culture of domestic, let alone international, mobility. This derives from a tradition of home ownership (as opposed to renting) and a strong attachment to family and locality. This cultural tradition reflects a Spanish concern for a "work–life balance" and a desire to remain socially integrated in one's family and community.

Practically all the subsidiaries in our research developed internal labor market approaches through the intensive use of corporate systems. However, the financial difficulties and restructuring suffered by most of the firms allowed for a more relaxed implementation of these corporate initiatives, and the case-study companies aimed both to "make" and to "buy" managerial talent.

Culture transmission

Among the different Spanish subsidiaries analyzed, we observed a high degree of importance given to an employee's understanding as well as his or her sense of agreement with dominant work beliefs and values. This trend represents a significant difference between these companies and most Spanish-owned firms. In reference to the culture, employees in these subsidiaries had difficulty articulating key beliefs but they "felt" that their parent company had its own cultural identity. As a manager pointed out:

> We are not provided with any manual of company culture, I cannot describe it, although definitely you can feel it, you "just know" that it exists.

Furthermore, we found many different mechanisms for transmitting corporate culture including: values and mission statements, international staff exchanges, HR corporate guidelines, training programs, storytelling, and expatriate rotation (Mendenhall & Oddou, 1985; Schein, 2004).

Although Spain has been characterized by the "malleability" of its business system and for being very receptive to the adoption of "American management style" practices, the concept of malleability does not mean total compliance. We did find local cultural barriers that impeded the direct transfer of an "American style" to the Spanish context. A comment from an HR manager illustrates the issue:

> [O]ur corporate culture came directly from the US HQ. The main idea was that the business divisions were in charge of implementing those values and guidelines at a local level but, in practice, HQ decided everything beforehand. As a result, a number of business units showed some reluctance towards something they considered done without any sensitivity. They disagreed with the idea of total compliance.

Moreover, competitive and financial pressures test the real strength and soundness of such corporate culture arrangements. Over the past decade, for example, some subsidiaries in our study encountered major market transformation, owing to increasingly fierce international competition. Consequently, the prospect of being a prosperous and continuously expanding company could not be maintained. This led to conflict between employees and their representatives, especially concerning the company's traditional welfare capitalist (Jacoby, 1997) culture: "The market has changed, and the company has to change as well. However, the company is made of people, and these people have been living in the same corporate culture for a long period of time, for them it is difficult to change. So, how can you simultaneously balance both messages?" asked the HR manager of a chemical company.

In another company, regarded as a welfare capitalist firm, the organizational principles and values imprinted by its founder still remain visible. To handle market pressures and avoid a severe downsizing, the company undertook a different approach by reducing the pay of the worldwide workforce and by cutting managerial salaries by an even higher percentage. Despite these difficult changes, employees and their unions were willing to accept these measures. Such employee adaptation reflects the role of communication in explaining the need for these measures as means to avoid greater downsizing.

Thus, the recruitment and development process played a major role in maintaining the culture of the company. The company has since tried to recruit inexperienced candidates who embodied its beliefs: "People join the company with some clear personal values, which are further developed. Selection and promotion policies allow us to perpetuate the company culture," according to the development manager at a prestigious pharmaceutical company. The company has a code of conduct that iterates an open-door policy and the importance of communication, as well as stressing the importance of this corporate culture in noting that, "The first and foremost responsibility of each employee around the world at the firm is to abide by the company's policies on business conduct."

The introduction of distinctive corporate cultures by US MNCs clearly had different consequences in Spanish subsidiaries and in the management of their HR practices. Nonetheless, the sophistication with which the issue of culture was handled in all the subsidiaries represented a notable difference compared with local companies.

Workforce diversity

The term "workforce diversity" usually means the provision of the same opportunities for all employees. The USA has placed special emphasis on this term given its history of social and racial heterogeneity, which originated in slavery and mass immigration. A legislative program of civil rights legislation from the 1960s created a framework of equal employment opportunity. More recently, a broader business agenda of "diversity" has developed and reflects corporate unease in tapping into scarce labor talent owing to the need to serve diverse customer bases (Ferner et al., 2005). All the Spanish subsidiaries that introduced diversity programs in their business agenda did so as a result of corporate policy.

Although diversity is still seen in Spain as a "gender equality" issue, recent developments such as the rising phenomenon of large-scale immigration and the increasing emphasis on company policies and legislative initiatives for achieving "work—life balance" are deeply affecting the Spanish social and business environments which, in turn, highly impact female managers. Our research shows that these policies have only recently found an audience in Spain. Although analyzed subsidiaries had already established some diversity policies, they were seldom put into operation in the same way as at corporate headquarters.

Again, we found sociocultural differences between the USA and Spain. In one of the first companies to introduce "diversity" policies in Spain, the importance that its headquarters paid to this issue greatly influenced the Spanish subsidiary, which was characterized by a progressive approach and described as "tolerance" of employees' differences in terms of gender, culture, race, religion, and economic circumstances. However, in other Spanish subsidiaries, HR managers were skeptical about the compulsory introduction of diversity policy, but they also recognized the importance that it might have in the future. The following is an example:

> Perhaps diversity has no real sense in Spain today. However, in the near future, we will have to face the same problems that the US has now, and we'll understand the reasons for the diversity "campaigns." As a subsidiary, we must understand the societal context of the diversity policies, which is why companies have been pushed to adopt those measures.
>
> (Recruiting manager)

The following quotation, from the HR manager at a consultancy company, is a good example of the difficulties in a direct implementation of American corporate diversity policies:

> Recruiting departments of US MNCs have to hire some percentage of black people, Hispanics, and other immigrant populations. The same is happening here. We are supposed to hire people who belong to different social classes. This is an impossible target to reach mainly due to the lack of a high level of education of this people. In HQ they

must be aware that in Spain there is a problem due to the cultural disparity which exists between the different regions. Top HQ executives do not realize this until they come to Spain. With regards to women, there is no real discrimination because of gender, but the corporate goals for female partners are far from being accomplished.

On the question of whether the subsidiary had room to make decisions without explicit authorization from headquarters in hiring women, this same manager answered that headquarters asked for statistical information while failing to understand that the subsidiary's objective was to hire engineers, and a lower percentage of women chose to study this subject. When then asked by headquarters why they did not therefore hire students of law or history to fill these vacancies, the subsidiary resisted on the grounds that such students would not meet its needs. Headquarters also made enquiries about the recruitment of gays and lesbians. The manager responded that it was not permissible under the Spanish constitution to ask people about such issues.

At an important IT subsidiary, there was a requirement to employ the same proportion of men and women in the Spanish subsidiary. However, they were not subject to pressures from headquarters to hire more women because they already had a good proportion of women (34 percent). This could also be seen as a preemptive adaptation by the subsidiary in order to avoid future pressures from headquarters. It also felt that the appointment of a young woman as the new Spanish CEO, which surprised many employees, had been done for "implicit diversity reasons" and had sent a direct message to all subsidiaries abroad.

Conclusions

As previously stated, the analysis has demonstrated the relevance of the relationship between Spanish institutional and cultural systems and related effects on Spanish companies. The Spanish case is particularly specific because of the Spanish business context, which has been growing slower than in other European countries owing to isolation caused by the Franco dictatorship. Moreover, direct foreign investment in Spain and the profile of Spanish companies (paternalism under family ownership) have served to slow the pace of HR development practices in Spain, especially in the case medium- and small-sized companies.

We have shown that the Spanish labor market presents a set of features that exert a specific influence on companies. It was characterized by rigid regulation until the late 1980s and the deregulation of the

Spanish labor market in the 1990s; it is still characterized by a complex web of legal regulation that constrains the ability of companies to introduce new practices. Despite this, the HR function in Spain is experiencing a quick evolution, shifting from a previously technical function to a more strategic one. Another factor behind this evolution is the movement of large-sized companies, which are currently increasing their HR functions and range of developed HR practices. This increase has been influenced heavily by foreign companies operating in Spain.

Finally, we have reported the general findings of one research study to understand better what can be learned about the evolution of HR in Spain and its current situation. As to the practical implications of this analysis, although our research study covers a comprehensive range of HR policy and practice issues at the level of the MNC organization, we focused on the developmental aspects to complement the purpose of this book. Overall, "American" policies have been well accepted by Spanish managers as a way of improving company performance. In most of the cases, successful implementation of HR corporate policies has been achieved because of some degree of malleability and openness within the Spanish business system, and the legitimacy given to managerial HR practices originating in the USA. It can be argued that it is likely that subsidiary management plays a key role in configuring its HRD and IR policies and practices. The evidence concerning foreign MNCs in Spain more generally also shows that there is a degree of openness to new practices, which can in turn establish new norms in the host country (Dickmann, 1999; Ferner et al., 2001; Muller-Camen et al., 2001).

Acknowledgments

We are very grateful to the editors of this volume, Yih-teen Lee and Carol D. Hansen, for their helpful comments. This chapter draws on a research project funded through grants by the Ministerio de Educación y Ciencia within "Convocatoria de ayudas a proyectos de I+D 2005" (ref. SEJ2007-03096, award 01/10/2006) and Fundación BBVA (ref. 216/06).

Notes

1 "Barómetro de los negocios norteamericanos en España." The American Chamber of Commerce In Spain and ESADE (2008).
2 "The proliferation of regional legislation means that, in some cases, companies have to abide by 17 different regulatory frameworks in their domestic market, posing obstacles and higher costs." (Confederación Española de Organizaciones Empresariales) (CEOE).

References

Aguilera, R. "Corporate Governance and Labour Relations: Spain in the European Context." In Pendleton, A. & Gospel, H., *Corporate Governance and Labour Management. An International Comparison* (Oxford: Oxford University Press, 2005).

Almond, P., Clark, I., Colling, T., Edwards, T., Ferner, A., & Holden, L. *US Multinationals and the Management of Human Resources in Britain.* Leicester Business School, November. (Leicester: DMU, 2003).

Amuedo-Dorantes, C. "Work Transitions into and out of Involuntary Temporary Employment in a Segmented Market: Evidence from Spain." *Industrial and Labour Relations Review,* 53(2) (2000) 309–26.

Banco de España Productive Investment in the Recent Cycle. *Economic Bulletin,* October 2002.

Baruel, J. "Spain in the Context of European Human Resource Management." In T. Clark (ed.), *European Human Resource Management* (Oxford: Blackwell, 1996) 93–117.

Campa, J. M. & Guillen, M. "A Boom from Economic Integration." In J. H. Dunning & R. Narula (eds) *Foreign Direct Investment and Governments* (New York: Routledge, 1999) 207–9.

Crouch, C. *Industrial Relations and European State Traditions.* (Oxford: Clarendon Press, 1993).

Dickman, M. *Balancing Global, Parent and Local Influences: International Human Resource Management of German Multinational Companies.* Ph.D.Thesis, Birkbecvk College, University of London (1999).

Dore, R. *Japan at Work: Markets, Management and Flexibility.* (Paris: OECD, 1989).

Evans, P., Lank, E., & Farquhar, A. "Managing Human Resources in the International Firm: Lessons from Practice." In P. Evans, Y. Doz & A. Laurent (eds) *Human Resource Management in International Firms* (London: Macmillan, 1989).

Ferner, A., Almond, P., Clarck, I., Trevor, C., Edwards, T., Holden, L., & Miller, M. The Transmission and Adaptation of American Traits in US Multinationals Abroad: Case Study Evidence from the UK. *Paper for conference on Multinational Companies and HRD: Between Globalisation and National Business Systems,* De Monfort University Graduate School of Business (2001).

Ferner, A., Almond, P., Clark, I., Colling, T., Edwards, T., Holden, L., & Muller-Camen, M. "The Dynamics of Central Control Subsidiary Autonomy in the Management of Human Resources: Case-study Evidence from US MNC in the UK." *Organization Studies,* 25(2) (2004) 327–56.

Ferner, A., Almond, P., & Colling, T. "Institutional Theory and Cross-National Transfer: The Case of 'Workforce Diversity' Policy in US Multinationals." *Journal of International Business Studies,* 36(3) (2005) 304–21.

García Delgado, J. L. "Etapas y rasgos definidores de la industrialización español." In J. L. García Delgado, R. Myro, & J. A. Martínez (eds) *Lecciones de Economía Española* (2nd ed.) (Madrid: Civitas, 1995) 21–47.

Guillén, M. *El auge de la empresa multinacional española.* (Madrid: Marcial Pons—Fundación Rafael del Pino, 2006).

Hamann, K. "Spanish Unions: Institutional Legacy and Responsiveness to Economic and Industrial Change." *Industrial and Labour Relations Review*, 51 (1998) 424–44.

Handy, C., Gordon, G., Gow, I., & Raddlesome, C. *Making Managers*. (London: Pitman, 1988).

Jacoby, S. *Modern Manors. Welfare Capitalism since the New Deal*. (Princeton, NJ: Princeton U.P., 1997).

Köhler, C. & Woodard, J. "Systems of Work and Socio-Economic Structures: A Comparison of Germany, Spain, France and Japan." *European Journal of Industrial Relations*, 3(1) (1997) 59–82.

Marginson, P. & Guglielmo M. European Union Enlargement and the Foreign Direct Investment Channel of Industrial Relations Transfer, *Industrial Relations Journal*, 37(2) (2006) 92–110.

Martin Artiles, A. "Sirve la formación para tener empleo?" *Papers. Revista de Sociología*, 58 (1999) 39–73.

Martínez, M. (1998) "Spain: Regulating Employment and Social Fragmentation." In A. Ferner & R. Hyman (eds) *Changing Industrial Relations in Europe* (Oxford: Blackwell) 426–58.

Martinez Lucio, M. Legitimar el Mercado. El neoliberalismo y el "juego" de la integración monetaria en España. *Cuadernos de Relaciones Laborales* n 15. (1999).

Muller-Camen, M., Almond, P., Gunnigle, P., Quintanilla, J., & Temple, A. "Between Home and Host country: Multinationals and Employment Relations in Europe." *Industrial Relations Journal*, 32(5) (2001) 435–49.

Pérez Díaz, V. & Rodríguez, J. C. "Inertial Choices: An Overview of Spanish Human Resources, Practices and Policies." In R. Locke, T. Kochan & M. Piore (eds) *Employment Relations in a Changing World Economy* (Massachusetts: MIT, 1995) 165–96.

Quintanilla, J. *The Configuration of HRD Policies and Practices in Multinational Subsidiaries: The Case of European Retail Banks in Spain*. Unpublished document. Doctoral Thesis (1998).

Quintanilla, J. *Dirección de Recursos Humanos en empresas multinacionales. Las subsidiarias al descubierto*. (Madrid: Financial Times, Prentice Hall, 2001).

Quintanilla, J., Sánchez-Runde, C., & Cardona, P. *Competencias de la dirección de personas. Un análisis desde la alta dirección*. (Madrid: Pearson/Prentice Hall, 2004).

Schein, E. "*Organizational Culture & Leadership*." NetLibrary (2004) roysmithtraining. co.uk.

Selmer, J. & de Leon, C. T. 'Parent Cultural Control of Foreign Subsidiaries Through Organizational Acculturation: A longitudinal study,' *International Journal of Human Resource Management*, 13(8) (2002) 1147–65.

Valle, R. La gestión estratégica de los Recursos Humanos, Addison-Wesley Iberoamericana, EEUU (1995).

8

Asian Reversalism: An Alternative Approach to Career Development

Yih-teen Lee and Carol D. Hansen

In recent years, Western models of career planning have typically promoted the "fast track," an accelerated approach to career development (CD) that encourages new recruits to advance quickly through their company's functional and managerial hierarchies in pursuit of high positions of rank and authority (Hall & Moss, 1998; Reitman & Schneer, 2003). The model is especially attractive to novice, yet talented, employees who seek to accelerate the upward movements and paths of their careers. However, is rapid upward career movement the optimum way for employees and their organizations to consider the issue of CD? The aim of this chapter is to challenge both the linear direction and the anticipated speed of the fast-track approach.

We look to Asia and its ancient Taoist philosophy to propose a new concept that we call "reversalism" as an alternative approach to the issues of time and direction. Although numerous studies document the relationship between time orientation and CD (Hesketh, 2002; Lennings, 1994), little research has explicitly suggested that a nonlinear (with few exceptions such as Bierema (1998) and Buzzanell & Goldzwig (1991)) and a slower approach to functional and managerial growth should be considered in the creation of CD policy and systems. As a result, for most employees, a speedy approach is traditionally considered a route to personal success that will bring better opportunities and benefits than those awarded to employees who advance at a more moderate pace.

Schein (1984) identified the way in which a culture can impact the perceptions and directions of individuals' careers. This important work argued that the predominant view of CD in the United States was linear and that within the Western business culture, a primary focus was placed on career speed. Our notion of reversalism upends the traditional Western timeframe by suggesting that fast can become slow and slow can become fast. Although this sounds like a contradiction, the central premise of reversalism points to a common phenomenon: the intense and exclusive focus on one extreme goal may actually lead to an unexpected and opposite result. Many of us have experienced the frustration of making mistakes or making superficial judgments in racing to meet a deadline. Career-wise, a fast tracker may not always achieve better long-run growth if he or she accepts a higher paying job at the expense of enlarging his or her skill base. Furthermore, some scholars (Latack & Dozier, 1986) suggest that job loss may become an opportunity for career transition and personal reflection, which generates future career growth. Thus, when the issue of time takes precedence over one's depth of understanding and ability to develop an effective strategy, then speed and vertical linearity may not always be the best approach in business and in CD.

This chapter is organized into three sections. First, we lay the foundation for our introduction of reversalism by reviewing traditional and emerging concepts of career advancement. Second we present our concept of reversalism and its theoretical origins in Taoism. Third, we conclude by explaining the characteristics and advantages of reversalism in the real-world task of CD.

Theoretical frame

The fast tracker and CD

CD is a key area of HRD practice and research as defined in studies where HRD practitioners described their role and functional scope in American corporations (McLagan, 1983/1989, 1996, 1997). The results were used by the American Society for Training and Development to produce a set of professional HRD competencies that were adopted by them and by the Academy of HRD to frame professional membership and scope. Studies about survival on the fast track (Kovach, 1988) typically concern upwardly mobile employees in major US corporations. The assumption that one must move quickly forward is embedded in American culture; the implications being that upward mobility is a good thing and that derailment is something to be avoided if possible. Underlying this belief is that people want to move up, will like the next higher post, and that they have control over their ability to progress (Kovach, 1989).

HRD in general, and CD in particular, first became a distinct occupational specialty with its own rules and employee development practices in the United States during the 1970s (DeSimone & Harris, 1998; Pace et al., 1991). Culturally framed societal assumptions directly influence the management of career models, and these ideals prescribe the norms for career paths and promotional opportunities. Prior study suggests that career norms are more influenced by societal bonds than by individual background differences or organizational affiliation (Hofstede et al., 1990). For example, Americans, as seen in Handy's (1988) work, place high value on corporate training as an investment in one's career. Along with Stewart and Bennett (1991), he linked this educational orientation to a "still flourishing frontier mentality"—one where almost anything is possible, and above all, that every individual has the chance to influence their destiny (p. 53). However, research by Hansen (2003) and Hansen and Wilcox (1997) counters the cross-cultural transferability of the American myth that anyone can be a manager if given the right management development training and mentoring.

A departure from the traditional

Not only is the American-founded view of fast-track career advancement culturally biased, there are problems with its sense of reality and application. Traditionally, this view of career progress was defined in terms of promotion and pay increases within one organization (DeSimone et al., 2002). However, these authors note that organizations can no longer promise that they will stay in business, that an employee's job will continue to exist, or that there will be room for promotion. "Challenged by rapid change, increased competition, globalization, employee relationships have shifted from long to short term and less loyalty-based connections to new, flatter, and less hierarchical organizational structures" (p. 453). Given the flattening of organizational hierarchies, some plateauing is inevitable (Feldman & Weitz, 1988) and as a result advancement opportunities narrow (Kovach, 1989). Additional issues of politics or demographics may be beyond the individual's control as they attempt to advance (Hall, 1986; Hall & Mirvis, 1996). Kovach (1989) also questions if people will experience greater satisfaction by moving up and notes that increased visibility can increase the likelihood of both praise and criticism from a vastly increased sector of the world at large where there is greater pressure to succeed.

Most scholars of CD now suggest that all fast trackers will experience derailment at some point, most probably during the executive transition. So, how can and should HRD specialists encourage CD without upward mobility? Patience can be a virtue, and a single-minded approach to CD may not be good for all employees. Although a downturn typically leads to disappointment, it can also lead to more employee growth through greater individual reflection and tolerance along with recognition that change is uneven. Although job slowdown may be associated with stress and disruption, stressful life events can lead to growth because they spur people to consider new alternatives, to develop new competencies, and to restructure their lives in positive directions (Latack & Dozier, 1986; Leibowitz & Schlossberg, 1981).

Other scholars have discussed career growth from job loss in the same light and indicated that many individuals see positive aspects to this event (Hartley, 1980; Kovach, 1989; Latack, 1984). Zikic et al. (2005) indicated that job loss or involuntary career transitions can eventually lead to further identity development and growth through conscious personal and career explorations. Kovach (1989) found that a clear slowdown in any career prompts a period of questioning oneself and one's relationship to others. In fact, some period of perceived derailment may have prompted the inner reflections that now appear to be at the core of the philosophic worldview that is held by senior statesmen. Soul searching and personal reflection appear to accompany derailment and are a critical part of the senior statesmen's approaches to the world. In a speech addressed to the graduates of Stanford University, Steven Jobs, CEO of Apple Computer, confirmed this view by saying: "I didn't see it then, but it turned out that getting fired from Apple was the best thing that could have ever happened to me. The heaviness of being successful was replaced by the lightness of being a beginner again, less sure about everything. It freed me to enter one of the most creative periods of my life" (Stanford Report, June 2005). Thus, senior fast trackers are reflective as well as active; implying that derailment and learning may necessarily be intertwined by providing a more mature orientation to oneself and others. Tichy (1986) identifies influential and successful executives as being lifelong learners.

New models that do not necessarily reflect the main stream of CD are emerging and are pluralistic, cyclical, and ongoing (Bloch, 2005; Driver, 1994; Inkson, 2004; Templer & Cawsey, 1999). Brousseau et al. (1996) reflect this new perspective by arguing that although a traditional model of career management has favored individuals with a linear or expert career focus, shifts going on in the world of work now tend to favor those with a transitory or spiral career approach. In addition, pluralistic models now exist which suggest there may be a multiplicity of career paths. For example, employees may choose to advance through a management or a non-management path (Tucker et al., 1992). It is with these thoughts in mind that we too offer an alternative approach to CD through the philosophy of Taoism and our concept of reversalism.

The Tao of reversalism

Opposites, relativity, and return

Our theoretical frame for reversalism is founded in Taoist philosophy and principally reflects the thinking of the classic writings of Lao Tzu (circa 400–320 BC). Etymologically, the term *Tao* means "the ways or roads to follow." Figuratively, it was used in ancient Chinese philosophy to depict the will of Heaven and the ultimate rules of the universe. Lao Tzu's manuscript *Tao De Jing* suggests that humans should behave in a way that is in harmony with the *Tao*. His writing emphasizes what Taoists call "the force of return." For example, when behavior proceeds too far in a given direction it will reverse itself in order to avoid extremism and maintain a natural sense of cyclic order and balance. Based on the Taoist principle of "returning," we define reversalism as the mechanism or force that drives action, in an abstract or philosophical sense, to change its path and direction when it reaches a point of the extreme in a given direction.

Lao Tzu perceived the universe as composed of opposites. These apparently opposing forces are linked to his sense of environmental relativity, which is an important feature of the *Tao*. Oppositions, instead of being in competition, are both at peace with and complete each other. For example, being and non-being, difficult and easy, long and short, high and low, before and after, derive meaning in how they relate to one another and thus become relative, rather than absolute, concepts (Lao Tzu Chapter 2; Qian, 1995). Furthermore, Lao Tzu argues that opposite pairs are not fixed in their initial position. Rather, they are in constant movement and change toward the other side (Lao Tzu Chapter 77; Qian, 1995). As a result, the Taoist view causes the absoluteness of things to lose its value because everything becomes relative to its opposite. This principle does not view the process of change as linear nor human history and its development as constant progress toward a better world. Big empires, for example, are bound to decline once they reach their peak.

The concept can be visualized as the movement of a bow (Lao Tzu Chapter 77): to shoot an arrow, the archer pulls the bowstring taut until the bow reaches its most extreme arch, yet this point of extremity is what sends the bow back into its original, resting position.

Yin-Yang

The Tao of reversalism is heavily grounded in a concept of ancient Chinese philosophy known as *yin–yang*, which holds that a pair of

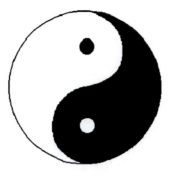

Figure 8.1 The yin–yang.

complementary and opposite elements such as fast and slow, will make a whole. This idea of the balancing nature of opposites is illustrated in the famous symbol of *yin–yang* shown in Figure 8.1. The black and white portions of the circle designate the *yin* and the *yang*, which together represent any pair of opposing forces. The *yin–yang* symbol shows how two opposing elements are contrasting yet also complementary; it takes both halves, dark and light, to complete and unify the circle. Furthermore, the *yin–yang* philosophy emphasizes the cyclical nature of opposing elements. The *yin* and the *yang* are in constant change and relative movement toward each other, so that no one element continually dominates the other and all elements change into their opposites in an eternal cycle of reversal. Drawing on this Chinese philosophy, our concept of reversalism thus blurs the distinction between opposing concepts (such as good and evil, high and low, strong and weak, and fast and slow) in our conventional thinking and instead, underscores the cyclical and constant movement of opposite forces.

Based on the perspective of the *yin–yang*, Lao Tzu considered the linear vision (Figure 8.2a) of opposing elements as incomplete. Opposing phenomena, such as fast and slow, are not situated on a continuum, with speed on the right-side and slowness on the left-side. Rather, the two opposites are *one*, and they form a cyclic round in which each element is constantly moving toward its opposite (Figure 8.2b). The linear and dichotomous view of the world captures only part of the universe understood through the *yin–yang* philosophy as cyclical. By focusing solely on a linear view of all principles in the universe, we fail to see that the flat continuum is actually a section of a very large circle (Figure 8.2c).

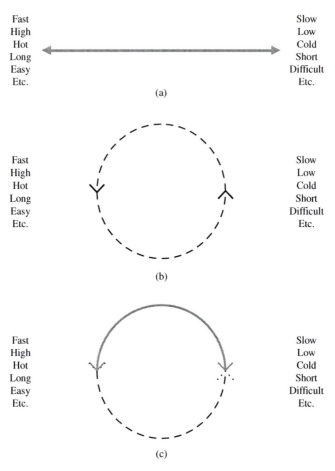

Figure 8.2 (a) Linear/dichotomous view of opposing phenomena; (b) Cyclic/returning view of opposing phenomena; and (c) Linear/dichotomous view as partial vision of the cyclic/returning view of opposing phenomena.
Source: Adapted from Qian (2000, p. 25).

Applying reversalism to CD

The philosophy of Taoism and our concept of reversalism clearly challenge the present popularity of the rapid forward movement of "the fast-track upwardly bound employee." In this section, we apply the concept of reversalism to the present-day career setting by showing that it is advantageous to CD. We will highlight two aspects of reversalism that we believe to have valuable applications to CD. First, reversalism values the process, not merely the end result, of moving or maturing from one extreme to another. Thus, the theory of reversalism encourages a holistic or global perspective of the universe. Second, reversalism emphasizes flexibility and a subjective approach to movement and growth. In this aspect, reversalism reveals the importance of personal flexibility in determining the appropriate time to make a specific career move.

Pathways to career maturity

Our notion of maturity is that time and direction are necessary elements in the *process* of arriving at a final stage or reaching an end result. Maturity takes into consideration the dynamic and developmental nature of CD, and it legitimizes the time for growth. Pursuing speed without taking into account the notion of maturity might result in rushed moves and a "harvest before maturity." That is, promotions and greater responsibilities might be conferred within short time periods, whereas the results might not be favorable, and might even cause adverse effects to both the individual and the organization in the long term. Taking time to proceed cautiously or return to a given step of development may seem tedious, but the final results may prove this method to be more effective than rapid advancement. Indeed the ultimate objective may be achieved at a faster pace because there may be fewer career mishaps that must be corrected.

This concept of maturity has been applied to the CD process and referred to as "the individual's ability to make a career decision and the degree to which one's choices are both realistic and consistent over time" (Levinson et al., 1998), or the "competence that individuals demonstrate in coping with CD tasks at various life stages" (Lennings, 1994, p. 243). However, prior research leaves this concept incomplete in two aspects. First, the concept of career maturity often refers to the idea of individual competence or knowledge to make appropriate career choice. It does not truly consider if the individual has the more global aspects of maturity such as the actual development of the skills and competence necessary to perform well in the job or position under consideration. As a result, maturity is generally not seriously considered as an important criterion when individuals are able to make career decisions, which leads them to chase after fast, upward promotion.

Second, the concept of career maturity has typically been applied exclusively to situations in which adolescents search for their first jobs (Flouri & Buchanan, 2002; Levinson et al., 1998; Patton & Creed, 2001). Yet maturity can also be applied to more general situations such as the transitional periods between different stages in an individual's CD. More precisely, for each transition step, one should pay attention to the *process* and the time needed for developing one's skills and knowledge (achieving the maturity) so as to meet the necessary requirements in going from one position to another as well as from one stage to the next.

Echoing Lao Tzu's teaching and reversalism, we suggest that one should adopt a broader view on maturity, and take into consideration the time needed to achieve maturity in CD. Rushing for career advance without reaching corresponding maturity (in terms of experience, expertise, network, and so on) for the position may hinder one's longer-term CD opportunities. Prior studies have evidenced the importance of relevant experience (Backhaus, 2003), expertise (Van der Heijden, 2002), and social networks (Higgins, 2001; Hesketh, 2002; Kram & Isabella, 1985; Seibert et al., 2001) for successful future career transition and development. All these require a certain amount of time to develop, and cannot be achieved overnight. Applying a reversal approach to CD, rather than focusing solely on the attainment of an advanced and established career, an individual might benefit by achieving a higher level of maturity and by valuing, and not overlooking, the entire process.

As one conceives of CD as a process taking into account of the effect of maturity, CD can further be thought of as an evolution of tasks, each characterized by different, although linked, functions and features (Greenhaus et al., 2000). To accomplish one task, there is generally a set of preceding stages (see Levinson et al. (1978) and Super (1957) for models of stages of CD). If one fails to consider the entirety of the development process, one risks bypassing essential tasks and thus leaving critical gaps in the process, which may, in turn, impact one's readiness to move forward. For instance, without reaching this maturity, as Hall and Chandler (2005, p. 159) argued, "task success can lead to psychological failure." By viewing CD more *holistically*, one may more appropriately allocate one's time and resources among various stages and thus, better accomplish one's goals.

Holding a global and *holistic* approach to CD indicates a long-term perspective because one does not concentrate only on immediate gain in the present stage. This attitude can affect beneficial outcomes for individuals. Marko & Savickas (1998) point to this idea when they suggest that increasing an individual's orientation to the future can be beneficial to that individual's career. Similarly, Hesketh (2002) stresses the importance and long-term benefits of an individual's taking the time needed in each stage of development to build a social network of influence and participate in training practices that will improve long-term skills. Although investment of time in these activities may delay movement to successive stages, one may expect a more promising career path in the long run. The value of reversalism based on a global view is supported by Lennings (1994, p. 245): "People entering the work force with long-term goals and a capacity to view the passage of time positively . . . are able to plan for the future more realistically, have a more positive attitude toward work and the temporal environment, and, presumably, achieve at a higher level."

Appropriate timing

The second illustration of an inverse view of speed lies in the idea of timing. In the domain of management and organization studies, this principle has been explored in finance (Brockman & Chung, 2001; Bartolini et al., 2001), new product launching (Dröge et al., 2000; Kohli, 1999), and foreign direct investment (Blandón, 2001), although it is still relatively underdeveloped in HRM and HRD. Following the same vein of the above-mentioned research, we define timing as the choosing of exactly the right moment to act to obtain the best effect. The point is that the right moment is not necessarily the earliest or the most immediate. Timing is in fact an art that requires evaluating a situation and determining the right moment to act. The art of timing and the choice of an appropriate pace represent an analytical frame that simultaneously takes into consideration the external environment and the internal resources impacting any decision. The timing to make the right career move should reflect the result of a comprehensive analysis of personal situations such as career maturity, personal ambition, job aspiration, work–life balance (Hall & Chandler, 2005; Hyman & Summers, 2004; Seibert et al., 2001), organizational situations like promotion rules, sociocultural norms in the enterprise, political games and struggles (van Vianen & Fischer, 2002; Vaughn & Wilson, 1994), and general socioeconomic contexts such as job-market opportunities. Consequently, fast, upward moves are neither always possible nor always the best solution for individuals.

Reversalism provides a useful insight by inviting people to strategically analyze the best time and direction to move rather than adopt a simplistic mental scheme which favors only fast-pace and unidirectional career moves. Rather than being driven by the rigid, but sometimes blind, drive to go always fast and upwards, an individual benefits from embracing greater *flexibility* and consciously considering the "right moment" to act in his CD so as to achieve the best results.

Moreover, reversalism invites us to question whether speed and appropriate timing can truly be measured in absolute terms. In the ancient writings that inform our concept of reversalism, Lao Tzu adopts a subjective view of time. According to his perspective, what is *appropriately* fast and slow depends on the subjective perception of each individual, which might in turn affect individual and collective behaviors. Durkheim (1965) noted the importance of social context in determining the subjective nature of time (Brislin & Kim, 2003; Rämö, 2002). Sorokin (1943) also argued that it is the subjective time perceptions that determine meaning attributed to specific events within a sociological system. This vein of studies allows individuals to think about new ways to conceive time and speed through the lens of intersubjectivity based on their own needs, and so the ideas of fast and slow are no longer perceived as absolute measurements of time. Recent studies on psychological career success echo this line of thinking (Hall & Chandler, 2005).

Conclusion and future research

Our discussion of reversalism begins to answer a need identified by Hesketh (2002): "time is a critical component of all strategic HR and individual career decisions, and we need to understand the way in which it affects choices" (p. 33). Today, in the typical organizational setting, many employees are eager to jump on the "fast track" to CD. As individual success within a company is commonly measured by how far and how quickly one advances, employees are pushed, and are themselves pushing, to join the collective race up the corporate ladder. In this popular view of CD, time is a scarce resource. While acknowledging that people do not simply race blindly up the career ladder without thinking, we suggest that the notion of reversalism could help to broaden the scope of time consideration and render workers more conscious about the consequences of the career decisions they may make. To maximize profits for both itself and its workers, the typical organization tends to focus on fast, forward movement; any length of individual or organizational downtime is viewed as a fiscal loss.

There often exists a tendency for human beings to choose only one of a pair of opposing forces (strong, fast, easy, and so on). However, Taosim stresses a balance of opposing elements, and for an individual, focusing on only one of a pair of opposites may be disadvantageous. Derived from this principle, the Tao of reversalism suggests that, in reaching a certain goal, speed may not always be favorable; rather, some backtracking or movement in a horizontal zigzag may strategically be more advantageous (Lao Tzu, 1963; Sun Tzu, 1993).

The objective of this article is not to claim that slow is better than fast in CD. Our purpose is to expand the picture by providing an alternative perspective that HRD practitioners might consider in counseling their employees and organizations about the pace and directionality of CD practices and policies given today's work challenges. Clearly, our model identifies the potential risks of moving too quickly in one direction as a means of achieving one's career hopes and dreams. We believe that individuals and organizations should create work cultures that allow flexibility and subjectivity in the CD process: those that take reversalism into account. Concretely, individuals may philosophically apply the principles of reversalism to their CD path to make the best decisions for their long-term interests. HRD professionals may apply these principles by advising top management not to pursue "fast track" CD exclusively, but also to consider and reward alternative career routes. HRD may help organizations to set up CD systems incorporating the view of reversalism and be prepared to council individuals who might opt for alternative career pathways, which reflect higher strategic values to them.

Despite its thought-provoking insight, key arguments in this chapter are mainly philosophical. We hope that future research will explore the following questions: (1) Will this ancient philosophy work in present day Asia? (2) Will it work in non-Asian cultural contexts? We encourage scholars to tackle these questions with various methodologies. For example, ethnographies can lead to the development of hypothetical propositions that can be tested with positivistic methods. We believe that there is much that organizations in general, and HRD in particular, can learn by backtracking and considering the historical Tao of the East.

Acknowledgments

We thank our research assistant, Ms Susan Walker.

References

Backhaus, K. "Importance of person-organization fit to job seekers." *CD International*, 8 (2003) 21–27.
Bartolini, L., Bertola G., and Prati A. "Banks' reserve management, transaction costs, and the timing of Federal Reserve intervention." *Journal of Banking and Finance*, 25 (2001) 1287–317.

Bierema, L. L. (ed.). "Women's CD across the lifespan: Insights and strategies for women, organizations and adult educators." *New Directions for Adult and Continuing Education*, No. 80. (San Francisco: Jossey-Bass, 1998).

Blandón, J. G. "The timing of foreign direct investment under uncertainty: Evidence from the Spanish banking sector." *Journal of Economic Behavior and Organization*, 45 (2001) 213–24.

Bloch, D. P. "Complexity, chaos, and nonlinear dynamics: A new perspective on CD theory." *CD Quarterly*, 53 (2005) 194–207.

Brislin, R. W. and Kim, E. S. "Cultural diversity in people's understanding and uses of time." *Applied Psychology: An International Review*, 52 (2003) 363–82.

Brockman P. and Chung, D. Y. "Managerial timing and corporate liquidity: Evidence from actual share repurchases." *Journal of Financial Economics*, 61 (2001) 417–48.

Brousseau, K. R., Driver, M. J., Eneroth, K., and Larsson, R. "Career pandemonium: Realigning organizations and individuals." *Academy of Management Executive*, 10 (1996) 52–66.

Buzzanell, P. M. and Goldzwig, S. R. "Linear and nonlinear career models: Metaphors, paradigms, and ideologies." *Management Communication Quarterly*, 4(4) (1991) 466–505.

DeSimone, R. and Harris, D. *Human Resource Development*, 2nd ed. (Fort Worth, TX: The Dryden Press, 1998).

DeSimone, R. L., Werner, J. M., and Harris, D. M. *Human Resource Development*, 3rd ed. (Fort Worth, TX: Harcourt, 2002).

Driver, M. J. "Workforce personality and the new information age." In J. A. Auerbach and J. C. Welsh (eds) *Aging and competition: Rebuilding the U.S. workforce.* (Washington, DC: National Council on the aging and the National Planning Association, 1994) 185–204.

Dröge, C., Jayaram, J., and Vickery, S. K. "The ability to minimize the timing of new product development and introduction: An examination of antecedent factors in the North American automobile supplier industry." *Journal of Product Innovation Management*, 17 (2000) 24–40.

Durkheim, E. *The elementary forms of the religious tile* (New York: Free Press, 1965, first published in 1915).

Feldman, D. C. and Weitz, B. A. "Career plateaus reconsidered." *Journal of Management*, 14 (1988) 69–80.

Flouri, E. and Buchanan, A. "The role of work-related skills and career role models in adolescent career maturity." *CD Quarterly*, 51 (2002) 36–43.

Greenhaus, J. H., Callanan, G. A., and Godshalk, V. M. *Career Management*, 3rd ed. (Fort Worth, TX: Harcourt College Publishers, 2000).

Hall, D. T. and Mirvis, P. H. "The new protean career: Psychological success and the path with a heart." In D. T. Hall (ed.), *The Career is Dead—Long Live the Career: A relationational approach to careers.* (San Francisco, CA: Jossey-Bass, 1996) 15–45.

Hall, D. T. and Moss, J. E. "The new protean career contract: Helping organizations and employees adapt." *Organizational Dynamics*, 26 (1998) 22–37.

Hall, D. T. and Chandler, D. E. "Psychological success: When the career is a calling." *Journal of Organizational Behavior*, 26 (2005) 155–76.

Hall, E. "A conception of adult development." *American Psychologist*, 41 (1986) 3–13.

Handy, C. "The United States." In C. Handy, C. Gordon, I. Gow, and C. Randlesome (eds) *Making Managers* (New York: Pitman, 1988) 51–81.

Hansen, C. "Cultural myths in stories about human resource development: Analyzing the cross-cultural transfer of American models to Germany and the Côte d'Ivoire." *International Journal of Training and Development*, 6 (2003) 16–30.

Hansen, C. and Wilcox, M. K. "Cultural assumptions in career management: Practice implications from Germany." *CD International Journal*, 2 (1997) 195–201.

Hartley, J. F. "The impact of unemployment upon the self-esteem of managers." *Journal of Occupational Psychology*, 53 (1980) 147–55.

Hesketh, B. "Time-related issues in training and CD." *Australian Journal of Management*, 27 (2002) 31–38.

Higgins, M. C. "Changing careers: The effects of social context." *Journal of Organizational Behavior*, 22 (2001) 596–617.

Hofstede, G., Neuijen, B., Ohayv, D. D., and Sanders, G. "Measuring organizational cultures: A qualitative and quantitative study across twenty cases." *Administrative Science Quarterly*, 35 (1990) 286–316.

Hyman, J. and Summers, J. "Lacking balance? Work-life employment practices in the modern economy." *Personnel Review*, 33 (2004) 418–29.

Inkson, K. "Images of career: Nine key metaphors." *Journal of Vocational Behavior*, 65 (2004) 96–111.

Kohli, C. "Signaling new product introductions: A framework explaining the timing of preannouncements." *Journal of Business Research*, 46 (1999) 45–56.

Kovach, B. E. *Survival on the fast track*. (New York: Dodd and Mead, 1988).

Kovach, B. E. "Successful derailment: What fast-trackers can learn while they're off the track." *Organizational Dynamics*, 18 (1989) 33–47.

Kram, K. E. and Isabella, L. A. "Mentoring alternatives: The role of peer relationships in CD." *Academy of Management Journal*, 28 (1985) 110–32.

Lao Tzu, *Tao Te Ching*, Translated by D. C. Lau (London: Penguin Books, 1963).

Latack, J. C. "Career transitions within organizations: An exploratory study of work, non-work, and coping strategies." *Organizational Behavior and Human Performance*, 34 (1984) 296–322.

Latack, J. C. and Dozier, J. B. "After the ax falls: Job loss as a career transition." *Academy of Management Review*, 11 (1986) 375–92.

Leibowitz, Z. and Schlossberg, N. "Training managers for their role in a CD system." *Training and Development Journal*, 35 (1981) 72–9.

Lennings, C. J. "An investigation of the effects of agency and time perspective variables on career maturity." *Journal of Psychology*, 128 (1994) 243–53.

Levinson, D. J., Darrow, C. N., Klein, E. B., Levinson, M. H. and McKee, B. *The seasons of a man's life*. (New York: Knopf, 1978).

Levinson, E. M., Ohier, D. L., Caswell, S., and Kiewra, K. "Six approaches to the assessment of career maturity." *Journal of Counseling and Development*, 76 (1998) 475–82.

Marko, K. W. and Savickas, M. L. "Effectiveness of a career time perspective intervention." *Journal of Vocational Behavior*, 52 (1998) 106–19.

McLagan, P. A. *Models for excellence: The conclusion and recommendations of the ASTD training and development study*. (Alexandria, VA: ASTD, 1983/1989).

McLagan, P. A. "Great ideas revisited: Creating the future of HRD." *Training and Development*, 50 (1996) 60–64.

McLagan, P. A. "Competencies: The next generation." *Training and Development*, 51 (1997) 40–47.

Pace, R. W., Smith, P. C., and Mills, G. E. *Human Resource Development: The field*, Englewood Cliffs. (NY: Prentice Hall, 1991).

Patton, W. and Creed, P. A. "Developmental issues in career maturity and career decision status." *CD Quarterly*, 49 (2001) 336–51.

Qian, M. *History of Chinese thoughts* (in Chinese). (Taipei: Student Bookstore, 1995).

Qian, M. *Posthumous papers on Chinese academic thoughts* (in Chinese). (Taipei: Lan-Tai, 2000).

Rämö, H. "Doing things right and doing the right things: Time and timing in projects." *International Journal of Project Management*, 20 (2002) 569–74.

Reitman, F. and Schneer, J. A. "The promised path: A longitudinal study of managerial careers." *Journal of Managerial Psychology*, 18 (2003) 60–75.

Schein, E. H. "Culture as an environmental context for careers." *Journal of Occupational Behaviour*, 5 (1984) 71–81.

Seibert, S. E., Kraimer, M. L., and Liden, R. C. "A social capital theory of career success." *Academy of Management Journal*, 44 (2001) 219–37.

Sorokin, P. A. *Sociocultural causality, space, time*. (Durham, NC: Duke University Press, 1943).

Stanford Report, "'You've got to find what you love', Jobs says", June 2005. http://news-service.stanford.edu/news/2005/june15/jobs-061505.html.

Stewart, E. C. and Bennett, M. J. *American cultural patterns: A cross-cultural perspective*. (Yarmouth, USA: Intercultural Press, 1991).

Sun Tzu, *The art of warfare*, translated by R. T. Ames. (New York: Ballantine Books, 1993).

Super, D. *The psychology of careers*. (New York: Harper, 1957).

Templer, A. and Cawsey, T. F. "Rethinking career development in an era of portfolio careers." *Career Development International*, 4 (1999) 70–76.

Tichy, N. *The transformational leader*. (NYC: John Wiley, 1986).

Tucker, R., Moravec, M., and Dieus, K. "Designing a dual career-track system." *Training and Development*, 46 (1992) 55–58.

Van der Heijden, B. I. J. M. "Individual career initiatives and their influence upon professional expertise development throughout the career." *International Journal of Training and Development*, 6 (2002) 54–79.

Van Vianen, A. E. M. and Fischer, A. H. "Illuminating the glass ceiling: The role of organizational culture preferences." *Journal of Occupational and Organizational Psychology*, 75 (2002) 315–37.

Vaughn, R. H. and Wilson, M. C. "Career management using job trees: Charting a path through the changing organization." *Human Resource Planning*, 17 (1994) 43–55.

Zikic, J., Richardson, J., and Church, R. "Unlocking careers following job loss: The interplay between individuals' cognitive appraisal and resources on career exploration processes." paper presented at EGOS Annual Colloquium 2005, Berlin (2005).

Part III

9

The Cultural Context of Organizational Identity: How Belief Systems Can Frame the Practice and Role of Human Resource Development

Sheila L. Margolis

The concept of identity has been studied at the individual level, the group level, and more specifically on the organizational level (Ashforth & Mael, 1996). The identity of an organization captures its spirit, its meaning, and its enduring attributes. Identity answers the question, "Who are we?" "Identity goes to the core of what something *is*, what fundamentally defines that entity" (Ashforth & Mael, 1996, p. 20). The organization has an identity; it is the essence of the organization, a source of stability and definition for its members and a basis for action (Albert & Whetten, 1985; Ashforth & Mael, 1996). Organizational identity is greater than a metaphorical device; it is "a phenomenon experienced by organizational members, perceived by outsiders, and central to social processes with real outcomes in organizational contexts" (Corley et al., 2006, p. 89).

Organizational identity and organizational culture are distinct but closely related constructs (Corley et al., 2006). As stated by Hatch and Schultz (2002, p. 991), "identity is embedded in cultural understandings." Culture provides the context within which identity is established and maintained (Hatch & Schultz, 1997). Fiol (1991) suggested that organizations manage culture by focusing on identities rather than solely manipulating behavior. Culture and identity are a part of a system of meaning and sense-making that provides definition.

Because culture is a powerful force driving organizations, this relationship between identity and culture must be better understood. In addition, because identity has the capacity to impact organizational potential, organizational identity must be better defined and managed. The HRD professional takes center stage in leading this effort. With the role of being the cultural steward for the organization (Grossman, 2007), the HRD professional has an obligation to guide members in the process of clarifying the organization's identity within the context of the culture and aligning actions with those identity attributes. During times of change, the HRD leader has the vital role of ensuring that the most fundamental essence of the organization—its identity—is sustained, unless the continuation of this identity threatens the viability of the organization. Managing the organization's identity—first by defining those attributes and then by filtering those attributes throughout the culture so that actions are aligned with the organization's identity—is central to the HRD function and to the vitality of the organization.

Organizational identity dimensions

According to Whetten (2006, p. 220), "The concept of organizational identity is specified as the central and enduring attributes of an organization that distinguish it from other organizations." It is subjective—a self-definition—a view of the organization as a collective actor. Based on Albert and Whetten's (1985) seminal paper, the three defining criteria of organizational identity are claimed "central character, distinctiveness and temporal continuity . . . each necessary, and as a set sufficient" (p. 265). These criteria—central, enduring, and distinctive—have been referred to as the CED definition (Whetten, 2006).

The central character criterion means that identity "distinguishes the organization on the basis of something important and essential" (Albert & Whetten, 1985, p. 266). Centrality can have a range of perspectives; it can be viewed as being deep rather than superficial, as being widely shared, and as being the central node in a structural network (Corley et al., 2006). The central nature of organizational identity implies a core essence that is foundational and fundamental to the organization. According to Ashforth and Mael (1996), the central character criterion refers to the "system of pivotal beliefs, values, and norms—typically anchored to the organizational mission—that informs sense-making and action" (p. 24).

The second criterion of claimed distinctiveness refers to characteristics of the organization that are unique, that distinguish it from others (Albert & Whetten, 1985) even if the uniqueness is more perception than reality. Attributes that meet this criterion "have repeatedly demonstrated their value as *distinguishing organizational features*" (Whetten, 2006, p. 221) and are "essential for distinguishing the focal organization from others" (p. 223). Distinctiveness defines boundaries that serve as positive differences between themselves and other relevant organizations (Ashforth & Mael, 1996). These unique and positive attributes serve to justify the organization's existence in relation to other organizations doing similar work and to define it as a distinguished actor (Whetten, 2006, p. 223).

The third criterion, temporal continuity, is an essential aspect of identity that implies something enduring that has emerged over time and is resistant to change (Albert & Whetten, 1985). "Continuity is important because it connotes a bedrock quality, that the organization has sufficient substance, significance, support, and staying power to warrant the investment of one's participation and trust. Accordingly, continuity begets continuity" (Ashforth & Mael, 1996, p. 26). "Organizations are best known by their deepest commitments—what they repeatedly commit to be, through time and across circumstances" (Whetten, 2006, p. 224). The greater the consensus in perceptions of organizational identity, the more likely that the attributes will endure. Identity is a source of inertia (Bouchikhi & Kimberly, 1996). It serves as an anchor for its members.

Most of the literature on organizational identity is theoretical in nature (Foreman & Whetten, 2002), but there is growing body of research. Although the research offers varying perspectives and assumptions on the nature of organizational identity, the identity construct remains relevant to organizations, particularly "in conjunction with novel, controversial, consequential strategic choices, and/or threatened changes in the organization's self-defining social classification" (Whetten, 2006, p. 227). Additionally, "mistaken identity . . . can be a fatal flaw for organizations" (p. 223).

Construction of organizational identity

Organizational identity typically emerges at founding and is a product of the motives, skills, experiences, and personality of the founders and the context of the founding (Bouchikhi & Kimberly, 1996). It is a reflection of the powerholders of the organization (Ashforth & Mael, 1996). The type of people that a company hires is often influenced by the background and experiences of its founders and their values and vision for the organization (Kimberly & Bouchikhi, 1995). Hiring and promotion practices serve to solidify this consistency not only in style but also in perceptions of purpose and principles of the organization (Bouchikhi & Kimberly, 1996). Although founders define the organization's purpose, it becomes reinforced by members' choices and activities that affirm the identity. In time, that identity becomes the property of its members. Any extreme change is difficult to accomplish owing to barriers both within and outside the organization. Although there will be some variability in how different members view their organization, they will see it more similarly than non-members (Dutton & Penner, 1993). Ashforth and Mael (1996) explained, "There are limits to how far identity claims can deviate from perceptions of either external stakeholders or internal members" (p. 40).

Hunt and Benford (1994) agreed that identities are constructed, reinforced, and transformed by interactions with others. In their examination of identity talk in peace movement organizations, they discovered that collective identities are products of social interaction and contribute to collective action. Their research also pointed to identity alignment as a theme in their discourse which served to support consistent perceptions of the organization and cohesion within its membership.

Identity is a relational construct (Hatch & Schultz, 2002), a product of interactions, comparisons, and reflections. As Schein (1992, p. 12) described culture as "a pattern of shared basic assumptions that the group learned," so is identity a collective perspective that is learned.

There is a link between organizational identity and action (Sarason, 1995). Identity not only affects organizational action and strategic behavior but also is affected by members' perceptions of what the organization does. Members gain an understanding of the reality of the organization by observing its practices and activities on an ongoing basis.

Organizational identity is reinforced when its members align their actions with the attributes of that identity (Bouchikhi & Kimberly, 1996). This can be accomplished through hiring practices, investment decisions, policies, and management systems. Identity is "a context for and a consequence of members' actions and interactions" (p. 30).

According to Ashforth and Mael (1996), the lack of a mutually understood organizational identity can be debilitating to an organization. Leaders must actively attend to it to give its members "a coherent and salient sense of what they represent" (p. 34). There are many barriers to achieving consensus to those features that are core, distinctive, and enduring. Perceptions can vary based on one's frame of reference. Also, members do not dwell on aspects of identity if it is not a constant focus of top management and if it is not managed and presented as an integral, critical, and realistic picture of the heart of the organization.

Many managers do not understand the importance of building a sense of community (Ashforth & Mael, 1996). Self-definition must be followed by choices that are wedded in that definition, and action that brings that definition to life. Management must also be consumed with the active symbolic management of that identity in ways that are mutually reinforcing and that propel that identity into the spotlight on a continuous basis. No member should be able to escape the language, setting, norms, stories, events, traditions, and rituals that support those identity claims. Exposure to these organizational features reinforces identity and provides consistent meaning. The ultimate aim is to create an environment where the goals, beliefs, and values of the organization and its members are aligned. Consensus among peers builds confidence in perceptions and brings enhanced life to those perceptions. The human resource functions of recruiting, selecting, socializing, training, communicating, and supporting rewards and promotions of organizational members all contribute toward achieving strong identities that are mutually reinforced throughout the organization.

Ashforth and Mael (1996) view organizational identity as an evolving construct that is most significant and open to change at times of discontinuities. Often a change in identity is the result of the cumulative development of the identity where elements are added or removed in ways that are somewhat unnoticed (Bouchikhi & Kimberly, 1996). An extension of the business or new elements to the purpose or operating principles produce change that appears neither radical nor threatening. Usually greater resistance to change occurs in situations where divergent forces demand change that will result in the development of feelings of loss among members.

Small number of organizational identity attributes

Organizational identity constitutes only the most central and enduring attributes that distinctively define the organization. Research consistently presents the number of identity attributes as quite small, with identity acting as a fine thread of Core principles that weaves throughout the organization. Additional beliefs exist within the organization and may vary by group or location. The identity attributes serve as a linking set of attributes to produce a connected community.

A case study by Dutton and Dukerich (1991) investigated how members of the Port Authority of New York and New Jersey dealt with the homeless in their facilities. The research revealed six attributes that members used to characterize their organization. Only one of these attributes was described by all informants. The remaining five attributes were each suggested by fewer than half of the informants, ranging from 25 to 44 percent. A limited number of identity attributes were shared by most members.

Research by Gustafson (1995) on Intel also revealed a small number of shared organizational identity attributes. Of the twenty categories, only three included attributes that were shared by a majority of the members. From this research, he suggested that organizational identity is a shared construct. Even a few attributes that are global in nature can contribute to a powerful collective schema. Gustafson described a complex model of both shared and fragmented attributes. He stated that the "multiple distinct subidentities held by sizable minorities of members may be beneficial to organizations in hypercompetitive environments because they provide requisite variety that encourages change" (p. 185).

Organizational identity: The enduring essence of organizational culture

Based on a qualitative case study of an airline going through a merger to lose identity (Margolis & Hansen, 2002) and supported by application in dozens of organizations, the author has created the Five Ps Model of of Organizational Attributes to enhance the ability to define and manage identity in an organization (Figure 9.1).

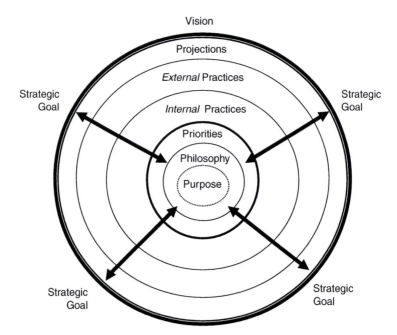

Figure 9.1   The Five Ps Model of Organizational Attributes.

In the Five Ps Model of Organizational Attributes, identity is at the core of the organization and at the center of the hierarchy of organizational attributes. Identity is the intangible substance that nurtures all other facets.

The model consists of a set of concentric circles representing an organization: the Purpose, Philosophy, Priorities, Practices (Internal and External), and Projections. This model presents the organization as a system of related and interrelated layers of beliefs, behaviors, interactions, and images. The attributes of each layer have the potential to impact each other. In this Five Ps Model, organizational identity is the two most central Ps: the Purpose and Philosophy. As a unit, Purpose and Philosophy provide the foundation for why the organization exists and the framework that directs how members behave. They are the enduring essence of the culture. By understanding this small set of attributes, members can build an organization that is guided by prime principles that are fundamental to and linked throughout the organization. The Purpose and Philosophy are the thread that guides behavior and unites the variety through a common bond. Identity allows for a diverse array of actions as long as they sustain an allegiance to this nucleus of prime principles. Organizational identity is the heart and soul of the organization's culture. The Purpose and Philosophy—as a unit—is its defining essence.

Purpose

Starting in the center of organizational attributes is the organization's Purpose. The Purpose defines why the organization exists. It's not the answer to the question: "What do members do?" Rather, it is the answer to the question: "*Why* is the work members do important?" Purpose is a complex message that inspires and motivates. It is the cause that encapsulates one's contribution to society. People seek meaning in their lives through their work. Most organizations exist to make a profit, but they also exist to make a difference. Through work, individuals can make a difference and be part of a meaningful legacy. The Purpose captures that legacy—it documents that contribution. An organization is a living entity, a vehicle for improving life and the world we live in.

The Purpose statement includes the few, most powerful words that communicate the organization's contribution. A crafted Purpose statement elicits an emotional connection to a cause. The statement is brief in length so members remember it and use it continuously to guide their actions. The Purpose statement transmits a sentiment that ignites dedication by those who have a passion for the cause. For example, the Purpose of The Coca-Cola Company is to benefit and refresh everyone it touches. The Purpose of The Carter Center is to advance human rights and alleviate unnecessary human suffering. A Purpose statement is also broad in scope. For example, Google is not just a provider of search technology; the organization's scope and scale are much broader. Google's Purpose is to organize the world's information. Google exists to make information universally accessible and useful. By having a broadly stated Purpose, it allows the organization to adapt over time to the needs of a changing world while remaining constant in its central focus. Guided by a broadly stated Purpose, members possess an expanded perspective that nurtures endless possibilities. The Purpose serves as a filter that has a broad lens.

When the Purpose is shared and genuinely owned by everyone in the organization, there is a feeling of unity and a collective spirit that propels the organization toward greater performance and heightened success. The Purpose must be conscious, discussed, and shared, or its impact may be diminished.

Philosophy

The second element of organizational identity that pairs with the Purpose is the organization's Philosophy. Philosophy is the prime value that distinguishes *how* members do their work. This fundamental and enduring belief has set the organization apart from others over the years. It's the reason two organizations in the same business feel different.

Philosophy is the essence of the organization's personality or character. As an individual has a personality, so does an organization. This personality—rooted in its Philosophy—is typically derived from the founder's personality or the skills or ideals that drove the organization's creation. Philosophy is the distinguishing and enduring character of the organization.

Purpose and philosophy

Where the Purpose provides the foundation for why the organization exists, the Philosophy provides the framework for how that Purpose is delivered in a distinctive way. The Purpose alone is not necessarily unique, but the Purpose combined with the Philosophy yields the distinctive and enduring essence of organizational identity. Since its founding in 1923, The Walt Disney Company has remained faithful in its commitment to producing unparalleled entertainment experiences based on its rich legacy of quality creative content and exceptional storytelling. Its Purpose is to make people happy, and they do it through their distinctive Philosophy of imagination. Entertaining through the Disney magic is the heart and soul—the identity—of this organization.

Linked by a passion for the vital Purpose and an allegiance to the distinctive Philosophy of the organization, members can form a community of workers who understand the uniqueness of their work and the valued contributions that they make. The first step in building a successful organization is to understand the organization's identity and use those defining principles as the basis for action.

Using strategic priorities to support identity: The components of core culture

Culture encompasses an array of attributes, ranging from the cherished beliefs of the organization to the observable behaviors of its members. Organizational identity is a small yet significant component of culture— it is the essence of the culture. Identity consists of the fundamental principle—the Purpose—defining why members do their work and the character-defining and enduring value—the Philosophy—that distinguishes how members do that work. Identity is essential to the organization and likewise, central to its culture. Understanding the basis for behavior and the foundational principles that ground culture requires understanding identity. Because of the enduring nature of identity, if either the Purpose or Philosophy of an organization changes, it will feel like a new organization to its members. This type of change is monumental because it attacks the essence of the culture. However, change is necessary to sustain the organization and its identity. Because sustainability requires adaptability, a strategic layer of values surrounds the identity core. In the Five Ps Model, the layer of organizational attributes outside of identity is a layer of additional values not as central in the hierarchy of attributes—values that do not have to be either distinctive or enduring. These strategic values are the organization's Priorities.

Priorities

Priorities are the values that guide how the organization's Purpose and Philosophy are put into practice in members' day-to-day activities. Priorities are guiding principles that enable the organization to be strategic. The Purpose and Philosophy are the organization's nature whereas the Priorities position the organization to sustain the identity and achieve its goals. There is a direct relationship between Priorities and the organization's strategy. Priorities guide "how" the organization will achieve the "what" of its strategy. These values must be carefully chosen because they become a filter to guide behavior so that all actions are grounded in these shared principles. Priorities are key standards for behavior that are relatively stable, but can be changed to enhance the organization's ability to compete and thrive. Strategy informs Priorities; therefore, whenever there is a strategy change, there is a need to reassess Priorities.

There are many Priorities that organizational members may believe sound good. The key is for members to identify the few values that are important to all areas of the organization and, if followed, will enable the organization to achieve its goals. Many Priorities are similar in nature, such as the values of teamwork, collaboration, partnerships, collegiality, and cooperation. However, each has a tone and connotation that must be considered to ensure that the chosen Priority captures the desired intent. Also, selecting a value that is "voiced" by members enhances its communication and understanding. For example, quality is one of the Priorities of a major food retailer. They have high standards and seek always to sell the highest-quality products they possibly can. They describe themselves as the buying agents for customers rather than selling agents for manufacturers. Another example is the Priority of safety at a pulp and paper company. Safety of employees, the environment, and the communities where they operate is one of their strategic values. They are serious about safety and have been named the safest forest products company in the industry year after year.

Core culture

The powerful pairing of Purpose and Philosophy supported by the strategic Priorities form the Core Culture of the organization. These central three Ps—Purpose, Philosophy, and Priorities—are the hub to guide action and the substance of the culture. This combination of enduring and strategic principles provides the foundation and framework for organizational action.

The role of HR

The HRD professional has a strategic role in ensuring that the organization's identity attributes—its Purpose and Philosophy—and it strategic Priorities are understood, shared, and practiced (Margolis, 2008). Consistency of actions reinforces the organization's defining identity and ensures that members behave in ways that sustain those prime principles and act strategically. Without a shared understanding of the Core Culture attributes, unity of action becomes more difficult and can compromise the success and sustainability of the organization. Members must know and use those principles to guide their daily activities.

In small organizations, the intent and emotion of the Core Culture principles may be expressed through just the presence of the leader—through the leader's words and actions. However, as an organization increases in size, there is a greater need to consciously define the Core Culture, share it, and align actions to it. Building a shared view requires a process of collecting perspectives of organizational members to determine the collective view of the organization's identity. In organizations with fragmentation and variation, the task of achieving a shared view can be challenging. However, without a shared understanding, there is no clear set of core, distinctive, and enduring beliefs or strategic values to guide practice. Clarifying the belief system that grounds and connects members of the organization is an essential first step in designing strategic HRD practices.

The strategy for bringing members together to share their views of the identity components—the Purpose and Philosophy—is the first step in managing identity and using those principles to guide behavior. Either through open dialogue or by collecting opinions through interviews, focus groups, or surveys, a united view can be constructed to serve as the organization's definition of itself. The HRD professional must guide a process that has leadership buy-in. In any identity-defining activity, leaders must understand the importance of the organization-wide initiative and be willing to speak and act in ways that support it.

In addition to leading the process to define the identity attributes, the HRD professional must ensure that the culture supports the organization's strategy. Priorities are the strategic values that support the outcomes of strategic planning; therefore, the HRD professional must guide the organization in deciding the Priorities that will enable the organization to achieve its goals in a way that is in accord with the organization's identity. Those strategic values become the organization's Priorities. With a shared view of the Purpose, Philosophy, and Priorities, the organization has a well-defined Core Culture that maps the principles that will yield success. The next step in the role of being a cultural and change steward is for the HRD professional to guide the organization in auditing the alignment of current practices with each attribute of the Core Culture and then develop and implement changes to enhance alignment with the Core Culture.

Alignment of practices and projections to core culture

Core Culture serves as a foundation and framework to guide organizational behavior. Once these attributes are defined, they must be managed. When the Core Culture principles are explicit, members can be more conscious in aligning their behaviors to produce consistency in action that will yield the continuation of those Core attributes. Alignment keeps the Core Culture principles alive. Without alignment, an organization may have intentions but does not reflect those intentions through daily activities.

In the Five Ps Model of Organizational Attributes (Margolis & Hansen, 2002), surrounding the organizational identity components of Purpose and Philosophy and the strategic Priorities are the remaining Ps: the Practices and Projections of the organization. These attributes of the organization must be audited and aligned with the Purpose, Philosophy, and Priorities to ensure that valued principles are sustained and strategy is achieved.

Practices

Practices are the behaviors and actions that keep the Core Culture alive. Practices are either Internal—within the organization—or External—with those outside the organization.

Internal Practices are the inner workings of the organization that affect employee relationships, interactions, and accomplishments. Most of these areas are the domain of human resources; therefore, the HRD professional is key to ensuring that these Internal Practices are aligned with the organization's identity—its Purpose and Philosophy—as well as with the organization's strategic Priorities. Internal Practices are where beliefs become behaviors, where words become actions. Beliefs are meaningless if they are not infused in workplace practices and demonstrated by employees and leaders alike. When actions match principles, the consistency produces reinforcing behaviors that sustain those beliefs and nurtures their maintenance. When HRD practices link to the Core Culture attributes, the organization exhibits a consistent image that promotes actions aligned to those attributes. Internal Practices include the structure of the organization, how work is organized, and the systems and processes for accomplishing the work; recruitment and selection practices; training and development; performance management; internal communications; and technology (Figure 9.2).

HRD professionals must ensure that the Internal Practice of organizational structure, work design, and the systems and processes for doing work align with and support the Core Culture. The structure of organizations will vary. Some are very static with clearly defined job descriptions and reporting structures with work organized around functions. Others are more fluid—where teams emerge around projects on a short-term basis, and job titles have little relevance. For example, in some organizations that nurture a Priority of innovation, they intentionally have

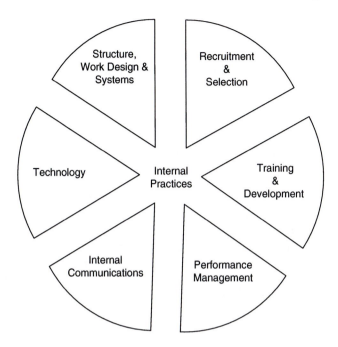

Figure 9.2 Internal Practices to be aligned with Core Culture.

few management layers or titles and members are allowed discretionary time to work on projects that they choose. They believe that having a loosely held structure, not limited by bureaucratic layers, facilitates innovation. The structure—no matter if it is a centralized, top-down militaristic structure, or an egalitarian, bottom-up structure—must align with the Purpose, Philosophy, and Priorities. Likewise, employees' daily activities and the systems for doing work must support the Core Culture principles, keeping them alive. At an airline known for their service culture, members strive to enhance their systems for loading and unloading planes to achieve a quick turnaround time. And central to the Core Culture of a technology company are the values of speed and accountability. They use teams to get the job done. They believe it's hard to dodge accountability when your team is small enough to be fed with one pizza. Again, the aim is to have a structure and processes that nurture the culture that is valued. HRD has the role of sustaining the Core Culture by working with members to find new and better ways to align the organization's structure, systems, and processes so they support those principles.

The next Internal Practice of recruitment and selection must be aligned with the organization's Core Culture. Finding the right people for an organization and retaining them are key to effective HRD practices. HRD professionals nurture the continuation of beliefs through rigorous efforts to ensure that candidates understand those beliefs, personally connect with them, and want to live by them. Many companies set up portals at their company website for prospective employees that communicate their Core Culture beliefs at the first step of the recruitment process. Organizations screen applicants for their passion for the Purpose and their natural ability to live by the Philosophy and Priorities. By using past actions and observable behaviors, HRD professionals can gauge a candidate's genuine connection to those central attributes. Many organizations hire for attitude and train for skills. Hiring employees who naturally value the Core Culture principles of the organization contributes to their practice. For example, one technology company highly values intelligence—it's a component of their Core Culture. Therefore, they administer a variety of tests to ensure that they hire smart individuals to support their Philosophy of intelligence. And in a communications company that highly values talent, members are selected based on past employment and prestigious on-air experience. Talent is part of their culture and critical in their selection processes.

To retain talent and ensure understanding of the culture, the HRD professional can provide new employees with a quick start through a comprehensive orientation program that includes the identity beliefs and the strategic Priorities and how to practice those principles effectively. This foundational knowledge jumpstarts employee success on the job by inculcating the principles that drive the organization and imparting the systems, processes, and practices employees should follow to support the Core beliefs. An effective orientation starting with an overview of the organization's Core Culture as well as the organization's strategy helps new employees assimilate faster, which promotes commitment and dedication. Many companies take pride in the array of training options that newly hired staff receive to enhance their immersion into the culture. Effective orientations reduce costly turnover and have a positive impact on the bottom line.

HRD also uses the Internal Practice of ongoing training and development to sustain the organization's beliefs and enhance their practice. Training is valuable for honing skills and enabling employees to practice the identity beliefs at the expected high levels of performance. By helping employees increase their skills and build on their strengths, the organization enhances the individual's worth and ability to contribute to practicing the principles that will bring continuity to the organization and enhance it strategically. People want to develop and achieve through their work. When employees have opportunities for personal growth, they are more engaged in their work and more committed to the organization because it provides this development. Organizations that are serious about preserving their Core Culture ensure that members are trained to practice those principles. For example, an entertainment company structures their training program to mix employees of different departments to support their collaborative culture while a hotel known for its quality customer service pairs new employees with departmental trainers to ensure that they perform at expected high standards.

When performance standards are aligned to the Purpose, Philosophy, and Priorities, employees have a clear picture of how well they live the Core Culture principles. This Internal Practice of performance management is more than an HRD tool; it is a means for helping members see how well their actions support the organization's identity and strategic Priorities. Living the Core Culture beliefs is one area for evaluation when an organization is serious about sustaining those beliefs. For example, in one healthcare organization, employees have 90-day action plans linked to delivering quality service which is valued at their Core. Another organization chose incentive pay rather than merit pay to align compensation more effectively with their entrepreneurial Philosophy. HRD professionals must ensure that everyone has clear standards to measure how well each person practices the Core Culture principles. In an organization that has integrity at its Core, pay and promotions are not based solely on delivering results but also on how well managers model this principle. Successful performance management practices include ongoing communication of performance expectations with feedback and support. Recognizing employee contributions in a variety of ways that are meaningful to individual employees builds commitment and dedication to the organization.

The Internal Practice of two-way flow of information is essential for creating a feeling of inclusion, understanding, and ownership. Regular conversations and exchanges about the Purpose, Philosophy, and Priorities communicate their importance throughout the culture. Effective communication starts at the top with leaders who provide broad messages that flow throughout the organization, and supervisors who reinforce the message and apply it to the specifics of their group. Communication involves listening as well as providing information.

Ongoing dialogue through a variety of channels heightens the workforce's understanding of the principles and their importance. In one organization, the leader does everything from walking around and talking with employees about the Core Culture to producing sophisticated videos on demand to ensure that the Core principles are emphasized. Communication—upward, downward, and lateral—must be effectively managed to share information and nurture the Core Culture.

The Internal Practice of technology should also align with the organization's Core Culture. Technology facilitates work, enabling effective, efficient practice of the Core beliefs. A proper investment in the appropriate software and equipment can help members practice and track data on how well they live those prime principles. For example, in an Internet company with a service-focused culture, much effort is directed at having the best technology to respond to customer questions and facilitate the buying process. Ensuring speed of service and customer satisfaction is prime to this organization, which is willing to make costly investments in technology to nurture those values.

Outside of Internal Practices are the organization's External Practices. Although External Practices are less central to the HRD professional's work, these practices have a direct link to the Core Culture attributes. External Practices are the activities an organization undertakes that deal with outsiders—like the customers an organization has, the products and services it provides, and its suppliers/vendors and partners—all must be aligned with the organization's Core Culture. Although further removed from the central three Ps in the Model of Organizational Attributes, these External Practices must still be aligned with those Core Culture attributes. Target customer and market segments where the organization will best compete. Strengthen relationships through shared values. Assess past customers, current customers, and potential customer groups to build a customer base that understands and values the organization's unique culture. Reflect the traits that make the organization special in the products and services that are offered. Also, screen suppliers, vendors, and partners to ensure that they uphold the principles that the organization holds dear. For example, in one organization that has safety as a Priority, they expect their subcontractors to learn their safety rules and have their same high standards. Their safety culture depends on their partners sharing their values. Shared interests and values ensure that Core beliefs will be strong. Manage these external relationships through activities to sustain the Core Culture principles.

Projections

Projections are the final P and must be aligned with the Purpose, Philosophy, and Priorities. Projections are not the substance of the organization's culture, but rather the reflections of it to the public. These projected representations of the organization are designed to influence outsiders although they have the capacity also to impact member views. Projections include the name of the organization; its logo and other corporate symbols; the location of corporate head-quarters; the image of the leader; the design and appearance of offices and stores; employees' dress or uniforms; marketing, public relations and advertising; and community activities. Each of these areas must be aligned with the organization's Core Culture principles to portray an image consistent with those prime principles. In most organizations, changes in Projections are relatively easy to manipulate, but Projections are very important because they are symbolic and emotionally relevant to employees. Changes in Projections can have an impact on how employees feel about the organization. In addition, any inconsistencies between projected images and actual experiences of customers can have a negative impact on the organization and the ability to drive business success. The alignment process requires filtering each Projection through the Core Culture attributes of the organization. The objective is to ensure that all Projections support and reflect the organization's principles.

Using core culture beliefs to guide organizational change

"Organizational cultures are neither static, stable, nor linear" (Hansen & Kahnweiler, 1995, p. 48). Often, it takes events like a merger or acquisition or leadership change—times when members "are grappling with profound, fork-in-the-road, choices" (Whetten, 2006, pp. 220–21) to make members stop and reflect on their organization's identity. Identity ambiguity (Corley & Gioia, 2004) can exist as a prelude to identity change.

At times of change, identity must be understood and managed. In the Five Ps Model, managing change requires a delicate balance of preserving the Purpose and Philosophy, if possible, while implementing changes in other aspects of the culture. Changing either the Purpose or Philosophy constitutes identity change; therefore, it will increase the magnitude of the change as perceived by its members. As a change agent, the HRD professional guides change by ensuring that changes are linked to the strategy of the organization as well as the organization's Purpose and Philosophy. Changes require auditing current practices to ensure that they are aligned with the change. Where current practices are not in alignment, recommendations for change must be discussed, planned, and implemented. Communicating the facets of the change, why it is necessary, and how it will impact members' work can lessen the ambiguity and reduce the tensions of change. Effective management of identity beliefs—by preserving the Purpose and Philosophy and guarding against changes that will damage these identity principles—enables members to feel a sense of stability while in the midst of change. Typically, Priorities, Practices, or Projections are the aspects of the culture that are targeted for change. These changes may not be inconsequential, particularly if they do not align with the Purpose and Philosophy. If changes are not linked to sustaining the identity, then those identity attributes will also change over time. Understanding this systems view and the relationship between the Five Ps of the organization is a responsibility of the HRD leader.

The HRD professional must understand the organization from its broadest view—as an entity grounded by its identity and guided by Priorities that nurture its strategy. Linking all HRD practices to the Core Culture and strategy ensures that the work of HRD practitioners contributes to organizational success. Understanding the "why" of Purpose, the "how" of Philosophy, and the "what" of strategy is the first step in being a strategic HR leader. Additionally, the HRD professional must understand the importance of linking the Priorities to the strategic goals and then aligning Practices, particularly Internal Practices, to the Core Culture and the strategy of the organization. To build a culture of distinction, the HRD professional can follow an iterative, phased process of: (1) defining organizational identity—the Purpose and Philosophy; (2) clarifying strategy and ensuring that the Priorities nurture the achievement of the strategy; (3) auditing all Practices—both Internal and External—and Projections to ensure that they support and reflect the central three Ps of Core Culture and the strategy; (4) planning for ways to achieve greater alignment; and (5) monitoring the execution of the alignment plan. This process of defining and managing the organization's culture ensures the sustainability of an organization so that it continues its unique legacy of contribution. Belief systems are fundamental to the organization Understanding, defining, and managing those Core Culture principles is central to the practice and role of HRD.

References

Albert, S., & Whetten, D. A. (1985) "Organizational identity." In L. L. Cummings, & B. M. Staw (eds), *Research in organizational behavior*, 7 (Greenwich, CT: JAI Press) 263–95.

Ashforth, B. E., & Mael, F. A. (1996) "Organizational identity and strategy as a context for the individual." In P. Shrivastava, A. S. Huff, & J. E. Dutton, (Series eds) & J. C. Baum & J. E. Dutton (vol. ed.), *Advances in Strategic Management:* vol. 13. *The Embeddedness of Strategy* (Greenwich, CT: JAI Press) 19–64.

Bouchikhi, H., & Kimberly, J. (1996) "The nature and dynamics of organizational identity." Paper presented at the INSEAD Conference on Organizations in the Marketplace: Implications of Sociology for Business Policy Research.

Corley, K. G., & Gioia, D. A. (2004) "Identity ambiguity and change in the wake of a corporate spin-off." *Administrative Science Quarterly*, 49, 173–208.

Corley, K. G., Harquail, C. V., Pratt, M. G., Glynn, M. A., Fiol, C. M., & Hatch, M. J. (2006) "Guiding organizational identity through aged adolescence." *Journal of Management Inquiry*, 15(2), 85–99.

Dutton, J. E., & Dukerich, J. M. (1991) "Keeping an eye on the mirror: Image and identity in organizational adaptation." *Academy of Management Journal*, 34, 517–54.

Dutton, J. E., & Penner, W. J. (1993) "The importance of organizational identity for strategic agenda building." In J. Hendry & G. Johnson with J. Newton (eds), *Strategic thinking: Leadership and the management of change.* (Chichester, England: John Wiley & Sons) 89–113.

Fiol, C. M. (1991) "Managing culture as a competitive resource: An identity-based view of sustainable competitive advantage." *Journal of Management*, 17, 191–211.

Foreman, P., & Whetten, D. A. (2002) "Members' identification with multiple-identity organizations." *Organization Science*, 13(6), 618–635.

Grossman, R. J. (2007) "New competencies for HR." In *HR Magazine*, 52(6), Society for Human Resource Management, 58–62.

Gustafson, L. T. (1995) "The structure and content of organizational identity in hypercompetitive environments." Unpublished doctoral dissertation, Arizona State University.

Hansen, C. D., & Kahnweiler, W. M. (1995) "Organizational tension and occupational scripts: Stories form HR professionals and top executives." *Human Resource Management Review*, 5(1), 25–51.

Hatch, M. J., & Schultz, M. (1997) "Relations between organizational culture, identity and image." *European Journal of Marketing*, 31(5/6), 356–65.

Hatch, M. J., & Schultz, M. (2002) "The dynamics of organizational identity." *Human Relations*, 55(8), 989–1018.

Hunt, S. A., & Benford, R. D. (1994) "Identity talk in the peace and justice movement." *Journal of Contemporary Ethnography*, 22(4), 488–517.

Kimberly, J. R., & Bouchikhi, H. (1995) "The dynamics of organizational development and change: How the past shapes the present and constrains the future." *Organization Science*, 6(1), 9–18.

Margolis, S. L., & Hansen, C. D. (2002) "A model for organizational identity: Exploring the path to sustainability during change." *Human Resource Development Review*, 1(3), 277–303.

Margolis, S. L. (2008) "Building a culture of distinction: Activities and tools to lead organizational change." (Atlanta: Workplace Culture Institute).

Sarason, Y. (1995) "A model of organizational transformation: The incorporation of organizational identity into a structuration theory framework." Best Papers Proceedings of the Academy of Management, Vancouver, 47–51.

Schein, E. H. (1992) *Organizational culture and leadership*. (San Francisco: Jossey-Bass).

Whetten, D. A. (2006) "Albert and Whetten revisited: Strengthening the concept of organizational identity." *Journal of Management Inquiry*, 12(3), 219–34.

10
The Culturally Distinct Role of Human Resource Development in Nonprofit Organizations

Ava Wilensky

In May 2005, *The NonProfit Times* noted a landmark occasion: the Internal Revenue Service reported the registration of over 1.5 million nonprofit organizations. Today, just a few years later, reports (including those nonprofit organizations that operate without an official designation) estimate the total to be closer to 2 million. Moreover, research shows that nonprofit organizations have been growing at a rate of approximately 90,000 organizations per year, and the total number has double over the past ten years (Cohn, 2005).

More nonprofit organizations have necessitated more nonprofit workers. Notwithstanding the small decrease in employment numbers that followed the tragedy of 9/11, employment in the sector has steadily increased. The number of Americans working in the voluntary sector has doubled in the past 25 years. Over 12 million people are currently employed in nonprofit organizations, representing approximately 7.1 percent of US employees— more than those who work in fields such as construction, transportation, finance, insurance, or real estate. Moreover, 84 million American adults volunteer in the nonprofit sector annually, in addition to an unidentified number of teenagers who give their time and efforts to charities individually or through religious or school organizations (Independent Sector, 2002b, 2007; Salaman & Sokolowski, 2006).

With revenues approximating $900 billion and assets exceeding $2 trillion, it is undeniable that the nonprofit sector has come to play a significant role in the American social and economic landscape (Independent Sector, 2007). Yet, this unprecedented growth has not reflected an increase in the presence of HRD in nonprofit organizations (Irons & Bass, 2004; Watson & Azbug, 2005). Moreover, there is a lack of academic research, and relatively little more in practitioners' literature, dedicated to the nature and necessity of HRD in the sector. Given that the cultures of nonprofit organizations are grounded in missions dedicated to serving the public good and therefore people, this lack of HRD presence in the sector is particularly paradoxical (Watson & Azbug, 2005; Wilensky & Hansen, 2001; Zdenek, 1998). Why has HRD not become a central function in this "people-first" culture?

Several circumstances contribute to the current state of HRD in this sector. HRD, like all occupational subcultures, is influenced by the organizational culture in which it operates (Hansen, Kahnweiler, & Wilensky, 1994; Margolis & Wilensky, 2006; Schein, 1992; Trice & Beyer, 1993; Wilensky & Hansen, 2001). The beliefs, values, and assumptions that drive nonprofit organizations emerge from fundamental functional and structural issues that are unique to the sector. "Congested schedules, underfunded programs, endless client needs, irregular financial cycles, and demands for reports of accountability, are among the never-ending pressures that crowd out the nonprofit's ability to focus on the critical human dimension" (Watson & Abzug, 2005, p. 625). Thus, it may not be surprising that within this complicated and demanding environment, nonprofit organizations focus on the people outside the organization—their clients—rather than the people inside the organization.

However, the extraordinary rate of growth in the sector thus far, and the predicted growth over the next two decades, will demand more qualified workers and dedicated leaders along with efficient and sophisticated organizational systems to support them (Cornelius, Corvington & Ruesga, 2008; Tierney, 2006; Toole, 2008). How will the sector prepare for this impending need? This is the expertise of the HRD professional. Three nonprofit issues provide a natural portal for HRD into the nonprofit organization: restrictions based on organizational size, the complexity of managing volunteer workers, and a complicated leadership and governance structure. By examining these issues and the cultural assumptions that accompany them, HRD can understand the unique nature of the sector and thus help nonprofit organizations optimize the strengths of their people to foster organizational excellence and ensure mission success.

A brief cultural context

History has a profound effect upon belief systems and therefore upon the culture of a sector. In the case of the nonprofit sector, the historical groundings are a unique blend of religious, political, and economic influences (Herman & Heimovics, 2005; Wilensky & Hansen, 2001; Zdenek, 1998). From its inception, America's spirit yielded settlers who banded together to create socially and religiously directed support systems. These early roots soon solidified and served as the basis for what was eventually instituted as the national nonprofit tax designation in the late nineteenth century. In contrast to the government sector's program and policy orientation, or the for-profit business sector's revenue focus, the nonprofit organization was prescribed to be mission driven to benefit the public good by addressing a wide range of issues and challenges not fully managed by other elements in society (Block, 1987; Scrivner, 1990).

Stemming from this simple idea, today the Internal Revenue Service (IRS) Code 501(c) 3 provides for 27 categories of tax-exempt organizations, forming a complex group of varying and multifaceted concerns that include healthcare organizations, educational institutions, social and human welfare concerns, arts organizations, religious groups, civic and fraternal organizations, and foundations. Although each of these subsectors is distinct, their shared history provides the cultural expectation to serve the public good. Conversely, although there are overarching and fundamental cultural consistencies, it is imperative to remember that each organization reflects the unique passions and allegiances that spurred that nonprofit into being.

HRD and nonprofit organizational size

Organizational size plays a predominant role in the presence and impact of HRD, not only in nonprofit organizations, but in all organizations. Research and practitioners generally suggest that until an organization reaches a certain size, organizational leaders do not consider a dedicated HR professional or function as necessary (La Piana Associates, 2007; Watson & Azbug, 2005). Although each organization has its own criteria, critical mass is generally considered to range from 50 employees to 100 employees (Hodgson, 2000; Klineman, 2004; Winning, 2008). This presents a fundamental problem for HRD in the nonprofit sector. Over 85 percent of all nonprofit organizations have fewer than 50 employees, and more than 73 percent of nonprofit organizations report total budgets of less than $500,000 (HR Council for the Nonprofit & Voluntary Sector, 2007; Independent Sector, 2002a, 2007). Small staffs and small budgets necessitate placing resources toward the mission and client-base, rather than investing in and building human resource potential.

Initially, it may be understandable that organizational capacity building is far down the list when placed in balance with feeding hungry children or housing homeless families. Of course, in the long term, this strategy works against the nonprofit where turnover and burnout are common-place (Azbug, 2007; Pierce, 2006; Pynes, 2004). Employing and keeping the right people in the right jobs allows an organization to run efficiently. Because the nonprofit organization ultimately depends on its people's abilities and commitment to implement its mission, investing in creating the best possible staff would seem to be a wise and beneficial expenditure (Watson & Abzug, 2005). Moreover, when staff are few and workloads are extensive, the loss of even one employee can lead to difficulty in maintaining adequate workflow and delivery of services to clients. The cost of replacing staff is time-consuming and expensive, and the ability to find good employees is further diminished owing to relatively lower salaries in the nonprofit sector compared with those in for-profit or government sectors (Nonprofit World, 1998; Wereschagin, 2007).

Thus, leaders of smaller organizations who may believe they can justify not meeting the needs of their employees because they must meet the needs of their clients, are actually short-changing their human resource potential and the potential of their organizations. It is important for HRD professionals to debunk this cultural assumption and show that even in nonprofit organizations with small staffs, investment in HRD systems serves to keep effective and valued employees and ultimately benefits program success and organizational continuity (Grant & Crutchfield, 2007; Pierce, 2006).

HRD and the volunteer workforce

Volunteers are a unique group of employees typical only to the non-profit sector. Four out of five nonprofit organizations use volunteers to assist in meeting organizational demands (Hager & Brudney, 2004a). In many nonprofit organizations, volunteers outnumber paid staff more than three to one. These unpaid workers, therefore, provide the primary human resources that allow the organization to exist and to accomplish its mission.

In 1999, over 109 million Americans volunteered in nonprofit organizations (Independent Sector, 1999). In 2007, the estimated per-hour dollar value of a volunteer was $19.51 (Independent Sector, 2008). These record-setting numbers represent a boon for the nonprofit sector. Not only do volunteers provide needed human power, greater organizational diversity, and increased community support, but their assistance saves the nonprofit organization salary and program dollars, resulting in a healthier bottom-line (Pynes, 2004). Moreover, volunteers serve as a natural donor base for the nonprofit organization. Happy volunteers are more likely to contribute financially to an organization to which they are connected and committed (Hager & Brudney, 2004b; US Department of Health and Human Services; 2005).

It would be misleading, however, to state that volunteers are literally "free" labor for the nonprofit organization. Volunteers, like paid employees, require support and guidance to be efficient and effective (McCurley, 2005; US Department of Health and Human Services, 2005). Historically, HRD practices for volunteers have not been applied consistently across the nonprofit sector. Moreover, research shows that the probability that a nonprofit organization will implement a HR volunteer management system depends on multiple organizational factors including budget, size, and subsector (Grossman & Furano, 2002; Hager & Brudney, 2004c).

Given the impact and importance of volunteers in the sector, it is intriguing that nonprofit organizations traditionally invest minimally in this work group. It is clear that the more volunteer management practices a nonprofit organization adopts, the greater the organizational benefit (Barbeitotto, 2004; Hager & Brudney, 2004b). In contrast, a deficient volunteer HRD program has been shown to result in ineffective work, discontented volunteers, increased rates of turnover, and potential harm to the organization and its mission (Grossman & Furano, 2002). Moreover, studies show that bringing in community helpers without clearly identifying how they will work with paid employees and how they will directly support a particular organizational objective, can lead to organizational dysfunction and dissatisfaction for both paid and volunteer employees (Ellis, 2002; McCurley, 2005).

Two cultural assumptions may explain the lack of attention to volunteer development by nonprofit leadership. First, nonprofit leaders tend to view volunteers as transient or temporary workers. With no contract or salary to bind them, volunteers can leave the organization without notice. Devoting hard-won and limited dollars to unpaid helpers that may not stay long-term could seem like a poor business decision. However, this is limited perspective.

Volunteers are certainly more likely to leave a nonprofit organization if they are dissatisfied with the environment (Davila de Leon, 2007; Hager & Brudney, 2004a). Using proven HRD practices for volunteer management directly affects volunteer satisfaction and, therefore, retention (Grossman & Furano, 2002; Hager & Brudney, 2004a). A well-designed

HRD volunteer management system provides volunteers with a sense of meaning and fulfillment and motivates them to stay longer and effectively contribute to the organization. After all, volunteering is a reciprocally advantageous act benefiting the volunteer, the nonprofit organization, and the recipient (Grossman & Furano, 2002; Watson & Abzug, 2005). Like paid workers, community volunteers do best when they feel they are integrally connected to the workplace culture, a place where their work is appreciated and valued (Margolis & Wilensky, 2006). Using HRD practices to keep talented volunteers engaged in the organization, as well as not having to re-select and re-train on a continual basis, is cost-effective and helps maintain program continuity.

Second, nonprofit organizations hold the belief that accomplishing the mission is sole priority of the organization; this concept translates into a client-focused environment. From the nonprofit perspective, if dollars are to be spent, they should be allocated to the program recipients, not program workers. Considering that most nonprofit organizations do not provide HRD support for their paid workers, investing in programs for "free workers" would appear highly irrational. However, not providing support and development opportunities to volunteers ultimately diminishes the likelihood that the nonprofit will benefit from their volunteers (Grossman & Furano, 2002). Moreover, research shows that financial investment alone does not yield the full benefit from community workers. A well-implemented HRD program is necessary to properly support and enhance volunteer capabilities (Hager & Brudney, 2004a). Grossman and Furano (2002) have identified three primary HRD issues necessary for a successful volunteer program: selection, orientation-training, and management.

Volunteers are often in short supply and, because they donate their time, expertise, and services, the competition to acquire the best and the brightest can be keen among nonprofit organizations (Pynes, 2004). Selecting the best volunteer for the right position promotes volunteer satisfaction and decreases the likelihood of turnover (Davila de Leon 2007). Frequently, however, nonprofit organizations do not take full advantage of volunteer capabilities and instead, choose to place them in low-level, clerical positions (US Department of Health and Human Services, 2005). In some cases, this practice may be the result of liability concerns. Working with young and special needs clients, as well as with confidential and sensitive issues, may demand rigorous administrative oversight for insurance or governmental requirements. With legal and confidentiality issues at stake, using volunteers in higher level positions may be a risk that the nonprofit organization cannot afford to take.

Alternatively, below-par placement may be simply due to a lack of established HRD systems. The safety of the recipients, the skill of the volunteer applicant, the time commitment necessary to do the work, as well as the time the volunteer candidate has available should all be priority considerations during the selection process. Moreover, volunteer job descriptions must be in place to help community workers understand how their work contributes to organizational goals and to help paid staff understand the limits and boundaries of volunteer efforts (Barbeito, 2004; McCurley, 2005). Having clear job expectations that suit volunteers' skill and interest levels increases the likelihood that they will be satisfied with their work and committed to the success of the organization's mission (Davila de Leon, 2007; Grossman & Furano, 2002).

An orientation-training program for volunteer workers is essential. Frequently, new volunteers are simply handed off to experienced volunteers to learn about the organization and their position. This is a missed opportunity for the nonprofit organization. Volunteers come to a nonprofit organization to contribute and be part of an endeavor that makes a difference to the larger community. Providing orientation secures the connection between the volunteer and the nonprofit organization's mission; it allows volunteers to understand how their jobs fit into the organization as a whole and serves as a way to welcome the newcomer into the nonprofit "family" (US Department of Health and Human Services, 2005). Once oriented, the nonprofit organization must maintain its relationship with the volunteer through ongoing training. Because staff are stretched, budgets are small, and client and program requirements are pressing, nonprofit organizations frequently do not address training needs on a consistent basis and frequently rely on "on-the-job" training. Recent studies show that only 25 percent of nonprofit organizations use ongoing training practices, most taking place in organizations with budgets over $5 million (Grossman & Furano, 2002). In many cases, nonprofit organizational success depends upon how well an organization can leverage its volunteers. HRD professionals are uniquely positioned to help these organizations design and administer effective training programs.

Once a volunteer is oriented and trained, management and supervision is imperative. Many nonprofit organizations handle this situation by simply assigning a staff member as the "go-to" person for potential questions or problems. This, however, often leaves volunteers feeling unsettled, unappreciated, and undervalued. Only 12.5 percent of nonprofit organizations have designated staff members devoted to full time volunteer management (Moore, 2004; Wereschagin, 2007).

Research shows that volunteer management is the most crucial element in a successful volunteer program, and that consistent two-way communication is the key to building a positive relationship between the supervisor and the volunteer, as well as between the volunteer and the organization (Hager & Brudney, 2004a; Grossman & Furano, 2002).

Thus, despite the transitory nature of volunteers, directing dollars toward building their capacity ultimately benefits the program and its recipients. HRD must confront the cultural assumptions of the sector and show that leveraging volunteer talent can be a powerful vehicle for the nonprofit organization to extend its reach beyond what might otherwise be restricted financial and human resources (Brudney, 2005; Grossman & Furano, 2002; Hager & Brudney, 2004b; McCurley, 2005).

HRD and nonprofit leadership

Like organizations in all sectors, the role of leadership is paramount. Today, the role of the nonprofit leader is in peril (Cornelius, Corvington & Ruesga, 2008; Tierney, 2006; Toole, 2008). Internal and external forces have created the probability of a vast leadership deficit in the sector. HRD is well positioned to strengthen leadership and find solutions to the nonprofit leadership predicament. Three principal issues present a natural fit for HRD expertise: the complicated nature of the nonprofit governance structure, the potential pitfalls of founder-leaders, and the critical need for leadership development in the sector.

Nonprofit governance

The governance structure of the nonprofit sector is distinct. Leadership authority in a nonprofit is a bifurcated system that includes the Executive Director as the paid, formal leadership professional and a Board of Directors (also call the Board of Trustees) headed by a Board Chairperson and comprised of volunteer leaders. Thus, nonprofit organizations have a governance structure that includes two primary leadership entities—one a volunteer, one paid; one part-time, one full-time; and one with a temporary term, and one that holds a position until he or she chooses to leave or is terminated.

Together, the Executive Director with the Board Chair and Directors govern the nonprofit organization. Legally, the Executive Director serves at the discretion of and reports directly to the Board of Directors. "A central paradox of the nonprofit is that the Board of Directors holds ultimate power but does not ordinarily wield it operationally unless the organization does not have paid leaders" (Axelrod, 2005, p. 134).

In other words, the Executive runs the nonprofit organization, but the Board of Directors is actually in charge on paper. In a 501(c)3 organization, this governance structure provides an inherent safeguard. Unlike a for-profit company that depends on its stockholders to vote and act as an external check on the actions of the CEO, the nonprofit organization uses its volunteer Board of stakeholders to monitor and maintain financial and management oversight. Today, in an era of strict financial audit concerns, Board supervision is a pivotal and essential responsibility.

Although no monetary consideration is given, each Board member has a legal and fiduciary responsibility to the organization. As fiduciaries, Board members are expected to ensure that the organization acts to benefit the public. Board members are charged with three standards of behavior: Duty of Care, Duty of Loyalty, and Duty of Obedience. The Duty of Care obliges Board members to take reasonable care when making decisions for the organization. Board members must stay well informed about the organization's practices, must be knowledgeable about the nonprofit's mission, services, and programs, and must be well prepared for business meetings. The Duty of Loyalty demands that Board members always act and make decisions in the best interest of the organization and guard against using, or be perceived as using, the nonprofit organization's information for personal gain. The Duty of Obedience compels the Board of Trustees to support the organization's mission at all times and to ensure that the nonprofit organization acts consistently within its mission and bylaws (Watson & Abzug, 2005).

There is not one specific governance model that works in all nonprofit organizations (Axelrod, 2005; Bradshaw, Hayday, Armstrong, Levesque, & Rykert, 1998; Watson & Abzug, 2005). Traditional models of governance tend to separate the roles of the Board and the Executive, whereas other models support a more mutually shared format to ensure increased accountability and Board effectiveness (Bradshaw, Hayday, Armstrong, Levesque, & Rykert, 1998). Some models suggest that the Executive Director, as the paid professional, must primarily direct the organization and manage the Board, whereas others suggest that a more collaborative approach is preferable (Axelrod, 2005; Herman & Heimovics, 2005). Of course, practitioners and researchers agree that the best nonprofit governance model is the one that elicits the most effective working environment for a particular organization.

In addition to the organization's governance structure, the personalities of the Executive Director and Board members impact the tenor of nonprofit governance. Whether it is a Board of a large nonprofit comprised of high-powered for-profit CEOs, or the Board of a new nonprofit organization filled with passionate communitarians, the relationship between the Board and the Executive Director can be stressful and require constant attention. The Executive Director of a nonprofit organization must be flexible enough to shift with each new Board Chair's term and must learn how to leverage the talent that each new Board member brings to share with the organization. Each new Board Chair must discover how to assert the responsibilities of the Board and maximize its members to forward the organization without stepping over the line into the Executive Director's domain (Anthony & Young, 1988; Axelrod, 2005; Herman & Heimovics, 2005; Wilensky, 1995)

The leadership "dance" that takes place in a nonprofit organization is unique to the sector. The crux of the dilemma between the Board and the Executive Director lies in the distinction between leadership and management. At their best, the Board Chair and the Directors evaluate the relevant landscape and work to set strategy and policy for the organization. The Executive Director provides the essential data that enables the Board to set this direction, and then enacts that direction through management practices. Both parties can easily cross these boundaries. This political quagmire leaves the nonprofit organization in a never-ending quest for leadership balance (Axelrod, 2005; Herman & Heimovics, 2005).

It is apparent from this brief overview that governance issues present a host of predicaments for nonprofit leadership. Because HRD professionals can solve organizational problems systemically, they can play a vital role in assisting the Executive Director and the Board in defining a governance structure that advances the organization's mission and supports its core values. Defining and clarifying roles and responsibilities within that structure can further improve collaboration and can allow leaders to focus on work and strategic alliances rather than be distracted by interpersonal matters or political drama. Further, helping Boards and Executive Directors develop the trust to work as a team allows the nonprofit organization to capitalize on individual strengths and resources for which the organization is the beneficiary.

Organizational genesis and "the" founder's syndrome

The potential for leadership challenges in the nonprofit sector emerges even as the organization first comes into existence. In many cases, a nonprofit organization's life begins with a group of passionate and dedicated citizens seeking to make a difference by ameliorating a societal problem. At the helm of this devoted group is an entrepreneurial, charismatic leader that embodies the essence of the organization and draws this small initial group together. As the nonprofit organization develops, others join the calling—serving on the Board, working on specific projects, generating funds, or providing direct services to recipients. In this nascent organization, all revenue typically is applied directly to the mission of the nonprofit organization and no member of the working Board receives compensation (McNamara, 1998).

Soon the nonprofit organization and its services grow to a critical mass and the decision is made to allocate funds for a salaried Executive Director or CEO. Many times, nonprofit Boards opt to allow their founder to become the Executive Director (Aggarwal, Evans & Dhananjay, 2007). From the Board's perspective, this may look like a reasonable decision; this individual is the heart and soul of the organization; who better to lead it to its next phase? Moreover, keeping the founder in place ensures that the culture will remain consistent and protects the group's identity. Unfortunately, this decision often leads to a problem characterized as founder's syndrome (Block & Rosenberg, 2002; McNamara, 1998).

Founder's syndrome occurs when a nonprofit organization maintains operations based on the personality and style of the founder rather than adopting management practices that will propel the organization to the next level. Founder–leaders tend to be more reactive than proactive. They are generally resistant to instituting formal budgets and guidelines, prefer to make decisions without Board input, and like to handle staffing and Board appointments based on likeability or relationship rather than expertise. In due course, these practices can stunt a nonprofit organization's growth and potentially lead to the its demise (McNamara, 1998).

There are two solutions for the dilemma of founder's syndrome. In one situation, the founder–leader can accept that the dream has become a reality and, having accomplished the goal, may choose to leave. This might be the case if the innovative and entrepreneurial founder–leader finds it too difficult to shift to a structure based on formal budgets and specific guidelines that demand the sharing of information and power with a fully empowered Board. Once the founder–leader steps down, the Board is free to hire a new Executive Director. Research shows that, after the departure of a founder–leader, Boards tend to hire a new leader who "is likely to have more experience and skill in efficiently managing and maintaining an organization" than the founder–leader (Block & Rosenberg, 2002, p. 364).

The alternative is for the founder–leader to embrace change and learn to adopt management skills to continue to lead the nonprofit organization.

Similarly, the founder–leader can choose to stay in the organization in an advisory or volunteer position. One study found that 33 percent of founders had served in a leadership role with their organization for 10–20 years (Block & Rosenberg, 2002). Whether the founder–leader remains as the Executive Director or finds another position within the organization in which to serve, personal ownership must be relinquished so that the nonprofit organization can grow and thrive.

Finding the right leader for the right time is a formidable task. Today's nonprofit executive must be a systemic leader, managing staff to excel, enabling the Board to succeed, and envisioning the change and innovation that will bring the nonprofit organization closer to accomplishing its mission (Herman & Heimovics, 2005). The HRD professional must be at the forefront of this endeavor, assisting nonprofit organizations in effectively managing organizational and leadership transitions while leveraging the founder's strengths to ensure that future challenges are met.

Leadership succession in nonprofit organizations

Perhaps no issue is more crucial in the current nonprofit climate that the impending deficit of leaders in the coming decade. Recent studies conclude that it will be necessary for the nonprofit sector to attract and develop 330,000 to 640,000 nonprofit leaders over the next 10 years. Competition with the for-profit and governmental sectors for the brightest and most talented leaders will be a formidable contest (Tierney, 2006; Toole, 2008).

There are three primary reasons for this impending leadership demand. First, as previously stated, the number of nonprofit organizations is growing at an unprecedented rate—as many as 90,000 per year. The total number of nonprofit organizations has tripled over the past 20 years (Independent Sector, 2007). Each new nonprofit organization represents the necessity for the availability of more highly skilled managers. Second, the baby-boomer generation is turning 60 and poised to leave the workforce; the effect on the nonprofit sector will be twofold. Not only will this age group indicate the retirement of capable nonprofit leaders, but the needs of this aging generation will require more nonprofit services (Cornelius, Corvington, & Ruesga, 2008; Tierney, 2006; Toole, 2008).

Third, and most disturbing, nonprofit organizations are experiencing a record increase in leadership attrition and transition (Cornelius, Corvington, & Ruesga, 2008; Tierney, 2006; Toole, 2008). Why, especially in this time of great need, are nonprofit executives exiting nonprofit organizations? Essentially these leaders report leaving high-stressed, underpaid positions for more attractive opportunities both within and outside the sector. Research shows that this is due to a pervasive, if not insidious, cultural belief in the sector that work in nonprofit organizations should "happen at a discount"—less pay for more hours (Cornelius, Corvington, & Ruesga, 2008, p. 3). Salaries in the non-profit sector lag behind those in the for-profit and governmental sectors (Cornelius, Corvington, & Ruesga, 2008). Moreover, the increasing focus on accountability and the competition for donor dollars has compelled nonprofit organizations to comply with funder demands that dona-tions be primarily directed to client services. These high standards for donor dollars leaves little funding for management support or salaries. Future leaders are also influenced by the impact of this cultural bias. Because nonprofit executives report burn-out, those down the manage-ment pipeline are not attracted by the potential of more responsibility and stress for fewer rewards (Cornelius, Corvington, & Ruesga, 2008; Tierney, 2006; Toole, 2008).

"Leadership capacity is what matters most to the long-run effective-ness of any organization, including nonprofits" (Tierney, 2006, p. 19). Although funding can be an important consideration, not attending to the critical nature of the leadership shortfall can be more dangerous. Recent research suggests that fewer than 10 percent of nonprofit organizations engage in succession planning (Santora, Caro, & Sarros, 2007). Moreover, nonprofit organizations have "neither the size nor the resources to develop large numbers of managers internally, as their for-profit counterparts do. The sector also lacks robust management-education and executive search capabilities" (Tierney, 2006, p. 3).

To be competitive, HRD professionals must be engaged to help even the smallest nonprofit management team learn how to grow and nur-ture new leaders from within. Moreover, HRD can assist the sector in creating management compensation packages that truly compete with the other sectors. Economic incentives, improved benefits, and the promise of sufficient retirement instruments, contribute toward making the case for nonprofit executive leadership. Despite reports that non-profit cultures are more accommodating of personal or family matters, recent studies shows that, because of the extended hours and stress, nonprofit executives feel their personal lives are significantly compro-mised by their workload (Lobell & Connolly, 2007). Although incen-tives and rewards cannot fully compensate for time and work pressures, if executives are paid well they can more easily justify their personal sacrifice and dedication to a mission (Tierney, 2006).

Finally, the nonprofit sector is in need of new resource possibilities for leaders. Traditionally, nonprofit organizations have found leadership referrals through professional networks and personal relationships. Although this tactic has worked in the past, competition among the sectors demands a professional and pointed approach. HRD professionals can help nonprofit leaders create efficient selection strategies to explore alternative and innovative leadership sources.

Meeting the leadership needs of nonprofit sector over the coming years will be demanding. While nonprofit organizations can survive for the short-term, ultimately, the well-being of nonprofit organizations—and their ability to deliver against their missions' promise—is at risk. The HRD professional is the optimum resource to help this nonprofit sector dispel cultural limitations and secure the necessary executive management for the next generation. Whether it is building the most advantageous governance structures, assisting with organizational and leadership transitions, or developing systems to address the need for future leadership, HRD has the fundamental capabilities to help the nonprofit sector continue to accomplish their vital social mission.

Conclusion

The unprecedented growth of the nonprofit sector over the past two decades presents a challenging quandary for today's nonprofit organizational leaders. How does the sector—focused on the delivery of services to its recipients and hampered by severe financial restrictions—attend to the inherent organizational needs of its staff and volunteers, while protecting the authenticity of its mission? When does spending dollars on the people who support the organizations detract from spending dollars on the people who depend on the organization? The cultural imperatives of the nonprofit sector have too long held its organizations in human resource captivity. Staff, volunteers, and leadership are the reason that the nonprofit organization can deliver its mission. To maximize outcomes, to create high-performance organizations, to attract the highest caliber leaders, the nonprofit sector must assess and confront those beliefs, values, and assumptions that have restricted the development of the people who dedicate their energies to their cause.

Likewise, HRD cannot sit casually by and wait to be invited into nonprofit organizations. Engaging a three-pronged approach, HRD professionals must demonstrate that their expertise brings definitive value to the sector—both the people and the bottom-line. First, cultural perspectives that have underrated or denied the need for organizational and individual development must be exposed, disputed, and realigned. Secondly, using price-sensitive products and services, HRD must demonstrate that investing in the people of the organization not only yields engaged staff, talented leaders, and committed volunteers, but also enhances client delivery services and funder satisfaction. Finally, more academic research must be conducted to explore and define how leveraging HRD expertise can strengthen and advance the nonprofit sector's capacity.

The nonprofit sector is ripe with organizational concerns; HRD holds the key to discovering the solutions. In the end, it will be up to the HRD profession whether it will challenge the nonprofit culture and assert its knowledge and capabilities, or continue to remain a relatively untapped resource for the sector.

References

Aggarwal, R. K., Evans, M., & Dhananjay, N. (2007) Nonprofit boards: Size and managerial incentives. [Electronic version]. Retrieved July 20, 2008, from http://faculty.chicagogsb.edu/workshops/accounting/pdf/nanda.nonprofit.pdf.

Anthony, R. N. & Young, D. W. (1988/1990). "Characteristics of nonprofit organizations." In Gies, D. L., Ott, J. S., & Shafritz, J. M. (eds) *The nonprofit organization* (Pacific Grove, CA: Brooks/Cole Publishing Company) 126–37.

Axelrod, N. R. (2005). Board leadership and development. In Hermann & Associates (eds), *The Jossey-Bass handbook of nonprofit leadership and management.* (San Francisco: John Wiley & Sons, Inc.) pp. 131–53.

Azbug, R. (2007) "Wishful thinking about nonprofits." *Transactional Social Science and Modern Society*, 44 (3) 45–47.

Barbeito, C. L. (2004) *Human Resource policies and procedures for nonprofit organizations.* (Hoboken, NJ: John Wiley & Sons Inc.).

Block, S. R. (1987/1990). "A history of the discipline." In Gies, D. L., Ott, J. S., & Shafritz, J. M. (eds) *The nonprofit organization* (Pacific Grove, CA: Brooks/Cole Publishing Company) 126–37.

Block, S. R. & Rosenberg, S. (2002) "Toward an understanding of founder's syndrome: An assessment of power and privilege among founders of nonprofit organizations." *Nonprofit management & leadership*, 12, 353–68.

Bradshaw, P., Hayday, B., Armstrong, R., Levesque, J., & Rykert, L. (1998) Nonprofit governance models: Problems and prospects. [Electronic version]. Retrieved May 20, 2008, from http://www.buildingmovement.org/artman/uploads/nonprofit_governance_models.pdf.

Brudney, J. L. (2005). Designing and managing volunteer programs. In R. D. Hermann & Associates (eds), *The Jossey-Bass handbook of nonprofit leadership and management.* (San Francisco: John Wiley & Sons, Inc.) pp. 310–44.

Cohn, T. (2005) Each 501(c) (3) is now. *The nonprofit times.* Retrieved April 1, 2007, from http://www.nptimes.com/May05/npt3.html.

Cornelius, M., Corvington, P., & Ruesga, A. (2008) A. Ready to lead? Next generation leaders speak out. Compass point. [Electronic version]. Retrieved May 20, 2008, from http://www.meyerfoundation.org/downloads/ready_to_lead/ReadytoLead2008.pdf.

Davila de Leon, M. C. & Fuertes, F. C. (2007) "Prediction of longevity of volunteer service: A basic alternative proposal." *The Spanish Journal of Psychology*, 10, 115–21.

Ellis, S. J. (2002) *The volunteer recruitment (and membership development) handbook.* (3rd ed.) (Philadelphia: Energize Books).

Grant, H. M. & Crutchfield, L. R. (2007) Creating high-impact nonprofits. *Stanford Social Innovations Review.* [Electronic version]. Retrieved July 23, 2007, from http://www.ssireview.org/articles/entry/creating_high_impact_nonproftis/.

Grossman, J. B. & Furano, K. (2002) Making the most of volunteers. [Electronic version]. Retrieved April 28, 2008, from http://www.ppv.org/ppv/publications/assets/ 152_publication.pdf.

Hager, M. A. & Brudney, J. L. (2004a) Volunteer management practices and retention of volunteers. [Electronic version]. Retrieved April 25, 2008, from http://www.urban.org/url.cfm?ID=411005.

Hager, M. A. & Brudney, J. L. (2004b) Balancing act: The challenges and benefits of volunteers. [Electronic version]. Retrieved April 25, 2008, from http://www.urban.org/url.cfm?ID=411125.

Hager, M. A. & Brudney, J. L. (2004c) Volunteer management capacity in America's charities and congregations. [Electronic version]. Retrieved April 25, 2008, from http://www.urban.org/url.cfm?ID=410963.

Hansen, C. D., Kahnweiler, W. M., & Wilensky, A. S. (1994) "Human resource development as an occupational culture through organizational stories." *Human Resource Development Quarterly*, 5(3) 253–68.

Herman R. D. & Heimovics, D. (2005). Executive leadership. In Hermann & Associates (eds), *The Jossey-Bass handbook of nonprofit leadership and management* (San Francisco: John Wiley & Sons, Inc.) pp. 153–70.

Hodgson, J. F. (2000) Human relations in a start-up environment.[Electronic version]. Retrieved July 18 from http://www.shrm.org/hrresources/whitepapers_published/CMS_000293.asp.

HR Council for the nonprofit & voluntary sector. (2007) Workforce statistics. [Electronic version]. Retrieved April 21, 2008, from http://www.hrcouncil.ca/about-the-sector/stats-sector.cfm.

Independent Sector (2002a). Balancing the scales: Measuring the roles and contributions of nonprofit organizations and religious congregations July 1, 2008, from http://www.independentsector.org/PDFs/ npemployment.pdf.

Independent Sector (2002b). The nonprofit almanac: Facts and findings. [Electronic version]. Retrieved April 21, 2008, from http://www.independentsector.org/PDFs/ npemployment.pdf.

Independent Sector (1999). Volunteering: Volunteer levels and the number of hours Recorded: 1999 National Survey. [Electronic version]. Retrieved April 21, 2008, from http://www.independsector.org/ gandv/svolu.htm.

Independent Sector (2007). Facts and figures about charitable organizations. [Electronic version]. Retrieved April 21, 2008, from http://www.independentsector.org/programs/research/Charitable_Fact_Sheet.pdf.

Independent Sector (2008). Value of volunteer time. [Electronic version]. Retrieved April 21, 2008, from http://www.independentsector.org/programs/research/ volunteer_time.html.

Irons, J. S. & Bass, G. Trends in nonprofit employment, earnings 1990–2004. [Electronic version]. Retrieved July 21, 2008, from http://www.ombwatch.org/article/articleview/2347.

Klineman, J. (2004) Human resources from scratch. [Electronic version]. Retrieved June 21, 2008, from http://philanthropy.com/free/articles/v17/i04/04002501.htm.

La Piana, Associates (2007). A case study in the creation of an effective human resources function: Yosemite National Institutes. [Electronic version]. Retrieved May 21, 2008, from http://www.lapiana.org/consulting/cases/yni.html.

Lobell, J. R. & Connolly, P. M. (2007) "Peak performance: Nonprofit leaders rate highest in 360-degree reviews." *Nonprofit Quarterly*. (December 21, 2007). Retrieved from http://www.nonprofitquarterly.org/content/view/165/1/.

Margolis, S. L. & Wilensky, A. S. (2006) *There is no place like work: Seven leadership insights for creating a workplace to call home*. (Layton, Utah: Gibbs Smith, Publisher).

McCurley, S. (2005). Keeping the community involved. In R. D. Hermann & Associates (eds), *The Jossey-Bass handbook of nonprofit leadership and management*. (San Francisco: John Wiley & Sons, Inc.) pp. 587–622.

McNamara, C. (1998) "Founder's syndrome: How founders and their organizations recover." *Nonprofit World*, 16, 38–41.

Moore, C. (2004) Charities must learn to manage volunteers, study finds. The Chronicles of Philanthropy. (March 18, 2004). Retrieved from http://philanthropy.com/free/articles/v16/i11/11003401.htm.

Nonprofit World. (1998) Nonprofit salaries still lowest. [Electronic version]. Retrieved May 21, 2008, from http://findarticles.com/p/articles/mi_qa5384/is_199803/ai_n21420112.

Pierce, G. (2006) "Developing managers to prevent staff burnout." *New Directions for Adult and Continuing Education*. 38, 77–86. [Electronic version]. Retrieved May 1, 2008, from http://www3.interscience.wiley.com/journal/112782825/.

Pynes, J. E. (2004) *Human resources management for public and nonprofit organizations*. (CA: Jossey-Bass).

Salaman, L. M. & Sokolowski, S. W. (2006) Employment in America's Charities. [Electronic version]. Retrieved April 21, 2008, from http://www.jhu.edu/ccss/research/pdf/Employment%20in%20Americas%20Charities.pdf.

Santora, J. C., Caro, M. E., & Sarros, J. C. (2007) "Succession in nonprofit organizations: An insider/outsider perspective." *SAM Advanced Management Journal*. [Electronic version]. Retrieved June 21, 2008, from http://findarticles.com/p/articles/mi_hb6698/is_200709/ai_n26562436.

Schein, E. H. (1992) Organizational culture and leadership (2nd ed.) (San Francisco: Jossey-Bass Publishers).

Scrivner, G. N. (1989/1990). "100 years of tax policy changes affecting charitable organizations." In D. L. Gies, J. S. Ott, & J. M. Shafritz (eds) *The nonprofit organization* (Pacific Grove, CA: Brooks/Cole Publishing Company) 126–137.

Tierney, T. J. (2006) The nonprofit sector's leadership deficit. The Bridgespan Group. [Electronic version]. Retrieved February 15, 2008, from http://www.bridgespangroup.Org/LeadershipDeficitWhitePaper.pdf.

Toole, T. F. (2008). CEO Succession: An urgent challenge for nonprofits. Enter for Community Engagement. [Electronic version]. Retrieved May 31, 2008, from http://www.cce-rochester.org/documents/ceo_succession_survey_report.pdf.

Trice, H. M. & Beyer, J. M. (1993) *The cultures of work organizations*. (Englewood Cliff, NJ: Prentice Hall).

U.S. Department of Health and Human Services. (2005) Successful strategies for recruiting, training and utilizing volunteers (HRS-SAMHSA Faith—Based and Community Initiative (DHHS Publication No. (SMA) 05-4005. Rockville, M. [Electronic version]. Retrieved April 21, 2008, from http://www.samhsa.gov/fbci/Volunteer handbook.pdf.

Watson, M. R. & Abzug, R. (2005). Finding the ones you want, keeping the ones you find. In R. D. Hermann & Associates (eds), *The Jossey-Bass handbook of nonprofit leadership and management*. (San Francisco: John Wiley & Sons, Inc.) pp. 623–59.

Wereschagin, M. Women (2007) paid less than men in nonprofit work. Pittsburgh Tribune-Review. [Electronic version]. Retrieved January 28, 2008, from http://www.pittsburghlive.com/x/pittsburghtrib/news/cityregion/s_490525.html.

Wilensky, A. S. & Hansen, C. D. (2001) "Understanding the work beliefs of nonprofit executives through organizational stories." *Human Resource Development Quarterly*, 12(3) 223–39.

Wilensky, A. S. (1995) Understanding the culture of nonprofit executives through stories: A qualitative investigation. (Doctoral dissertation, Georgia State University). Dissertation Abstracts International 9541507.

Winning, E. A. (2008) When is an HR department necessary? [Electronic version]. (1995–2008). Retrieved April 23, 2008 from http://www.ewin.com/articles/whnHR.htm.

Zdenek, R. (1998) Organizational culture and nonprofits. *Public administration and management: An interactive journal*, 3. [Electronic version]. Retrieved February 15, 2008, from http://www.pamij.com/zdenek.html.

11
Culture Conflicts in Demonstrating the Value of Human Resource Development

Saul Carliner

Given that the concept of performance-based training has existed for over 30 years and several tools have arisen to demonstrate that it works, one might expect that, by 2008, both training culture and practice—that is, the value and belief system of people who design, develop, and deliver learning programs for the workplace—would seamlessly incorporate performance. That a promotion for a seminar by a major training magazine asks "Is performance-based training a trend or an approach that can truly deliver compelling business results?" suggests otherwise.

This schism between advocated cultural values and actual practice among training practitioners is especially evident in the demonstration of the impact of training programs. On the one hand, authors in the literature of training (which includes the literature on human resource development (HRD), training, instructional design, and human performance technology) advise training professionals to *Quick, Show Me Your Value* (Seagraves, 2004) and warn "The rule [should be] 'Always establish a return on investment that represents dramatic return for the client . . . ' and [failing to do that] is why internal training and human resource efforts continue to fade and lose credence while consulting business skyrockets" (Weiss, 2008). On the other hand, repeated studies through the years have shown that training departments still do not assess the impact (Arthur, Bennett, Edens, & Bell, 2003) and return on investment (ROI) of their work, leading one magazine columnist to advise for practical reasons, "Don't focus on ROI" (Galloway, 2007).

In this chapter, I explore this dichotomy. In it, I present evidence from two related studies of field practice that demonstrate the limited extent to which the training managers track and report the impact of their training programs. I then interpret the evidence to suggest why

179

demonstrating the impact of training programs has not become the practice that so many authors have recommended and even demanded. Before doing so, however, I first provide some background on the context of the studies.

Background

Performance-based training is "based on precise tasks learned in sequence and tested against a criterion of competent performance . . . improvement of employee performance is the main goal" (Belfiore, 1996, p. 42).

Thomas Gilbert introduced the concept of performance in his watershed 1978 book, *Human Competence: Engineering Worthy Performance*. By the late 1980s, the National Society for Performance and Instruction (now the International Society for Performance Improvement) adopted performance as its approach to training, and the larger American Society for Training and Development (ASTD) followed suit by the mid-1990s. Books like Dana and James Robinson's *Training for Impact* (1989) and *Performance Consulting* (1995), and a host of similar texts by other authors mainstreamed the concept of performance-based training in the training and development community. Since the mid-1990s, the concept has also been mainstreamed among the broader community of instructional designers (many of whom do not work in a training context), with its mention in most of the major textbooks on the subject, including later editions of the Walter Dick and Lou Carey's best-selling *Systematic Design of Instruction* (now in its sixth edition).

Not only have efforts been made to integrate the concept of performance into the culture of training and instructional design, but also, through a related effort, trainers have been encouraged to demonstrate that performance has actually improved as the result of a training program or similar intervention (Stolovitch & Keeps, 1992, 1999, 2004). The concept of training evaluation has been around since the earliest instructional design models were proposed in the 1940s (Deutcsch, 1992; Reiser, 2001). Those earliest models emphasized tests of learning as a means of evaluating training. In 1959, Donald Kirkpatrick (1998) proposed a more holistic four-level approach to training evaluation, which assessed not only learning (level 2 in his model), but also learners' satisfaction with the training program (level 1), their ability to transfer the behavior taught in the training program to the job (level 3), and the impact of the new behavior on the organization that sponsored the training (level 4).

Formula for Calculating ROI	Example in Words	Example in Numbers
Resulting impact on the training organization _____ Investment in training	As the result of a $15,500 training course, 900 workers have reduced scrap by $10/day each (900 workers saving $10/day and working 250 days a year is $21,600).	21,600 = 1.39 _____ 15,500 (That is, the ROI in this course after one year is approximately 1.39. It returned its cost, plus an additional 39 percent benefit.)

Figure 11.1 Calculation of return on investment.

Since the late 1990s, people writing about the field of training have focused on the importance of evaluating impact, especially in quantitative terms. At the least, impact can be quantified in terms of metrics already used to assess performance in the training environment (Kirkpatrick 1998, Swanson, & Holton, 1999), such as reduced dependence on user assistance staff, reduced errors in a manufacturing process, fewer displeased customers in a customer-service process, or increased sales of a new product. At the most, because so many of these impacts can be quantified in financial terms, impact can also be expressed financially terms. When computed as the ratio of the impact to the investment in training, impact is called the return on investment (ROI) in training (Phillips, 2003; Phillips & Stone, 2002; Swanson & Holton, 1999). In simplest terms, ROI involves calculating the return on investment in percentage terms (Phillips, 2003). Figure 11.1 provides a more in-depth explanation of ROI.

Because of its focus both on individual training programs (which, in practice, tend to be the focus of most training efforts) and reporting financial returns, ROI has dominated the discussion on demonstrating the performance of training. ROI is an extension of levels 3 and 4 of the Kirkpatrick methodology, but his description offers no advice on establishing a methodology for determining this. As a result, literature has emerged to fill this gap, led by Phillips' extensive publications on ROI (Phillips, 2003; Phillips & Breining, 2007; Phillips & Phillips, 2008; Philips & Stone, 2002), but also addressed by books like *Developing and Measuring Training the Six Sigma Way: A Business Approach to Training and Development* (Islam, 2006).

However, ROI is not the only scheme for demonstrating the impact of training, as noted by the other publications exploring additional methods of demonstrating value (Gargiulo, Pangarkar, Kirkwood, & Bunzel, 2006; Rothwell, Lindholm, & Wallick, 2003; Van Adelsberg & Trolley, 1999). These other methods focus on the impact of the group providing training (such as a training department or corporate university), not just the impact of a course. For example, ASTD's Workplace Learning and Performance (WLP) Scorecard (ASTD, 2006) tracks several performance metrics for an entire training unit, and Bassi & McMurrer's (2007) financial analysis system links publicly traded organizations' overall investment in training with the performance of their stocks.

The fact that the impact of training can be demonstrated at the department and course level, and using different methods, reflects the challenges in operationalizing the concept. One of the key challenges in doing so is terminology, as terms like *quality, value,* and *effectiveness* are used interchangeably with *impact,* even though some of these terms do not address impact. Consider quality. Bandes (1986) defines it as conformance to requirements. In the training literature, requirements are defined as learning objectives (Dick & Carey, 2008; Smith & Ragan, 2004), which can be assessed by criterion-referenced assessments, one of the means that Kirkpatrick suggests using to assess learning (level 2). In contrast, consider value. Shetty & Buehler (1988) define it as the ratio of quality to price. In concrete terms, that could mean getting as many things as possible for the money spent (such as when one can buy two suits for the price of one) or having a durable product or service that has long-lasting value (such as when one "invests" in a suit, hoping its durability will help the owner avoid the expense of replacing the suit). Both are a type of impact, but not the same type. Last, consider effectiveness. Its ultimate meaning is tied up not only in language, but also in beliefs about what constitutes effective training. For example, some people (most often executives who work outside training, but sometimes those who work inside the field) believe that a course that students rate as satisfactory is effective. That definition is unsatisfactory to others who assess the effectiveness of training as learning, financial impact, or the ability of learners to apply the lessons taught in training in their workplaces.

Although the methods for assessing impact differ in scope and definition, they share two common characteristics. The first is that they are prescriptive, focused on what training managers *should* be doing to demonstrate their value, but not on what they are doing. The second common characteristic is that, except for Kirkpatrick's level 1 (assessing reaction to training), empirical studies consistently show that training managers are not using these forms of evaluation. For example, several studies have shown that use of Kirkpatrick's levels 3 and 4 is below 10 percent (Arthur, Bennett, Edens, & Bell, 2003; Mattson, 2003). In other words, despite strong messages to adopt performance-based training and to demonstrate that training had the intended impact on performance, training managers are not using the most widely described and most thoroughly developed methods.

About the studies

So which aspects of training impact are managers tracking and reporting, if any? How are they doing so? Are there any common practices being followed? If so, how does actual practice vary from prescribed practice? The studies discussed in this chapter were designed to find out.

To conduct the research, terminology had to be operationalized. To make sure that the issue was explored from as many angles as possible, the concept was broken into two parts: *productivity*—that is, how much training was produced; and *effectiveness*—that is, how good was the training (D. Walmer, personal conversation, 1998).

In addition, initial beliefs that might color the research had to be identified. Without identifying them up front, these beliefs could bias research activities by guiding the research toward preconceived notion, rather than what the data was actually reporting. Five were identified through a frame interview. The first was that many training managers do not fully understand training evaluation in the first place. The second entering belief was that demonstrating the impact and ROI of training programs should be a widespread cultural practice among training managers but the methods described in the literature do not accurately reflect what these managers actually do. A third entering belief was that some of the newer schemes like the WLP Scorecard might assess training activity and impact more precisely and thoroughly, but are time-consuming and complex to use. The fourth entering belief was that, although the empirical literature suggests that training managers do not widely apply Kirkpatrick's levels, some might be collecting, analyzing, and reporting those measures of impact and ROI that are readily available to them , and their discovery (and resulting communication) might lead to widespread use. The last entering belief was that, because the work of trainers is similar to that of professional communicators (Carliner, 2000), perhaps the easily collected, analyzed, and reported measures that were sought might be found in the related fields of technical communication (which focuses producing documents for practical purposes, including user's guides, reference manuals, service guides, and training), and corporate communication (which primarily focuses on communicating internally within an organization such as through policies and procedures, employee newsletters, and internal meetings).

The original research plan involved conducting a series of related studies ultimately intended to discover and validate measures. The series would begin with a pair of descriptive studies that explored how organizations assess the learning and communication products they produce. The first would be a qualitative study to generate hypotheses about how managers in training, technical communication, and corporate communication track and report productivity and effectiveness. The second would be a quantitative study to confirm the hypotheses emerging from the first. Both studies would be conducted with managers in these fields. As a result of practical experience and awareness of demographics of the field, I was aware that management in each of these fields is likely to have not only varying years of experience, but also varying qualifications for their jobs (some working their way through a career ladder in the field, and others moving from other fields into their management positions). So only one assumption about managers' awareness of, much less acculturation in, their respective occupational cultures was made. That assumption was: as the legal representative of their groups, managers would need some understanding of accepted practices in the fields they were managing. The next sections describe these studies.

Study one: Generating hypotheses about how training managers assess productivity and effectiveness

In this qualitative study, I wanted to learn which metrics training, technical communication, and corporate communication managers tracked to assess the productivity of their staffs and the effectiveness of their work, how managers reported the results to their managers, and the extent to which the managers of these departments felt pressure from their executives and senior managers to track and report this information.

Participants in the study were purposely chosen to reflect a variety of industries, department sizes, and geographies in North America. Altogether I interviewed 16 managers, of whom five managed training departments, four managed technical communication departments, four managed corporate communication departments, and three managed departments that had responsibilities for two or more of these functions (two had responsibility for training). Of those that managed training groups, two were in the financial services industry, one in the consumer products industry, one each in the biotechnology, professional services, and retail industries, and one in a government-owned corporation. Of the seven managers responsible for training, two were based in eastern Canada, two in the mid-Atlantic region of the USA, one each in the southeastern USA, USA Midwest, and western part of the USA.

Although managers were not formally asked about their backgrounds as part of the interview process, most shared this information. All of the managers overseeing training had worked in the field for at least five years, and all as individual contributors (either as instructors, course designers and developers, or instructor–developers). Two specifically mentioned that they had graduate degrees in fields related to training (one in instructional design, the other in training management), and the rest were educated in other social-science disciplines. One specifically mentioned that she had an MBA. Communication managers had similar backgrounds, though one had not completed a bachelor's degree, and another had just completed a graduate degree in management. In most cases, then, participants' occupational values would have developed in the work environment rather than through formal education.

Interview questions addressed the portfolio of work managed (that is, the types of assignments their staffs worked on), resources in the department (human, technological, and financial), the metrics used to assess the productivity of their staffs, the metrics used to assess the effectiveness of the work of the staffs, the metrics that senior management sought from these managers, the method of reporting, and the level of importance that their staffs and management placed on tracking productivity and effectiveness. Data were analyzed using a modified approach to grounded theory analysis.

This analysis yielded several realizations and hypotheses about the methods that managers used to assess and report the productivity and effectiveness of their staffs, as well as the manner in which they reported this data.

The first realization was the limits on training managers' awareness of their department budgets. For example, one of the managers in the study provided a budget amount that could not even cover staff salaries. Upon probing the issue, she realized that the number she provided only represented her "core" training budget, which did not include funding from two other budgets: one to handle specific responsibilities for coordinating training among all training units in her corporation and the other for projects associated with special areas of corporate emphasis (like a program to increase employee engagement). One manager was fully aware of her budgets, though not because their organizations emphasized it; a unique situation demanded it. She oversaw an external training program that generated $US 1.2 million per year. Because her department was a cost center, the accounting system would not let the department directly receive its revenue. So she had to track the incoming revenue and make sure that her department received the credit—a "faith-based initiative" as she called it. The pattern of limited awareness of budgets was even stronger among communications managers. In fact, a weak pattern among them showed that managers did not even know their budgets. In one case, that was because the organization funded salaries and other departmental expenses in separate budgets, and managers only had awareness of and control over the budget with operational expenses.

The first hypothesis emerging from this study is that managers have no externally provided metrics for estimating and assessing productivity. In fact, two asked me, "how do *you* do it?" In the absence of external measures of productivity, managers used subjective assessments. Two of the managers interviewed estimated work by asking, "how long would it take me to do the same thing?"

The next several hypotheses pertain to effectiveness. The second is that the most common evaluation of the effectiveness of training programs is an evaluation of satisfaction (level 1 of the commonly used Kirkpatrick model). All managers interviewed used it. This finding is consistent with quantitative studies in the literature. Also consistent with the literature was the third hypothesis: that managers rarely perform evaluation of transfer (behavior) (Kirkpatrick level 3) and impact (Kirkpatrick level 4). In fact, the only manager who reported making extensive use of these types of evaluation was the manager of the largest training department, who oversaw 72 staff members.

Although the sample of training managers was too small and the department sizes too varied to identify a relationship between size of department and the types of measure tracked, when considered within the broader set of data that included communication managers, a sufficiently strong pattern generated a fourth hypothesis: that the larger the department, the more likely managers are to evaluate transfer and impact.

The fifth hypothesis was that several training managers feel only limited pressure to report measurements to their management.

Although four indicated that they felt a high level of pressure to report effectiveness, three felt the opposite, receiving very little pressure. One commented that her boss might think she was pressuring her, but this training manager did not feel that pressure. Managers generally indicated that they felt more pressure to report effectiveness than productivity. Perhaps that is because most managers do not receive concrete measures from their senior manager that they need to report. For example, one manager commented that she is assessed "entirely by what I tell" the manager. "They take my word for productivity," she added.

Indeed, some managers even believe that their own managers do not even know how to assess training. "That's a good question," one participant responded when asked which measures her manager requested that she track. "We're new working together so I don't know." Another responded that she provides "whatever [metrics] I tell her." Most managers reported that they felt they were assessed more on word of mouth. Many commented that they were assessed on the most recent experience with the department. "My boss assesses my group's skills and abilities through feedback from others," one commented. That managers are most commonly assessed by informal, word-of-mouth feedback is the last hypothesis emerging from this study.

Study two: Confirming hypotheses about how training managers assess productivity and effectiveness

To confirm the hypotheses emerging from the first study, I conducted a quantitative study. Once again, I sought participants who managed groups that produce learning and communications materials for the workplace. I used a convenience sample recruited through the local chapters of professional organizations serving trainers, technical communicators, and corporate communicators. The organizations included the American Medical Writers Association (AMWA), American Society for Training and Development (ASTD), the International Association of Business Communicators, the International Society for Performance Improvement (ISPI), and the Society for Technical Communication (STC).

Participants completed an online survey that had several parts. The first was a qualifying section, to ensure that participants had personnel responsibility. Those who did not meet the qualifying criteria were directed out of the survey. The second part sought information about productivity metrics. Because both the literature and the qualitative study suggested that managers in all three disciplines used the same terminology to discuss productivity issues, only one version of this section was prepared. The third section inquired about effectiveness metrics. Because both the literature and the qualitative study suggested that managers in the different disciplines used different terminology to discuss effectiveness, separate sections were prepared for each of the disciplines studied. For example, although trainers, technical communicators, and corporate communicators all track satisfaction with the materials they produce, the terminology and methodologies differ. Most training groups use a post-class survey whereas most technical communication groups use Reader's Comment Forms. Although preparing different sections would complicate comparisons among the three groups later, the use of terminology appropriate to the occupational culture would ensure more accurate collection of data. Managers who managed groups with only one of the three responsibilities would complete the section just once; managers who managed groups with more than one of the three responsibilities were prompted to complete the section separately for each of their responsibilities. The last part of the survey inquired about the reporting of metrics through the participant's management chain and was the same among all three groups.

The survey instrument was validated through two pilots. The data for the 62 managers who had responsibility for training (which included managers for whom training was their sole responsibility, as well as for those who also had responsibility for corporate and technical communications) was separately analyzed to determine whether the hypotheses emerging from the qualitative study were supported.

The quantitative study supported the first hypothesis: that managers have no externally provided metrics for estimating and assessing productivity. To use time effectively, managers make assigned deadlines and budgets work, rather than determining how much time a project really needs and what resources are really needed to design and develop it. Fewer than half (46.2 percent) used some sort of a project tracking system. More than half (54.8 percent) indicated that guesstimating was the dominant method for estimating projects. Only a small percentage (32.3 percent) tracked a productivity rate either for their departments or individual workers.

The quantitative study also supported the second hypothesis emerging from the qualitative study: that the most common means of assessing learning products is satisfaction surveys (level 1 of the Kirkpatrick scheme). Nearly all (96 percent) responding to this question indicated that they do so. (Note that 22.3 percent of participants did not respond to this question.) Although level 1 evaluations were common, participants primarily used it for classroom learning (93.7 percent). The next type of learning product most likely to be evaluated was online tutorials (56.7 percent). Some types of learning products, such as workbooks, seem to be rarely assessed (29.1 percent).

The quantitative study supported the third hypothesis: that managers rarely evaluate transfer of training or impact. On the one hand, 52 percent of respondents said that they conducted some sort of follow-up study of their training. However, a closer inspection suggested that such follow-ups happen infrequently. Of the respondents, 45.9 percent assessed transfer of training for just 25 percent or less of the learning materials produced; another 20.8 percent conducted it for 50 percent or less of the learning materials produced. In terms of assessing impact, 70 percent of respondents did not conduct this type of evaluation.

The quantitative study did not support the fourth hypothesis: that the size of the department was correlated with likelihood of conducting assessment of transfer and impact. What was correlated is the knowledge of the budget: that is, managers who know their departmental budget are more likely to conduct such assessments.

The quantitative study did not support the fifth hypotheses: that training managers do not feel that their own managers are pressuring them to provide measurements of effectiveness and productivity. Fifty-eight percent reported that they were expected to report the productivity and effectiveness of their staff. Only one manager in the quantitative study reported not knowing the metrics needed by senior management to assess the department.

However, the quantitative study did support the last hypothesis: that training managers are most commonly assessed by word-of-mouth feedback. The most commonly named metrics used to assess training groups, in order of frequency cited, were:

- Word of mouth (informal positive and negative feedback about staff)
- Reach—that is, the number of learners reached in a given year
- Student satisfaction surveys
- ROI
- Service quality—that is, how well staff service the requests that are received, such as turnaround time on requests
- Customer surveys
- Training administration (metrics about the entire training team)

The list also suggests that the metrics most likely to be used to assess the productivity or effectiveness of a training group are those that are easiest to collect: word of mouth, reach (which can be compiled from enrollment records), and student satisfaction surveys (the most commonly performed type of assessment).

Insights and implications for the culture of training

The data from both studies do not suggest that training managers feel an urgency to demonstrate the impact and ROI of the work of their departments. Both studies found that fewer than 10 percent of training programs are assessed for impact, and that training managers do not feel exceptional pressure to conduct such assessments.

Why don't they feel this way? To some extent, numbers offer an explanation, actually two sets of numbers. The first pertains to the time required to conduct the evaluations needed to demonstrate ROI, which is not calculated in project estimates. Indeed, the time required is not even part of most project-estimating formulas as described by participants in the qualitative part of this study. Most formulas for estimating projects (such as Hackos' (1994) estimator for documentation and training projects) assume a project ends upon general availability of a course. However, that is when the summative evaluation needed to determine ROI begins. Such estimating formulas only include formative evaluation, which occurs during development of a training program.

In some instances, organizations inappropriately use formative evaluations to calculate ROI, and one training certification program lets applicants submit such data as part of the skill demonstration. Methodologically, however, such data are not acceptable because the training program and evaluation instruments from which the data were collected are not yet validated (Carliner, 1997). This is significant because the formative evaluation might show that evaluation instruments might not be effectively collecting the data for which they are designed (Tessmer, 1993). That the practice continues indicates that demonstrating impact and ROI in methodologically credible ways faces obstacles even from within the profession. The second set of numbers pertains to the proportion of training expenditures to overall organizational expenses. Studies of practice suggest that organizations typically spend between 1 and 2 percent of total payroll (not total expenses, just total payroll expense) on training (Bassi & McMurrer, 2007; ASTD, 2005). In contrast, marketing expenses can represent 20 percent of an organization's costs. When addressing cost issues, then, organizations often focus on costlier areas. Put more bluntly, training investments are not very significant for most organizations. Therefore, their return is of similarly insignificant interest to executives.

Other explanations for the disparity between this recommended and actual cultural practice exist. One is a disconnect between training executives and other higher-level executives in organizations about the purpose of training. According to a 2005 study by ASTD that compared the perceptions of the training function among chief learning officers (CLOs) and other C-level executives (O'Driscoll, Vona, & Sugrue, 2005), other C-level executives felt that the raison d'être for training was to impart skills; CLOs felt it was to improve skills. If the top executives are not looking to trainers to improve performance, why would they ask trainers for measures of impact and ROI? Even if other C-level executives felt that the purpose of training is to improve individual and organizational performance, would the performance data provided by the training group seem credible to them? The primary methodology recommended for demonstrating performance improvements (impact) and, thus, calculating ROI is self-reported measures of savings or revenue generated (Phillips, 2003; Phillips & Stone, 2002). At the very least, self-reported measures pose credibility problems because people might under- or overestimate the savings. Even if the estimates are accurate, accounting systems can only handle expenditures and revenues that are actually incurred. So estimates of savings and additional revenue from training are "soft" at best (Redish & Ramey, 1995). These improvements do not represent actual savings or revenues that accountants could externally verify. Furthermore, given that most general investments in the markets return between 1 and 20 percent in a good year, the 400–500 percent ROI reported on some training programs seem so disproportionately high that they demand closer scrutiny by business leaders.

More than these numerical explanations, perhaps a more basic explanation exists for the difference between prescribed and actual practice, one rooted in different cultural orientations. While conducting the literature review for this study, some patterns in both the peer-reviewed and popular literature emerged. When classifying whether the literature was empirical or theoretical in origin, most material was identified as theoretical, both in professional and peer-reviewed publications. Upon closer inspection, most of the "theoretical" literature was further classified as opinion, rather than theory that was rooted in the literature: the authors' primary claims were substantiated only by their personal observations rather than theory or models from the peer-reviewed literature (much less empirical evidence).

This begged the question, who is writing these articles and where might their opinions come from? So an analysis of the authors of these articles was conducted in which the credentials of the authors of each of the articles in professional publications were analyzed. Material published in professional publications (such as *T&D* and *TRAINING* magazines) was chosen because it is more likely to be read by and aligned with the interests of professionals (Deadrick & Gibson, 2007) and, therefore, more likely to influence practice.

Of the 30 articles reviewed for the literature review, six were written by reporters for trade magazines, 23 were written by consultants, and only one was written by someone working in an internal training department. In other words, 97 percent of the articles advising trainers on this issue worked outside a training department. The authors of the other 23 articles were all independent consultants and contractors, each an entrepreneur of sorts. Although they consulted in the field of training, perhaps their roles as entrepreneurs and executives in their own enterprises took precedence over their roles as training professionals in shaping their worldviews of the business culture. In their 1995 study, Hansen and Kahnweiller found differences "with respect to values, beliefs, causal attributions, and priorities" (1995, p. 25) between executives and HRD (training) professionals. As such, these authors placed a high cultural value on the importance of demonstrating the impact of training because, as entrepreneurs, they too had to demonstrate an ROI in their own work or risk financial ruin.

This does not mean that training executives do not place a cultural value on the importance of demonstrating their impact. Indeed, most reported its importance. However, as Hansen and Kahnweiller also observed, "work beliefs and organizational practices are not synonymous." "During professional training, one's specific career creeds develop and are then reinforced by professional experiences" (1995, p. 44). As the data from these studies indicate, even if the cultural value of demonstrating the impact of training is imparted during professional training, it is not reinforced on the job. Not only was this conclusion reached in the studies described in this chapter, but Mattson (2003) reached a similar conclusion, noting that anecdotal evaluation was most frequently used in training. That the managers ever received formal training in the cultural value of demonstrating impact might be a false assumption. Although information about their training was not systematically collected as part of these studies, the data available from the qualitative study suggest much inconsistency in how managers learned about the profession of training. All seem to have learned most aspects of the work through their jobs, both current and past positions. Just two in the qualitative study learned about training from degree programs. Information from professional societies such as the Canadian Society for Training and Development suggests that many different college, university, and continuing education programs can formally prepare people for positions in training, including adult education, educational (instructional) technology, and HRD (which can be offered both through education and business faculties), as well as through related disciplines of HRM and technical communication. Although all of these disciplines prepare training professionals, each is based on a different body of knowledge and different sets of beliefs and values. Moreover, demographic studies of people working in the field of training suggest that these degree programs reach less than half of prac-ticing professionals (Canadian Society for Training and Development, 2008). With such varied roads to their management positions, people who share the job title training manager do not likely share knowledge bases, practices, value systems, and underlying beliefs.

In terms of demonstrating impact, at a minimum, the different backgrounds result in different approaches to impact, which are often culturally rooted. Those trained in adult education under the radical adult education philosophy (Driscoll & Carliner, 2005) are likely to have adopted a philosophy of education that rejects neoliberal economic concepts like ROI, and impact would be assessed, instead, in terms of social change promoted by the program. In contrast, those with busi-ness degrees are likely not only to be comfortable with the concept, but will have the training in finance and operations research to calculate ROI more effectively than students from most education disciplines, which have, at most, project and general management training, but no finance or operations management in their curricula. In other words, many training managers enter their jobs with varying cultural values on this issue, and the workplace reinforces all of them.

As a result, perhaps the professional literature on demonstrating the impact and ROI of training (at least, the professional literature) should be considered, at best, as a recommendation for cultural practice. The reliance of this literature on opinion from people working outside the training function explains its limited impact on behavior inside the training function. Even if the opinion is based on past work experience inside this function and recent consulting projects, the author's work externally could contribute significant biases.

Perhaps, then, the real issue is that the authors of the articles pro-moting ROI are responding to a different set of cultural cues than the internal training managers and, as a result, make too many assumptions about those managers. On a practical level, the authors might be making false assumptions about the extent of pressure that training managers feel to track performance and report ROI carefully. At a deeper level, these authors might be making false assumptions about the role of demonstrating the ROI of training in the value systems of HR managers and the senior management to whom they report. Until these issues are addressed, practices within training groups are not likely to change, even if attitudes become increasingly focused on demonstrating ROI. Demonstrating impact requires more than being an advocated cultural practice: it requires tangible resources, and only senior executives can approve them.

Acknowledgments

Thanks to Juan Carlos Sanchez Lozano and Adnan Qayyum for their assistance with data analysis.

References

Arthur, W. A., Bennett, W., Edens, P. S., & Bell, S. T. (2003) "Effectiveness of training in organizations: A meta-analysis of design and evaluation features." *Journal of Applied Psychology*, 88(3), 234–45.

ASTD. (2006.) WLP Scorecard Overview. Viewed at http://wlpscorecard.astd.org/. Visited September 6, 2008.

ASTD. (2005.) What do you spend on training? What *should* you be spending? T&D Magazine. 18, March 2005.

Bandes, H. (1986) "Defining and controlling documentation quality—part 1." *Technical Communication*, 33(1), 6–9.

Bassi, L. & McMurrer, D. (2007) "Maximizing your return on people." *Harvard Business Review*. 85(3), 115–25.

Belfiore, M. (1996) *Understanding Curriculum Development in the Workplace.* Toronto, ON: ABC Canada.

Canadian Society for Training and Development. (2008.) 2008 member survey. Toronto, ON: Canadian Society for Training and Development.

Carliner, S. (2000) "Different names, similar challenges: What's behind the rumored merger of instructional design and technical communication?" *Performance Improvement*, 39(6), 5–8.

Carliner, S. (1997) "Demonstrating the effectiveness and value of technical communication products and services: A four-level process." *Technical Communication*, 44(3), 252–65.

Deadrick, D. L. & Gibson, P. A. (2007) "An examination of the research–practice gap in HR: Comparing topics of interest to HR academics and HR professionals." *Human Resource Management Review*, 17(2), 131–39.

Deutsch, W. (1992) "Teaching machines, programming, computers, and instructional technology: The roots of performance technology." *Performance & Instruction*, 31(2), 14–20.

Dick, W., Carey, L., & Carey, J. (2008) *The Systematic Design of Instruction* (7th ed.) (Burlington, MA: Addison-Wesley).

Driscoll, M. & Carliner, S. (2005) *Advanced Web-Based Training: Adapting Real World Strategies in Your Online Learning*. (San Francisco: Pfeiffer).

Gargiulo, T. L., Pangarkar, A. M., Kirkwood, T., & Bunzel, T. (2006) *Building Business Acumen for Trainers: Skills to Empower the Learning Function*. (San Francisco: Pfeiffer).

Galloway, L. (2007) "Don't focus on ROI." *Training*, 44(10), 40–41.

Hackos, J. T. (1994) *Managing Your Documentation Projects*. (New York: John Wiley & Sons).

Hansen, C. D. & Kahnweiller, W. M. (1995) "Organizational tension and occupational scripts: Stories from HR professionals and top executives." *Human Resource Management Review*, 5(1), 25–51.

Islam, K. A. (2006) *Developing and Measuring Training the Six Sigma Way: A Business Approach to Training and Development*. (San Francisco: Pfeiffer).

Kirkpatrick, D. L. (1998) *Evaluating Training Programs: The Four Levels* (2nd ed.). (San Francisco, CA: Berrett-Koehler).

Mattson, B. W. (2003) "The effects of alternative reports of human resource development results on managerial support." *Human Resource Development Quarterly.* 14(2), 127–51.

O'Driscoll, T., Vona, M. L., & Sugrue, B. M. (2005) "The C-level executive and the value of learning." *T&D*, 59(10), 70–77.

Phillips, J. J. (2003) *Return on Investment in Training and Performance Improvement Programs* (2nd ed.) (Improving Human Performance) (Boston, MA: Butterworth-Heinemann).

Phillips, J. J. & Breining, M. T. (2007) *Return on Investment in Meetings and Events*. (Boston, MA: Butterworth-Heinemann).

Phillips, J. J. & Stone, R. (2002) *How to Measure Training Results: A Practical Guide to Tracking the Six Key Indicators*. (New York: McGraw-Hill).

Phillips, P. P. & Phillips, J. J. (2008) *ROI in Action Case Book (Measurement in Evaluation)*. (San Francisco: Pfeiffer).

Redish, J. & Ramey, J. (1995) "Adding value as a professional technical communicator." *Technical Communication*, 42(1), 26–39.

Reiser, R. A. (2001) "A history of instructional design and technology: Part II: A history of instructional design." *Educational Technology Research and Development*, 49(2), 57–67.

Robinson, D. and Robinson, J. (1989) *Training for impact* (San Francisco, CA: Jossey Bass.)

Rothwell, W. J., Lindholm, J., & Wallick, W. G. (2003.) *What CEOs Expect From Corporate Training: Building Workplace Learning and Performance Initiatives That Advance*. AMACOM.

Seagraves, T. (2004) *Quick, Show Me Your Value*. (Alexandria, VA: ASTD Press).

Shetty, Y. K. & Buehler, V. M. (1988) "Productivity and quality: The keys to competitive advantage." In Y. K. Shetty & V. M. Buehler (eds) *Competing through Productivity and Quality*. (Cambridge, MA: Productivity Press) 3–16.

Smith, P. L. & Ragan, T. J. (2004) *Instructional Design* (3rd ed.) (Upper Saddle River, NJ: Prentice-Hall Inc.).

Stolovitch, H. & Keeps, E. (2004) *Training Ain't Performance.* (Alexandria, VA: ASTD Press).

Stolovitch, H. & Keeps, E. (1999) "What is human performance technology?" In H. Stolovitch & E. Keeps (eds) *Handbook of Human Performance Technology: Improving Individual and Organizational Performance Worldwide* (2nd edition). (San Francisco: Jossey-Bass) 3–23.

Stolovitch, H. & Keeps, E. (eds) (1992) *Handbook of Human Performance Technology: Improving Individual and Organizational Performance Worldwide.* (San Francisco: Jossey-Bass).

Swanson, R. A. & Holton, E. F. (1999) Results: How to assess performance, learning, and perceptions in organizations. (San Francisco: Berrett-Koehler).

Tessmer, M. (1993) *Planning and conducting formative evaluations: Improving the quality of education and training.* (London: Kogan-Page.)

Van Adelsberg, D. & Trolley, E. (1999) *Running Training Like a Business: Delivering Unmistakeable Value.* (San Francisco: Berrett-Koehler).

Walmer, D. (1998). Personal conversation with Saul Carliner about early research in this area.

Weiss, A. (2008) "DO focus on ROI." *Training,* 45(2), 4.

12
The Influence of Organizational Culture on Training Effectiveness

Kay Bunch

Training has never been more critical for organizations determined to achieve and maintain a competitive advantage (Salas & Cannon-Bowers, 2001). Yet, despite a century of research on learning and training (Ford, 1997), effectiveness often is elusive (Salas & Cannon-Bowers, 2001). The extent of failure is unknown because few companies adequately plan or evaluate training (Roberson, Kulik, & Pepper, 2003; Saari, Johnson, McLaughlin, & Zimmerle, 1988), but one of the more optimistic estimates suggests no more than 15 percent of learning transfers to the job (Cromwell & Kolb, 2004). Along with wasting immeasurable time and billions of dollars, failed interventions contribute to the persistent undervaluing of the HRD/training profession (Shank, 1998), costly litigation (Eyres, 1998; Mitchell & Tetlock, 2006), and growing cynicism about the worth of any organizational change (Wanous, Reichers, & Austin, 2000).

Increasingly, organizational context is linked to training effectiveness, but the influence of culture has been virtually ignored (Palthe & Kossek, 2003). The purpose of this chapter is to explore the relationship between training effectiveness and organizational culture. First, I describe how the dominant culture shapes training practices and outcomes. Second, I identify the differential impact of various subcultures, especially in light of the relative weakness of the HRD/training function.

HRD encompasses many disciplines, but I focus on the training function for several reasons. First, despite divergent views on the HRD construct, there is general agreement that training is a core component of HRD (Nadler, 1984; Swanson, 2001). The argument that HRD has moved beyond *simplistic* training belies the historical meaning of training as "planned programs of organizational improvement through changes in skill, knowledge, attitude, or social behavior"

(Cascio, 1988, p. 348). I believe that Cascio's broad view of training fits within the HRD construct. Second, the "science of training" (Salas & Kosarzycki, 2003) is more comprehensive and accepted than other fields such as organizational development (Sammut, 2001). This may explain why HRD scholars frequently cite training literature related to design, implementation, and evaluation (Goldstein, 1990; Latham, 1988; Salas & Cannon-Bowers, 2001; Tannenbaum & Yukl, 1992). Third, exploring the relationship between organizational culture and training should elucidate culture's influence on other forms of HRD interventions (Eddy, D'Abate, Tannenbaum, Givens-Skeaton, & Robinson, 2006).

Much of the literature concentrates on training design, content, and evaluation. However, even a perfect intervention is doomed without organizational support. Training effectiveness, defined as the extent to which interventions "lead to the desired level of proficiency" (Ford, 1997), involves identifying what affects learning before, during, and after training (Ford, 1997; Salas & Cannon-Bowers, 2001). Organizational culture may play a role in each of the following forms of training failure: (1) unskilled practitioners provide flawed interventions; (2) skilled practitioners provide flawed interventions because they do not have the power or influence to design a valid program; (3) skilled practitioners provide valid interventions but learning does not transfer to the job; (4) skilled practitioners provide valid interventions that produce positive transfer, but effectiveness is not perceived (Bunch, 2007).

Organizational culture

Culture has been described as "one of the most powerful and stable forces operating in organizations" (Schein, 1996, p. 231). Definitions vary, but typically include concepts such as shared beliefs, values, and assumptions that are reflected in attitudes and behavior (Kopelman, Brief, & Guzzo, 1990). There has been considerable interest in the relationship between organizational culture and variables such as productivity (Kopelman et al., 1990), use of technology (Zammuto & O'Connor, 1992), employee retention (Sheridan, 1992), improvement initiatives (Detert, Schroeder, & Mauriel, 2000), discipline (Franklin & Pagan, 2006), absence (Martocchio, 1994), and knowledge management (Alavi, Kayworth, & Leidner, 2006). Several writers have considered a link between organizational culture and human resource management (HRM) practices (Aycan, Kanungo, & Sinha, 1999; Ferris, Arthur, Berkson, Kaplan, Harrell-Cook, & Frink,

1998; Kopelman et al., 1990; Palthe & Kossek, 2003; Sheridan, 1992), although the general focus is on HRM's influence on culture.

Several writers depict culture with multiple layers. Schein (1990) proposed three levels: artifacts, values, and underlying assumptions; whereas Rousseau (1990) envisioned five: artifacts, patterns of behavior, behavioral norms, values, and fundamental assumptions. Artifacts and patterns of behavior are observable manifestations that reflect and perpetuate underlying norms, values, and assumptions. I draw on Rousseau's model to examine the relationship between organizational culture and training effectiveness.

Artifacts

The most visible layer of culture (Schein, 1990), artifacts, is the "physical manifestations and products of cultural activity" (Rousseau, 1990, p. 157). They can convey organizational support for training through impressive training facilities, certificates of training success, graduation ceremonies, prominent involvement of organizational leaders in training activities, and the high hierarchical position of training leaders. Symbols determine the "values and norms used by organizational actors in judging and making choices" (Galang & Ferris, 1997), but the real meaning of artifacts may be misconstrued. An organization may use its impressive facilities or large budget to provide meaningless interventions. The goal of training may be to "pacify the masses" (Jermier, Slocum, Fry, & Gaines, 1991) or improve the organization's image. For example, many organizations frame diversity training as a symbol of management's support for equality when the real purpose is to avoid litigation (Schultz, 2003). Indeed, Heilman (1997) speculated that organizational interventions designed to reduce discrimination may actually "support and perpetuate it."

Patterns of behavior

Patterns of behavior are observable activities such as decision-making, communication, and new employee socialization that reflect underlying beliefs, values, and assumptions (Rousseau, 1990). For example, a clear link between training and an organization's career development and reward system signals that training leads to recognition and advancement (Santos & Stuart, 2003). Even seemingly minor events can influence perceptions (Rentsch, 1990). Simply labeling an intervention *voluntary* may imply irrelevance (Baldwin & Magjuka, 1997). On the other hand, supervisory behaviors such as encouraging subordinates before an intervention or praising new behavior enhance the reputation of the training/HRD function (Rouiller & Goldstein, 1993). Organizational leaders can trivialize training through symbolic behavior such as hiring unqualified practitioners, excluding training/HRD leaders from the strategic planning process, or reflexively firing trainers at the first sign of an economic slowdown (Ruona, Lynham, & Chermack, 2003).

Behavioral norms

Behavioral norms are the beliefs of organizational members that guide actions (Rousseau, 1990) and emerge from experience and cultural reinforcement (Church & Waclawski, 2001). New employees quickly learn about the consequences of behaviors through observations or stories that training is a frivolous endeavor (Bloor & Dawson, 1994; Cooke & Rousseau, 1988). Based on previous events, even competent trainers may admit the futility in conducting needs assessment and sophisticated evaluation if "training is perceived as a waste of time and as a way to avoid work" (Clark, Dobbins, & Ladd, 1993, p. 304).

Moreover, organizational members may support training in general, but reject a specific intervention that conflicts with cultural norms. Thus, if first-line supervisors earn bonuses for reducing labor costs through high turnover, practitioners will reject the need for employee development. To create an affirmative defense against charges of harassment, many organizations provide training that encourages reporting events to management. Yet, employees will not report harassment if they fear retaliation (Knapp, Faley, Ekeberg, & Dubois, 1997).

Values

Values are of significant importance given organizational aspects such as quality versus quantity (Rousseau, 1990). Although norms guide how to perform organizational activities, values influence which activities to perform. For example, norms affect the role of training in quality initiatives, but values determine if quality is a priority. Thus, training will not improve customer service if improving service is neither rewarded nor measured.

Values are difficult to identify because of discrepancies between espoused values and actual behavior (Pager & Quillian, 2005; Schein, 1990). Even if organization members support training in the abstract, previous events and perceived organizational constraints dictate behavior. Consequently, Orpen (1999) warned that it is "better not to offer training" if it is poorly designed or implemented because it creates or confirms the belief that training is inconsequential or worse.

Fundamental assumptions

Subconscious assumptions are the source for all other facets of culture. Schein (1990) explained that assumptions begin as values that are reinforced through experience until they become taken-for-granted. As a result, it is difficult to identify assumptions because individuals holding them are not mindful of their existence (Rousseau, 1990). This explains why managers may espouse great support for training but cut the training budget.

Assumptions determine the structure and content of the cognitive categories individuals use to encode, store, and retrieve information so that contradictory events may be ignored. This may be the greatest impediment to effective training. Because assumptions influence how individuals explain success or failure, even if an intervention is effective, improved performance may not be attributed to training (Hatch, 1993).

Subcultures

Saffold (1988) cautioned against presuming a unitary dominant culture or ignoring the impact of subcultures of different levels of power, status, and influence (Cooke & Rousseau, 1988; Trice & Beyer, 1993). Subcultures emerge from membership in various groupings including function, hierarchical level, line or staff, gender, and profession (Cooke & Rousseau, 1988; Helms & Stern, 2001; Schein, 1990). The shared values, beliefs, and assumptions of each subculture shape perceptions of and reactions toward the dominant organizational culture (Helms & Stern, 2001) and other subcultures (Plathe & Kossek, 2003). It is a formidable challenge to understand, much less accommodate, the various subcultural differences that Rentsch (1990) cautioned might require customized interventions. However, HRD's future is inexorably linked to confronting the causes and consequences of subcultural differences.

Repeated failure may create feelings of inevitability and futility. Hansen, Kahnweiler, and Wilensky (1994) surmised through subject-generated stories that some HRD professionals did not feel empowered, appreciated, or competent. These beliefs become self-fulfilling. Thus, practitioners acquiesce to organizational values and assumptions at odds with the "social consciousness" of HRD (Bierema & D'Abundo, 2004) when only "dominant groups get their values and goals accepted as legitimate" (Bloor & Dawson, 1994, p. 279).

Function

Differences based on elements such as technology, structure, and external influences contribute to the emergence of functional or departmental subcultures (Trice & Beyer, 1993). Members of these subcultures tend to share values and assumptions that support behavioral norms and artifacts unique to each department (Dansereau & Alutto, 1990; Trice, 1993). Perceived goal congruence between the function and the dominant organizational culture enhances the power and status of the department (Ferris, Perrewé, Ranft, Zinko, Stoner, Brouer, & Laird, 2007; Nauta & Sanders, 2001). Level of congruence, in turn, shapes perceptions of a function's performance and value to the organization (Welbourne & Trevor, 2000). In contrast to other departments, however, HRD/training has limited influence and prestige (Galang & Ferris, 1997). Often, it is "seen as part of a weak or discredited personnel department" (Hallier & Butts, 2000, p. 376) whose goals and values may seem at odds with other functions. Outsourcing (Cooke, Shen, & McBride, 2005) and devolution of many HR activities to line managers (McConville, 2006) reinforce perceived differences from the norm.

Even if there is general agreement among functions on stated organizational variables such as objectives and strategies, assumptions may vary (Welbourne & Trevor, 2000). The company motto, "Customers come first," has distinctive meanings for production, accounting, and marketing (Dansereau & Alutto, 1990). Perceived training needs (Santos & Stuart, 2003), as well as viewpoints on design and content (Mathieu & Martineau, 1997), vary across departments. For example, organizational leaders may support ethics training for accounting but not marketing.

Hierarchical level

Organization leaders create and sustain the *official* organizational culture (Jermier et al., 1991). Yet, different hierarchical levels can produce distinct subcultures (Trice & Beyer, 1993). Stevenson and Bartunek (1996) observed that organizational members at similar hierarchical levels share similar views of the dominant culture. Power, status, and reputation are all associated with hierarchical levels. Training managers rarely participate in strategic planning, in part, because of their hierarchical standing (Rothwell & Kazanas, 1990). Rather than be the "champions of change," individuals at lower hierarchical levels are more likely to support "conflict avoidance, competition, and dependence" (Cooke & Rousseau, 1988). In organizational hierarchies, groups "caught-in-the-middle" face conflicting demands from the powerful above and the powerless below (Smith, 1983). It is typical for the top hierarchy to reserve decision-making authority for themselves but to *delegate* the implementation of their decisions (Palich & Hom, 1992). If the implementation is successful, the "powerful" take credit; if the implementation fails, the powerful blame the *incompetent* middle (Palich & Hom, 1991).

On the other hand, practitioners may overestimate top management's sponsorship (McCracken & Wallace, 2000) or confuse "permission with support" (Baldwin & Magjuka, 1997). Although executives report more positive views of HR than line managers (Wright, McMahan, Snell, & Gerhart, 2001), it is a mistake to assume that espoused beliefs or survey responses denote values and assumptions (Pager & Quillian, 2005).

Line/staff

To some extent, conflict between line and staff is a fact of organizational life, especially in circumstances of low profit margin and intense competition (Church & Waclawski, 2001). Line functions have more power and resources because they more directly contribute to measurable outcomes (Lyness & Heilman, 2006). The rift between HR and line management often goes beyond the inherent conflict between line and staff (Koslowsky, 1990; Wright et al., 2001). Clashes have been long-standing and often acrimonious, as recently demonstrated when Hammonds (2005) issued his acerbic missive exploring "hatred" for HR, specifically mentioning training. He deplored what he viewed as the abuse of frazzled line managers by HR practitioners who "aren't the sharpest tacks in the box."

In most organizations, emphasis on the bottom line is a basic cultural assumption (Weick, 1979). The inability or unwillingness to demonstrate results that are "organizationally valued" hurts the credibility of training managers (Taylor & O'Driscoll, 1998). Supervisor support is crucial to achieving training effectiveness (Clark et al., 1993), but line managers often consider training a low priority (Santos & Stewart, 2003) or resent increased training duties (McConville, 2006).

Gender

The assumptions and values held by members of the dominant organizational culture and subcultures such as upper management and many professions are stereotypically masculine (Evetts, 2003; Richeson & Ambady, 2001). Women are concentrated in occupations, such as HRM, "where their 'softer' participatory style of management is viewed as better utilized" (Crampton & Mishra, 1999, p. 92). According to the US

Department of Labor (2006), women make up 73 percent of HR managers compared with only 29 percent of general and operations managers and 17 percent of industrial production managers. The growing percentage of women in HRD has been linked to a decline in the status and perceived value of training as a contribution to organizational effectiveness and as a career (Hanscome & Cervero, 2003). Lupton (2000) asserted, "this association with women stems from personnel's origins as a welfare function and has proved difficult to dislodge despite the more managerial and strategic orientation of the modern-day function" (p. 40). In general, males in HRM advance faster, have fewer qualifications, and tend to undervalue stereotypical female functions such as training as solutions to organizational problems (Lupton, 2000).

Profession

Professions are "the most highly organized, distinctive, and pervasive sources of subcultures in work organizations" (Trice & Beyer, 1993, p. 178). Members of strong occupational cultures often can dominate other subcultures. On the other hand, HRD is weak compared with professions such as medicine, law, engineering, accounting, or even HRM. For example, because of their rigorous education, difficult certification process, and meticulous performance measures, most engineers are neither willing nor expected to compromise professional ethics and standards just to please members of other groups. Yet, there are numerous depictions of corporate and government training fiascos in the popular press (Shank, 1998). The editor of *Industry Week* (Panchak, 2000, October 3) wrote a scathing column describing corporate training as "ridiculously silly at best and insultingly disrespectful of the workers' intelligence at worst." The author asserted, "Virtually every other area of management expenditures requires an analysis of the return on investment."

Characteristics of professional cultures include special knowledge, power to determine when and how to apply that knowledge, control over work, education standards of members, code of ethics, membership in professional associations, and reliance on other members as a reference group within the organization (Bloor & Dawson, 1994; Trice, 1993). A profession's strength is linked to issues such as "exclusive ownership of an area of expertise and knowledge and the power to define the nature of problems in that area as well as the control of access to potential solutions" (Evetts, 2003, p. 30). In contrast, members of weak professions are likely to share the beliefs and assumptions of a more dominate culture (Trice & Beyer, 1993).

Systematic body of knowledge and performance standards

True professions are organized around bodies of knowledge over which its members strive to have "monopolistic control" (Jacobs, 1990), but Short, Bing, and Kehrhahn (2003) asserted, "There is limited evidence that HRD has really moved far from the fad-ridden gutters of false short-term training panaceas" (p. 239). The unrelenting dispute over the theory and practice of HRD may be invigorating, but it is difficult to establish a systematic body of knowledge without consensus. Debate often centers on seemingly mutually exclusive core values. Bierema and D'Abundo (2004) chided HRD professionals for their misplaced loyalties to organizations and profits instead of employees. However, practitioners must weigh the consequences and feasibility of challenging profit driven cultures (McGuire, Cross, & O'Donnell, 2005).

Short et al. (2003) warned that HRD professionals cannot achieve status and power as long as many practitioners offer solutions "based on guesswork" instead of theory-driven research. There is a strong link between credibility of the profession and demonstrable effectiveness (Evetts, 2003; Galang & Ferris, 1997), but practitioners seldom assess needs, establish specific objectives, or evaluate beyond Kirkpatrick's (1976) reaction level (Arthur, Bennett, Edens, & Bell, 2003; Clarke, 2004; Sugrue, 2005; Swanson, 2001; Tannenbaum & Yukl, 1992). Even highly qualified practitioners may lack the perceived expertise to convince organizational leaders that evaluation is worth the time and expense (Camp et al., 1991; Ferris et al., 2007). On the other hand, some knowledgeable trainers resist evaluation to avoid exposure (Goldstein, 1980)

Standardized training and restricted membership

Individuals are more likely to maintain the values of their profession than submit to the values of the organization when they share similar training and socialization (Bloor & Dawson, 1994). However, there is no standardized program or fundamental level of knowledge for trainers. Instead, many practitioners learn on the job where the values and assumptions of the dominant culture guide behavior (Trice & Beyer, 1993). Kuchinke (2001) acknowledged that HRD was not yet an academic discipline but claimed this was an asset because it afforded more flexibility. Nevertheless, it is impossible to develop a curriculum without consensus on core competencies.

Some practitioners recognize that the slow pace of professionalization undermines the field's credibility (Ruona et al., 2003) whereas others dismiss attempts at certification or credentialing (Claus & Collison, 2004; Kaeter, 1995). A recent survey of HR professionals suggests that many decry their low credibility and autonomy, but "attach little importance" to education and credentialing (Claus & Collison, 2005). However, the number of unqualified or perceived unqualified trainers may be a greater obstacle (Gauld & Miller, 2004). The growing prevalence of the "accidental trainer" (Bartlett, 2003) harms the profession and ensures that effective training is accidental. It is foolhardy to demand autonomy and respect for a profession with a "low barrier to entry" (Claus & Collison, 2005).

Occupational associations and codes of ethics

There are several practitioner organizations, including the Society for Human Resource Management and the American Society for Training and Development. These organizations consistently call for and support greater professionalism. However, the failure, especially among HRD writers, to reach consensus on the regulation or even definition of the field promotes continuous, exasperating, and often unfathomable debates. For example, in yet another examination of the HRD field, Sambrook (2004) observed that in the face of considerable disagreement on its theory or practice, "we continue our attempts to investigate HRD, so that we may understand better, teach and practice it" (p. 612).

A professional code of ethics is a fundamental artifact of strong professions but requires a concrete theoretical foundation to be meaningful. This is especially important in the face of recent corporate scandals. Yet, efforts to define unethical HRD behavior (Hatcher & Aragon, 2000) are hindered by the ongoing debate over the core values of the profession. Should professionals offer training linked solely to improved productivity or profit margins? Is it ethical to conduct ineffective training if a decision-maker asks for it (Holton, 1998)? Moreover, discussions of ethics and morality often reveal an uncompromising tone that is dismissive of divergent points of view and the organizational realities of many HRD professionals (Krefting & Nord, 2003; McGuire et al., 2005).

Conclusion

Researchers investigate the pervasiveness of ineffective training and offer solutions, but practitioners appear undaunted (Cascio, 2003). Its complexity underestimated, training is "devolving" to line management (Heraty & Morley, 1995) and increasingly labeled a "dead end" occupation (Hanscome & Cervero, 2003). At first glance, achieving training success is a simple matter of following well-established guidelines derived from decades of research. However, I suggest that ill-conceived or poorly executed programs reflect more than incompetence or unwillingness. Training failure can be a manifestation of the values, beliefs, and assumptions shared by members of various levels of organizational culture. The disregard for sound practices is an immediate cause of failure but also a reflection of cultural barriers that can circumvent the best-designed program. Beliefs that training is simple, unimportant, or pointless generate behaviors such as employing incompetent trainers, rejecting the recommendations of competent trainers, discouraging transfer of learning to the job, and failing to recognize positive transfer.

Ultimately, training effectiveness depends on the power and status of the profession. Central to overcoming bias against training and HRD is improving the image of HRD. Real or perceived training failure hampers efforts to elevate the profession. Nothing is more critical than reaching agreement on core competencies. The pursuit of a grand theory should not preclude consensus on midrange theories including the social context of training effectiveness (Ferris, Hall, Royle, & Martocchio, 2004). HRD must define itself or leave the task to others.

References

Alavi, M., Kayworth, T. R., & Leidner, D. E. (2006) "An empirical examination of the influence of organizational culture on knowledge management practices." *Journal of Management Information Systems*, 22, 191–224.

Arthur, W., Jr., Bennett, W, Jr., Edens, P. S., & Bell, S. T. (2003) "Effectiveness of training in organizations: A meta-analysis of design and evaluation features." *Journal of Applied Psychology*, 88, 234–45.

Aycan, Z., Kanungo, R. N., & Sinha, J. B. P. (1999) "Organizational culture and human resource management practices." *Journal of Cross-Cultural Psychology*, 30, 501–26.

Baldwin, T. T., & Magjuka, R. J. (1997) "Training as an organizational episode: Pretraining influences on trainee motivation." In J. K. Ford (ed) *Improving training effectiveness in work organizations* (Mahwah, NJ: Lawrence Erlbaum) 99–127.

Bartlett, K. R. (2003) "Accidental trainers versus HRD professionals." *Human Resource Development Quarterly*, 14, 231–34.

Bierema, L. L., & D'Abundo, M. L. (2004) "HRD with a conscience: Practicing socially responsible HRD." *International Journal of Lifelong Education*, 23, 443–58.

Bloor, G., & Dawson, P. (1994) "Understanding professional culture in organizational context." *Organization Studies*, 15, 275–95.

Bunch, K. J. (2007) "Training failure as a consequence of organizational culture." *Human Resource Development Review*, 6, 142–63.

Camp, R. R., Hoyer, D. T., Laetz, V. B., & Vielhaper, M. E. (1991) "Training practitioner perceptions of the research agenda needed to improve training." *Human Resource Development Quarterly*, 2, 65–73.

Cascio, W. F. (1988) *Applied psychology in personnel management* (Englewood Cliffs, NJ: Prentice-Hall).

Cascio, W. F. (2003) "Invited reaction: The effects of alternative reports of human resource development results on managerial support." *Human Resource Development Quarterly*, 14, 153–58.

Church, A. H., & Waclawski, J. (2001) "Hold the line: An examination of line vs. staff differences." *Human Resource Management*, 40, 21–34.

Clark, C. S., Dobbins, G. H., & Ladd, R. T. (1993) "Exploratory field study of training motivation: Influence of involvement, credibility, and transfer climate." *Group & Organization Management*, 18, 292–307.

Clarke, N. (2004) "HRD and the challenges of assessing learning in the workplace." *International Journal of Training and Development*, 8, 140–56.

Cooke, F. L., Shen, J., McBride, A. (2005) "Outsourcing HR as a competitive strategy? A literature review and an assessment of implications." *Human Resource Management*, 44, 413–32.

Cooke, R. A., & Rousseau, D. M. (1998) "Behavioral norms and expectations: A quantitative approach to the assessment of organizational culture." *Group and Organization Studies*, 13, 245–73.

Crampton, S. M., & Mishra, J. M. (1999) "Women in management." *Public Personnel Management*, 28, 87–106.

Cromwell, S. E., & Kolb, J. A. (2004) "An examination of work-environment support factors affecting transfer of supervisory skills training in the workplace." *Human Resource Development Quarterly*, 15, 449–71.

Dansereau, Jr., F., & Alutto, J. A. (1990) "Level-of-analysis issues in climate and culture research." In B. Schneider (ed), *Organizational Climate and Culture* (San Francisco, CA: Jossey-Bass) 192–236.

Detert, J. R., Schroeder, R. G., & Mauriel, J. J. (2000) "A framework for linking culture and improvement initiatives in organizations." *Academy of Management Review*, 25, 850–63.

Eddy, E. R., D'Abate, C. P., Tannenbaum, S. I., Givens-Skeaton, S., & Robinson, G. (2006) "Key characteristics of effective and ineffective developmental interactions." *Human Resource Development Quarterly*, 17, 59–84.

Evetts, J. (2003) "The construction of professionalism in new and existing occupational contexts: Promoting and facilitating occupational change." *The International Journal of Sociology and Social Policy*, 23, 22–35.

Eyres, P. (1998) *The legal handbook for trainers, speakers, and consultants: The essential guide to keeping your company and clients out of court.* (New York: McGraw-Hill).

Ferris, G. R., Arthur, M. M., Berkson, H. M., Kaplan, D. M., Harrell-Cook, G., & Frink, D. D. (1998) "Toward a social context theory of the human resource management-organization effectiveness relationship." *Human Resource Management Review*, 8, 235–65.

Ferris, G. R., Hall, A. T., Royle, M. T., & Martocchio, J. J. (2004) "Theoretical development in the field of human resources management: Issues and challenges for the future." *Organizational Analysis*, 12, 231–54.

Ferris, G. R., Perrewé, P. L., Ranft, A. L., Zinko, R., Stoner, J. S., Brouer, R. L., & Laird, M. D. (2007) "Human resources reputation and effectiveness." *Human Resource Management Review*, 17, 117–30.

Ford, J. D. (1997) "Advances in training research and practice: An historical perspective." In J. K. Ford (ed), *Improving training effectiveness in work organizations* (Mahwah, NJ: Lawrence Erlbaum) 1–16.

Franklin, A. L., & Pagan, J. F. (2006) "Organizational culture as an explanation for employee discipline practices." *Review of Public Personnel Administration*, 26, 53–73.

Galang, M. C. & Ferris, G. R. (1997) "Human resource department power and influence through symbolic action." *Human Relations*, 50, 1403–26.

Gauld, D., & Miller, P. (2004) "The qualifications and competencies held by effective workplace trainers." *Journal of European Industrial Training*, 28, 8–21.

Goldstein, I. L. (1990) "Training in work organizations." In M. D. Dunnette & L. M. Hough (eds), *Handbook in industrial organizational psychology:* vol. 2: 2nd ed. (Palo Alto, CA: Consulting Psychologists Press) 507–620.

Goldstein, I. L. (1980). "Training in work organizations". *Annual Review of Psychology*, 31, 229–72.

Hallier, J., & Butts, S. (2000) "Attempts to advance the role of training: Process and context." *Employee Relations*, 22, 375–86.

Hammonds, K. H. "Why we hate HR." *Fast Company*. (2005). Retrieved July 27, 2005 from www.fastcompany.com/subscr/97/open_hr.html.

Hanscome, L., & Cervero, R. M. (2003) "The impact of gendered power relations in HRD." *Human Resource Development International*, 6, 509–25.

Hansen, C. D., Kahnweiler, W. M., & Wilensky, A. S. (1994) "Human resource development as an occupational culture through organizational stories." *Human Resource Development Quarterly*, 5, 253–68.

Hatch, M. J. (1993) "The dynamics of organizational culture." *Academy of Management Review*, 18, 657–93.

Hatcher, T., & Aragon, S. R. (2000) "A code of ethics and integrity for HRD research and practice." *Human Resource Development Quarterly*, 11, 179–85.

Heilman, M. E. (1997) "Sex discrimination and the affirmative action remedy: The role of sex stereotypes." *Journal of Business Ethics*, 16, 877–89.

Helms, M. M., & Stern, R. (2001) "Exploring the factors that influence employees' perceptions of their organisation's culture." *Journal of Management in Medicine*, 15, 415–29.

Heraty, N., & Morley, M. (1995) "Line managers and human resource development." *Journal of European Industrial Training*, 19(10), 31–37.

Holton, E. F. (1998) "Customer service is not the best model for HRD practice." *Human Resource Development Quarterly*, 9, 207–09.

Jermier, J. M., Slocum, Jr., J. W., Fry, L. W., & Gaines, J. (1991) "Organizational subcultures in a soft bureaucracy: Resistance behind the myth and façade of an official culture." *Organization Science*, 2, 170–94.

Kaeter, M. (1995, November) HRD degrees: Who needs them? *Training*, 32, 65–74.

Kirkpatrick, D. L. (1976) "Evaluation of training." In R. L. Craig (ed.), *Training and development handbook: A guide to human resource development* 2nd ed., 301–19.

Knapp, D. E., Faley, R. H., Ekeberg, S. E., & Dubois, C. L. Z. (1997) "Determinants of target responses to sexual harassment: A conceptual framework." *Academy of Management Review*, 22, 687–729.

Kopelman, R. E., Brief, A. P., & Guzzo, R. A. (1990) "The role of climate and culture in productivity." In B. Schneider (ed.), *Organizational climate and culture* (San Francisco: Jossey-Bass) 282–317.

Koslowsky, M. (1990) "Staff/line distinctions in job and organizational commitment." *Journal of Occupational Psychology*, 63, 167–173.

Krefting, L. A., & Nord, W. R. (2003) *"Ethics and HRD: A New Approach to Leading Responsible Organizations"*. *Academy of Management Review*, 28, 512–13.

Kuchinke, K. P. (2001) "Why HRD is not an academic discipline." *Human Resource Development International*, 4, 291–94.

Latham, G. P. (1988). Human resources training and development. *Annual Review of Psychology*, 39, 545–82.

Lupton, B. (2000) "Maintaining masculinity: Men who do 'women's work'." *British Journal of Management*, 11, 33–48.

Lyness, K. S., & Heilman, M. E. (2006) "When fit is fundamental: Performance evaluations and promotions of upper-level female and male managers." *Journal of Applied Psychology*, 91, 777–85.

Martocchio, J. J. (1994) "The effects of absence culture on individual absence." *Human Relations*, 47, 243–62.

Mathieu, J. E., & Martineau, J. W. (1997) "Individual and situational influences in training motivation." In J. K. Ford (ed.), *Improving training effectiveness in work organizations* (Mahwah, NJ: Lawrence Erlbaum) 193–221.

McConville, T. (2006) "Devolved HRM responsibilities, middle-managers and role dissonance." *Personnel Review*, 35, 637–53.

McCracken, M., & Wallace, M. (2000) "Exploring strategic maturity in HRD: Rhetoric, aspiration or reality?" *Journal of European Industrial Training*, 24, 425–37.

McGuire, D., Cross, C., & O'Donnell, D. (2005) "Why humanistic approaches in HRD won't work." *Human Resource Development Quarterly*, 16, 131–37.

Mitchell, G., & Tetlock, P. E. (2006). "Antidiscrimination law and the perils of mindreading." *Ohio State Law Journal*, 67, 1023–124.

Nadler, L. (1984) *The Handbook of Human Resource Development*. (New York: John Wiley & Sons).

Nauta, A., & Sanders, K. (2001) "Causes and consequences of perceived goal differences between departments within manufacturing organizations." *Journal of Occupational and Organizational Psychology*, 74, 321–42.

Orpen, C. (1999) "The influence of the training environment on trainee motivation and perceived training quality." *International Journal of Training and Development*, 3, 34–43.

Pager, D., & Quillian, L. (2005) "Walking the talk? What employers say versus what they do." *American Sociological Review*, 70, 355–80.

Palich, L. E., & Hom, P. W. (1992) "The impact of leader power and behavior on leadership perceptions: A LISREL test of an expanded categorization theory of leadership model." *Group & Organization Management*, 17, 279–96.

Palthe, J., & Kossek, E. E. (2003) "Subcultures and employment modes: Translating HR strategy into practice." *Journal of Organizational Change Management*, 16, 287–309.

Panchak, P. (2000) Viewpoint—The Great Training Hoax. *Industry Week*. (October 3, 2000) Retrieved June 25, 2005, from http://www.industryweek.com/Columns/asp/columns.asp?ColumnID=677.

Rentsch, J. R. (1990) "Climate and culture: Interaction and qualitative differences in organizational meanings." *Journal of Applied Psychology*, 75, 668–81.

Richeson, J. A., & Ambady, N. (2001) "Who's in charge? Effects of situational roles on automatic gender bias." *Sex Roles*, 44, 493–512.

Roberson, L., Kulik, C. T., & Pepper, M. B. (2003) "Using needs assessment to resolve controversies in diversity training design." *Group & Organization Management*, 28, 148–74.

Rothwell, W. J., & Kazanas, H. C. (1990) "Training: Key to strategic management." *Performance Improvement Quarterly*, 3(1), 42–56.

Rouiller, J. Z., & Goldstein, I. L. (1993) "The relationship between organizational transfer climate and positive transfer of training." *Human Resource Development Quarterly*, 4, 377–90.

Rousseau, D. M. (1990) "Assessing organizational culture: The case for multiple methods." In B. Schneider (ed.) *Organizational climate and culture*. (San Francisco: Jossey-Bass) 153–92.

Ruona, W. E. A., Lynham, S. A., & Chermack, T. J. (2003) "Insights on emerging trends and the future of human resource development." *Advances in Developing Human Resources*, 5, 272–82.

Saari, L., Johnson, R. T., McLaughlin, S. D., & Zimmerle, D. M. (1988) "A survey of management training and education practices in U.S. companies." *Journal of Applied Psychology*, 41, 731–44.

Saffold, G. S. III. (1988) "Culture traits, strength, and organizational performance: Moving beyond 'strong' culture." *Academy of Management Review*, 13, 546–58.

Salas, E., & Cannon-Bowers, J. A. (2001) "The science of training: A decade of progress." *Annual Review of Psychology*, 52, 471–99.

Salas, E., & Kosarzycki, M. P. (2003) "Why don't organizations pay attention to (and use) findings from the science of training?" *Human Resource Development Quarterly*, 14, 487–91.

Sambrook, S. (2004) "A 'critical' time for HRD?" *Journal of European Industrial Training*, 28, 611–24.

Sammut, A. C. (2001) "HR & OD turfwar: Highlighting the need to establish a clear definition of OD." *Organization Development Journal*, 19, 9–19.

Santos, A., & Stuart, M. (2003) "Employee perceptions and their influence on training effectiveness." *Human Resource Management Journal*, 13, 27–45.

Schein, E. H. (1990) "Organizational culture." *American Psychologist*, 2, 109–19.

Schein, E. H. (1996) "Culture: The missing concept in organization studies." *Administrative Science Quarterly*, 41, 229–41.

Schultz, V. (2003) "The sanitized workplace." *Yale Law Journal*, 112, 2061–194.

Shank, P. (1998) "No R-E-S-E-C-T? Five foolish things trainers do." *Training & Development*, 52(8), 14–16.

Sheridan, J. E. (1992) "Organizational culture and employee retention." *Academy of Management Journal*, 35, 1036–56.

Short, D. C., Bing, J. W., & Kehrhahn, M. T. (2003) "Will human resource development survive?" *Human Resource Development Quarterly*, 14, 239–43.

Smith, K. K. (1983) "Social comparison process and dynamic conservatism in intergroup relations." *Research in Organizational Behavior*, 5, 199–233.

Stevenson, W. B., & Bartunek, J. M. (1996) "Power, interaction, position, and the generation of cultural agreement in organizations." *Human Relations*, 49, 75–104.

Sugrue, B. (2005) *The 2006 ASTD state of the industry report.* (Alexandria, VA: American Society of Training and Development).

Swanson, R. A. (2001) "Human resource development and its underlying theory." *Human Resource Development International*, 4, 299–312.

Tannenbaum, S. I., & Yukl, G. (1992) "Training and development in work organizations." *Annual Review of Psychology*, 43, 399–441.

Taylor, P. J., & O'Driscoll, M. P. (1998) "A new integrated framework for training needs analysis." *Human Resource Management Journal*, 8, 29–50.

Trice, H. M. *Occupational subcultures in the workplace.* (1993) (Ithaca, NY: ILR Press).

Trice, H. M., & Beyer, J. M. (1993) *The cultures of work organizations.* (Englewood Cliffs, NJ: Prentice-Hall).

U.S. Department of Labor. (2006) *Women in the Labor Force: A Databook.* (Washington, DC: Department of Labor).

Wanous, J. P., Reichers, A. E., & Austin, J. T. (2000) Cynicism about organizational change. *Group & Organization Management*, 25, 132–54.

Weick, K. E. (1979). Cognitive processes in organizations. *Research in Organizational Behavior*, 1, 41–74.

Welbourne, T. M., & Trevor, C. O. (2000) "The roles of departmental and position power in job evaluation." *Academy of Management Journal*, 43, 761–71.

Wright, P. M., McMahan, G. C., Snell, S. A., & Gerhart, B. (2001) "Comparing line and HR executives' perceptions of HR effectiveness: Services, roles, and contributions." *Human Resource Management*, 40, 111–23.

Zammuto, R. F., & O'Connor, E. J. (1992) "Gaining advanced manufacturing technologies' benefits: The roles of organization design and culture." *Academy of Management Review*, 17, 701–28.

13

When Human Resources Practices and Organizational Culture Collide: A Performance Management Case Study

Kimberly Clauss Magee

Cabrera & Bonache (1999) noted that since the early 1980s, the literature on human resources has suggested that the competitive capacity of organizations can be increased by building strong cultures and effectively developing and managing people. "In other words, two key factors for success in today's competitive environment are continuously espoused to be an organization's culture and its human resource practices, both of which influence the behavior of organizational members" (p. 51).

Performance management is an organizational practice used to develop and manage people. A 1993 national survey of performance management practices (Rogers, Miller, & Worklan, 1993) and a follow-up survey in 1997 of 80 companies (Bernthal, Sumlin, Davis, & Rogers, 1997) found that most responding organizations had a company-sanctioned performance management process in place and planned to continue using it. Organizations use performance management systems and processes for various reasons and in various ways, but the primary espoused goal is to enable organizational performance (Rheem, 1995). Becker & Gerhart (1996) found that human resource decisions, including how to manage performance, could be crucial to maintaining and improving high organizational performance.

Performance management processes promise to enhance the quality of organizational and individual decisions, enhance the relationship between the individual and the organization, and provide a foundation for organizational development and change efforts (Murphy & Cleveland, 1995). Huselid (1995) found that performance management systems are a key work practice that can improve the knowledge, skills, and abilities of a company's current and potential employees; increase employee motivation; reduce shirking; and enhance retention of quality employees while encouraging non-performers to leave.

In their performance management practices survey, Bernthal et al. (1997) found that most CEOs surveyed believed their performance management system drives the key factors associated with business strategy. Almost 80 percent perceived their performance management system as driving the people or the cultural strategies that maximize human assets.

Yet, for all this promise, the performance management systems implemented in today's organizations generally fail to deliver the promised benefits and results despite significant investment of time and money. In their national survey, Rogers et al. (1993) reported that although 89 percent of organizations 'in their survey sample used a company-sanctioned performance management system or approach, overall satisfaction with the system or approach was low. Although manager and employee satisfaction with the overall effectiveness of performance management processes did improve between 1993 (Rogers et al., 1993) and 1997 (Bernthal et al., 1997), most managers and employees surveyed remained dissatisfied. Additionally, over 40 percent of the respondents indicated that their organizations planned to make significant changes to their systems or how the systems were implemented.

Ineffective performance management systems can be harmful to an organization in a variety of ways. For example, performance management systems can overemphasize the individual and underemphasize the contributions of teams (Nickols, 2007; Reilly & McCourty, 1998). This is particularly alarming in organizations that espouse teamwork as a stated corporate value. Others have criticized performance management as ignoring the reality of the organizational system (Deming, 1986); sending mixed messages to users of the performance management system (Cleveland, Morrison, & Bjerke, 1986); and becoming an unnecessary source of dissatisfaction and dissent (Heathfield, 2007; Murphy & Cleveland, 1995). The employee appraisal component of performance management has been specifically questioned and criticized (Deming, 1986; Heathfield, 2007; Nickols, 2007; Rasch, 2004). Coens and Jenkins (2000) and Gray (2002) concluded that companies would be better developing alternatives rather than trying to fix current performance appraisal systems and processes.

In short, most organizations use some semblance of a performance management process or system to increase organizational performance, but most of the people in those organizations, managers and employees alike, report that they do not think that process is entirely effective or that it delivers a reasonable return on investment. That investment can be significant when managerial and employee time is considered, plus system development, implementation, and maintenance costs (Nickols, 2007).

HRD practitioners are on the front lines to deliver training and development, career development, and organizational development programs to address performance deficiencies. In many instances, HRD resources are called upon to develop performance management systems, programs, and interventions to support organizational and individual performance. HRD practitioners often diagnose performance challenges through front-end organizational analysis and find that an understanding of the cultural context within which a performance management system must operate is critical before developing a solution. An understanding of the cultural context of the organization is also invaluable in determining how the solution may be accepted and implemented. This chapter contains a case study of a company's implementation of a performance management system that ultimately underdelivered expected benefits. This was, in large part, because the system was not aligned with significant aspects of the company's culture. The case is also used to highlight the important role HRD practitioners have in highlighting the need for culture change and influencing the alignment of human performance levers, including organizational culture and performance management, to business strategy.

Organizational culture as a contextual factor in performance management

Performance management is both a process defined by a set of rules that the organization prescribes and a set of manager and employee actions. Those actions may or may not follow the process rules. Despite training, coaching, senior management support, and employee communications, managers often conduct performance management in different ways than intended. Despite knowing how performance management should be implemented, managers choose to do things differently or sometimes not at all. Why is that? Certainly one of the reasons is a function of the organizational culture in which they are operating.

It cannot be easy for managers to make technical accuracy their goal in performance management when such accuracy conflicts with messages they receive from the organizational culture such as "keep the noise level down" or "keep people engaged and motivated." The definition of accuracy itself could have a culturally derived meaning for managers. Some organizational cultures may support distinguishing between individuals in terms of their performance; others may not. An organizational culture that stresses teamwork and group goals might discourage raters from distinguishing among individual subordinates. Cultures that stress individual achievement might more readily support performance management that recognizes individual differences in performance. Culture may also affect the power and authority structures of an organization, which may have implications for the acceptability of accurate ratings. Organizations with a clearly defined power structure and significant power differentials between levels of the organization may be more supportive of performance management systems designed to produce accurate ratings than organizations with very flat and democratic power structures (Murphy & Cleveland, 1995).

Characteristics of the organizational system such as culture are likely to play an important role in facilitating rating distortions (Kozlowski, Chao, & Morrison, 1998). If distortions are commonplace, the contextual factors influencing performance management politics, for example, are likely to go beyond features of the performance management system, implicating organizational culture among other factors. That is, there must be organizational mechanisms to rationalize, guide, and communicate distortion strategies. Under such circumstances, distortions of the formal performance management system may constitute an adaptive response by system users.

Performance management takes place within an overall organizational context. Murphy and Cleveland's (1995) four-component model of performance appraisal frames context as the starting point from which other components (judgment, rating, and evaluation) should be examined. A central assumption of their model is that performance appraisal outcomes are the results of a rater's goal-directed behavior. That behavior is shaped by the organizational context in which the ratings appear. The organizational context influences the judgment process, the rating process, the evaluation process, and the eventual uses of the rating data. The model can also be used to examine the broader notion of performance management (the overall process of identifying, measuring, evaluating, and developing employee performance) and not just the performance appraisal. Thus, organizational culture is an important part of the overall context in which the entire performance management process is performed, interpreted, and used. In fact, Murphy and Cleveland proposed that performance appraisal research on the rating context could profit from the consideration of intra-organizational factors such as organizational values and culture.

In reviewing performance management research to date, three things are apparent. One is that it is necessary to conduct research about organizational culture and performance management in organizations with organizational participants. There are relatively few studies of this nature because access into organizations willing to participate can be difficult. Secondly, there is a relationship between some elements of performance management and some elements of organizational culture as demonstrated by several quantitative studies. These studies are generally useful in establishing the relationship but contribute little to our understanding of it, because the analyses do not go beyond the descriptive level. Further, it is not clear that the commonly used culture surveys are sufficiently relevant or comprehensive in relation to the organizational culture under study. Thirdly, an examination of an organization's performance management process or system can tell us something about the organization's culture and how the culture is either supportive or hostile to the espoused goals of performance management.

There is a recurring issue in the literature about the lack of a universally accepted definition of organizational culture. However, there do appear to be four shared issues underlying the many definitions of organizational culture: organizational culture is relatively stable and resistant to change; it is taken for granted and less consciously held; it derives its meaning from the organization's members; and it incorporates sets of shared understandings (Langan-Fox, 1997).

In her book, *Cultural Knowledge in Organizations: Exploring the Collective Mind*, Sackmann (1991) uses the notion of sense-making to substantiate generic constructs to capture the essence of culture. People use cognitive devices to make sense of what they experience and perceive. These devices are such things as the labels used to describe or name things or events, explanations about an event structure, lessons learned from events, and reasons why these events happened. People use the devices, or cognitions, to make sense of things they experience. When a group in an organization holds cognitions in common, the cognitions become a part of the cultural knowledge that guides and shapes the behavior of the group.

Overview of this case study

In this case study, Sackmann's (1991) qualitative research methodology was adapted to develop a cultural knowledge map of an organization using performance management as the issue of focus. The cultural knowledge map was used as the basis for conclusions and theory development about culture as a contextual factor in performance management. Culture is derived from its members; to fully understand it, the researcher must work to capture the emic, or insider's, view in constructing cultural reality (Morey & Luthans, 1984; Pike, 1966) instead of imposing the researcher's constructions and interpretations *a priori* (Schein, 1990).

The study sought to answer three general questions: (1) What cultural knowledge of performance management did organizational managers have? (2) What was the impact of organizational culture on the way performance management was implemented in an organization? and (3) How did performance management perpetuate and challenge the organization's culture? These focus questions did not constitute testable hypotheses. Rather, they guided and helped to focus the study with the goal of generating, rather than testing, theory about how organizational culture impacts the implementation of performance management.

The site for this study was a large multinational Fortune 500 manufacturer, distributor, and marketer of consumer products in the food and beverage industry. The company owns over 400 brands, is a global leader in its industry, and has a presence in over 200 countries. The company was founded in the mid-1800s. In 2006, over 70 percent of the company's net operating income came from the company's international divisions.

Data were collected from managers at various levels in the North America divisions through ethnographic interviews. Schein's research (1992) on the influence of organizational leadership on work cultures guided the decision to collect data from managers who are charged with the responsibility of implementing performance management within their areas of control. Although managers may belong to several cultural frames (national, organizational, occupational, and gender), this study focused on the organizational, sub-organizational, and occupational frames. Additional data were collected through participant observation and related organizational documents.

Findings and implications for HRD research and practice

The findings from this case study research have theoretical implications for the study of organizational culture as a contextual factor in performance management in key areas of interest to organizational researchers: (1) organizational culture as a contextual factor in performance management; (2) purpose of performance management in organizations; and (3) need for alignment among strategy, culture, and HR practices including performance management.

Organizational culture: The context for performance management

The findings of this study further the development of Cleveland and Murphy's conceptual model (1995) of the appraisal aspect of performance management occurring not only in an immediate context but also in the cultural context of the organization (see Figure 13.1). That is, managers' goal-directed behavior in appraisal is shaped by an overall context that would include the manager and employee relationship, for example, and by the broader organizational culture in which managers and employees find themselves by being organizational members.

The expanded model of performance management in the broader context of organizational culture depicted in Figure 13.1 begins with the source of organizational culture in this organization, the leader–founder.

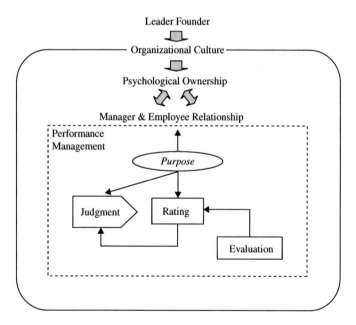

Figure 13.1 Performance management in the broader context of organizational culture.

In this case, an important aspect of organizational culture was that the culture engendered and reinforced feelings of psychological ownership among its members. Pierce, Kostova, and Dirks (2001) proposed the theory of psychological ownership in organizations. The theory posits the notion that under certain conditions, organizational members can develop feelings of ownership or possession toward an organization and various organizational factors. Such feelings were expressed by many participants in this study. The theory also holds that such ownership results in several organizational effects, including reasons why and the conditions under which organizational members promote or resist change. In this case, there was resistance to the performance management system because it represented imposed, revolutionary, and subtractive change to organizational members.

This phenomenon of psychological ownership impacted another important aspect in the culture: the relationship between a manager and a subordinate employee. Within the overall context of the organizational culture, performance management was implemented by the organization both for administrative and developmental purposes. The administrative purpose of performance management provided a more immediate context in which managers had to weigh the importance of their relationships with employees against the judgment and rating processes in which they had to engage.

Organizational culture, then, influences the judgment process, the rating process, the evaluation process, and the eventual uses of the rating data. This case study represents a unique perspective of organizational culture as an intra-organizational factor in performance management. The culture of an organization provides information and shapes the behavior and experiences of employees. Culture, by defining which behaviors are appropriate and which are not, serves to reduce the uncertainty of organizational members. At the time of this research, the organization was undergoing unprecedented changes that were challenging aspects of the organizational culture such as members' beliefs about their relationship to the organization.

This research supported the notion that organizational culture was an important contextual factor in the implementation of performance management. The prescribed performance management system in this organization featured objective setting in alignment with broader organizational goals, employee ownership of the process, focus on not only what is to be achieved but also how it is to be achieved, ongoing coaching and feedback, emphasis on development, and a pay for performance philosophy. Overall, the system contained elements often cited as "best practices" in performance management research. Yet, participants in the study generally agreed that the organization's performance management system was not particularly effective, mostly because some of its features were counter-cultural. Also, the performance management system was being used in an uncertain environment where the overall organizational strategy was not well defined or articulated.

One example of the performance management system's misalignment with the culture was the espoused intent of performance management to make employees responsible for their own performance and development. Managers, though, remained in control as the final decision-makers relative to objectives, development plans, performance ratings, and the associated financial outcomes of the ratings. Performance management, then, was actually a form of management control, characteristic of a patriarchal organization.

The perceived imposition of a structured and regulated performance management system was potentially threatening to the individual manager's sense of control and authority. Aspects of the performance management system that were counter-cultural were forcing changes to the status quo, including the self-continuity of organizational members. Also, the harsh realities of confronting poor performers and separating them from the organization were counter-cultural to the longstanding tradition of taking care of employees to retirement. Organizational members naturally resisted these changes because of consequent increased uncertainty. Said another way, the culture did not encourage the behaviors necessary for the organization to change and compete in a highly competitive market.

There were no data that indicated consideration of the organization's culture before implementation of the performance management system. This may explain some of the participants' disillusionment with the process. They were being asked to use a process that in many ways challenged what they believed to be the organization's norms. Feedback, for example, was an integral element of the performance management process, yet feedback was not an organizational norm. The performance management process mandated that underperforming employees should not be tolerated. Confronting poor performers requires direct feedback from managers that could result in conflict, yet the organization had neither a feedback culture nor a constructive approach to surface and resolve conflict. Direct feedback and conflict were seen as potentially damaging to all-important positive relationships within the organization.

The suggested distribution of performance ratings was another example of the performance management system's misalignment with the organizational culture. Participants in this study grappled with the notion of communicating, "You're average," to most of their employees, who would find the message de-motivating and potentially damaging to otherwise positive employee–manager relationships.

These findings suggest that when aspects of the performance management system are not aligned with the organizational culture, tension is created. Although managers may intellectually know that the organizational culture and their behavior must change, they instinctively cling to familiar norms rather than adopting new ones. This is especially true when they are personally uncomfortable with new norms and are uncertain about overall strategy and leadership in the organization.

Administrative versus developmental purposes of performance management

In this case, performance management had both administrative and developmental purposes. That is, the performance management system was used for pay decisions, for example, as well as to identify an individual employee's development needs and to create a plan to address them. In this organization, the administrative purpose of performance management took precedence over the developmental purpose, suggesting that dual-purpose performance management systems are not effective in achieving both aims. The direct link between an overall performance rating and specific financial rewards is consistent with a pay for performance philosophy. That link, though, minimizes other potential value of performance management such as employee development.

The administrative purpose of performance management has been found in other studies to predict both rating inflation (Kane & Lawler, 1979; Larson & Rimland, 1984; Mohrman & Lawler, 1983) and concerns for equity and fairness (Cropanzano & Greenberg, 1997; Folger & Greenberg, 1985). Both were found to be true in this organization. Participants in this study expressed frustration and concern about the company's suggested rating distribution guidelines and did not have confidence that poor performers were, in fact, receiving lower ratings. Additionally, most participants expressed concerns about equity and fairness, stemming from the belief that the performance management process was not being implemented consistently across the organization.

This company, like many others, uses a single performance management system for multiple purposes. Research on the functions of performance management (Alexander & Wilkins, 1982; Bretz, Milkovich, & Read, 1992; Ilgen, Fisher, & Taylor, 1979; Kluger & DeNisi, 1996; Schneier, 1989) cite several organizational purposes: performance improvement, coaching and guidance, feedback and communication, compensation, termination and legal documentation, staffing decisions, and professional development. The intent is to maximize results and more efficiently use the time that managers and employees spend on activities related to performance management. Combining or bundling these purposes, however, results in managers and employees not realizing the full range of potential benefits, because the multiple purposes undermine each other. A single process, no matter how well designed and implemented, simply cannot deliver against a diverse list of expectations. A process must be culturally fit for purpose, and organizations would be best served by focusing on the developmental purpose of performance management to build and sustain the necessary commitment from employees the future demands.

Alignment required: Strategy, culture, and performance management

Traditionally, organizational strategy, organizational culture, and the design of HR practices such as performance management have been studied as independent approaches for increasing organizational success. The findings of this research suggest that strategy, organizational culture, and HR practices such as performance management need to be complementary and aligned to enable change (Bennett, Fadil, & Greenwood, 1994; Cabrera & Bonache, 1999; Ehrlich, 1997; Schwartz & Davis, 1981).

The performance management system in this organization was implemented in the absence of clear organizational strategy and in the presence of substantive changes including cultural change. This lack of alignment caused anxiety and frustration for managers. Without a clearly defined and communicated business strategy, the performance management system had little chance of being fully leveraged to communicate and reinforce desired behavioral norms such as feedback.

In the past, this company had a defender strategy (Miles & Snow, 1984) supported by internal recruitment, a process-oriented performance management approach, and an internally consistent compensation system. It appeared to be adopting a growth strategy that would need to be supported by external recruitment, a results-oriented performance management approach, and an externally competitive compensation system. To current organizational members, these changes were viewed as imposed, revolutionary, and subtractive. As a result, the changes were resisted.

Semler (1997) defined organizational alignment as "the extent to which the strategy, structure, and culture of the organization combine to create a synergistic whole that makes it possible to achieve the goals laid out in the organization's strategy" (p. 27). Further, he conceptualized alignment as a correlational measure of degree ranging from −1.00, complete opposition, to +1.00, perfect harmony and synergy. Although perfect alignment of strategy, culture, and HR practices is more theoretical than practical, organizations such as the one in this study need to view strategy, culture, and HR practices holistically and systemically. Intentional change in one impacts the other two (Semler, 1997). The results of this study illustrate that overall strategy should drive culture and HR practices. Without strategy, organizational culture and the organization's HR practices, including performance management, can become barriers rather than enablers of necessary organizational change. Organizational culture provides the context in which HR practices are implemented. Both strategy and culture communicate messages to employees about the behavioral norms that enable the organization to achieve its overall strategic objectives.

Implications for HRD practitioners

This case study highlights several implications for HRD practitioners: (1) evaluating the administrative and developmental purposes of performance management and determining appropriate processes to fulfill those purposes; (2) uncovering and questioning the basic assumptions the organization has relative to performance management; (3) advocating a systems view of the organization to increase organizational effectiveness; and (4) providing appropriate performance management training and other performance support mechanisms for managers and employees.

There are several legitimate purposes of performance management that directly relate to the role and expertise HRD practitioners bring to an organization. These include performance improvement, coaching and guidance, feedback and communication, skill development, and career development. In organizations where performance management is tied to any of these purposes, it becomes important for the HRD practitioners to ascertain whether those purposes can be achieved through performance management. This research demonstrates that when performance management has administrative purposes such as determining pay, and developmental purposes like individual development planning, the administrative purposes are emphasized in the minds and actions both of managers and employees, and developmental processes are undermined. This confirms similar findings by Cleveland, Morrison, & Bjerke (1986). In such cases, then, HRD practitioners must be in a position to provide alternative, robust developmental processes to meet the learning needs of the employees and the organization.

Further, when an organization is designing or implementing a performance management process, HRD practitioners should play an influential role in decoupling administrative purposes from developmental purposes. Organizations, and the managers within them, may be inclined to expect that the performance management process should concurrently accomplish several things as efficiently as possible. This notion of economy may drive a bias toward one integrated process. Although that process may be efficient, it will not be effective in achieving a plethora of diverse goals. HRD practitioners should play a consultative role with organizational leaders and line managers in developing and implementing complementary processes to achieve administrative and developmental goals.

Additionally, HRD professionals have a role in facilitating discussion and debate about the underlying assumptions the organization holds about performance management practices and the implications of those assumptions. In their book, *Abolishing Performance Appraisals: Why They Backfire and What to Do Instead*, Coens and Jenkins (2000) noted: "The real culprit is underlying assumptions – the beliefs and messages the appraisal conveys about people, work, motivation, improvement, and supervision. These assumptions are not realistic or healthy, and they sharply clash with the values espoused by quality management organizations."

Questioning basic assumptions such as those held about organizational responsibility for employee feedback and development, managers' ability to evaluate and assess individual performance objectively and reliably, the motivational value of performance ratings, and the use of performance management in gaining employee commitment to the organization will help to uncover the underlying beliefs that exist about performance management as well as individual and organizational performance. These beliefs, then, must be contrasted with the values that the organization espouses and wants to promote. In short, the underlying assumptions about performance management must align with the organization's desired culture. It is inherently risky for HRD practitioners to develop, implement, or change an organization's performance management process and practice without understanding the organizational context. Proposed solutions that are out of the norm may be partly implemented, ineffectively implemented, or outright rejected by organizational members.

In addition to uncovering and understanding underlying assumptions about performance management, HRD practitioners must also be cognizant of underlying assumptions about employee development in general. To uncover these assumptions, HRD practitioners should ask several questions to get to organizational beliefs about employee development. The answers, often in the form of recipe knowledge about what should be in place, need to be triangulated with observations of management behavior around resource allocation and managerial support of employee development for validation.

What are examples of the kinds of questions HRD practitioners can use to uncover axiomatic or cultural knowledge about employee development? HRD practitioners should ask about management's willingness to free-up employee time for development and training experiences. Do managers support time away from the job with back-up resources or expect that employees will get the job done while also engaged in training and other developmental activities? Is on-the-job learning planned and monitored or just assumed to be taking place? A lack of rigor and discipline when it comes to employee development may be a good indicator that the organization does not see or has not realized any upside or downside to employee development.

Another area for HRD practitioners to probe for axiomatic cultural knowledge is management's attitude toward spending money on employee development and training. Is there clarity on training budgets and the process to allocate those resources? When and how is the training and development budget increased or trimmed throughout the year? Organizations that cut training and development budgets in lean times communicate something far different to their employees than those who maintain or even add investment to employee development during those times. Does leadership demonstrate interest in the immediate functioning of employees, without consideration for longer-term questions such as employability (Stoker & Van der Heijden, 2001)?

HRD practitioners should examine if and how senior management participates in and supports employee development. Are senior leaders expected to be faculty in development programs? Former General

Electric CEO Jack Welch served as leadership development faculty throughout his tenure. This helped set the tone that managers were teachers and needed to lead by example. Another interesting question is whether or not senior leaders spend time on their own development or view it as great for other groups of employees but not really applicable to themselves.

HRD practitioners should ask about and observe how management views the external competition and how benchmarking and best practices are viewed and used within their organization. Does management have a healthy respect for the competition and seek to learn competitive strategies for talent acquisition, development, and retention? Is benchmarking valued, and how are successful practices of other companies viewed and used?

Lastly, and perhaps most importantly, HRD practitioners should seek to understand the organization's fundamental philosophy and definition of employee development. Some organizations adopt a deficiency model: employee skill or competency gaps are identified and then addressed through interventions. Other organizations are using a strengths model (Buckingham & Clifton, 2001) grounded in the view that it is far more effective to identify and leverage employee strengths than continue to focus on their weaknesses. Still other organizations essentially have no organizational viewpoint on employee development. The answers to these types of question are indicators of the organization's readiness, willingness, and ability to leverage HRD strategies and initiatives to drive individual and organizational performance.

HRD practitioners also have a critical and unique role in influencing management to examine an organization as a system when trying to increase organizational effectiveness (Katz & Kahn, 1978). The organizational system comprises elements including culture and environment, people, materials, equipment, and methods and structures. A systemic perspective will direct time and attention to the system as a whole rather than to one component in isolation from the others. Optimizing an organizational practice such as performance management, for example, without considering the effects of the organizational culture and environment, is counterproductive, because the two are interdependent and a change in one impacts the other. A systemic organizational perspective facilitates discussion about the extent to which individual performance is determined by the system in which the work is done, or by individual effort and abilities.

HRD practitioners are often in organization development roles and should be part of organizational change initiatives, specifically focused on how the change will impact people in the organization. Who else will engage management in thinking about the human aspects of the change; what steps should be taken to engage people in the change; and a plan for creating, implementing, and sustaining the change? Using a systems perspective, HRD practitioners can focus on alignment of the various system components with the overall strategy and direction of the organization. For example, HRD professionals have the responsibility of ensuring that the organization's people practices are aligned and in support of the overall organizational strategy. HRD professionals can also help to develop and execute a meaningful communications plan to engage and update all stakeholders, including employees, about the change.

HRD has an important leadership role in the design, development, and delivery of performance management training and other performance support mechanisms for managers and employees. Training was shown in this case study to be an effective means of conveying dictionary ("what is") and directory ("how things are done around here") cultural knowledge about the organization's performance management process. Training, though, needs to go beyond just process and encompass coaching, feedback, and other developmental activities. HRD practitioners should develop and provide post-training performance support to managers and employees on a just-in-time basis. These performance support mechanisms could include such things as consulting services to managers, employees, and teams; online performance management help tools and skills practice sessions; and successful performance management practices forums.

Perhaps one of the most important implications of this research is that organizations, with leadership from HRD practitioners, must align organizational culture and organizational practices to an overall business strategy. Without a strategy to provide direction to the organization, the culture of an organization will seek stasis, and organizational members will resist necessary change. Performance management can be a lever for change, but only in the context of an organizational culture that is supportive of and aligned to the business objectives and values of the organization.

New directions for HRD research

Performance management is a prolific HR practice in organizations. Further research is needed to explore questions not only about how performance management should be implemented but also if it should be implemented. Such research could further examine the inherent assumptions underlying performance management processes and the extent to which such assumptions are valid and relevant in organizations, especially those cultures characterized by high employee commitment. Rasch (2004) advocates an alternative "professional growth model" with a "focus on employee success, a priority for leadership development training for supervisors, and a special performance process for those employees who need targeted focus in performance" (p. 407). This model might represent the next generation of performance management and merits further research.

Chehade, Mendes, & Mitchell (2006) posit the notion that "Culture plays a key role in organizational performance, but it's an outcome of the organizational system, not an input to the system. Adjust the building blocks, and you change the system. Change the system, and you change the culture. Change the culture, and you unlock strategy by enabling execution." We need research on how best to change and leverage the building blocks, including performance management, to drive organizational performance and the organizational culture needed to enable high performance. Research is also needed that examines the interaction of basic building blocks like recruitment practices, performance management, employee development initiatives and retention strategies, and how they are best combined to enable high performance.

Performance management might be one of the first places HRD practitioners new to an organization can look to understand a company's leadership philosophy, organizational people practices, and culture. Of course, there are clues about those elements during the recruiting process, and HRD practitioners being recruited are likely to hear about how the organization values employee development, how supportive leadership is of development programs, and how valuable and welcome their HRD skills and expertise will be as the organization focuses on developing capability and improving organizational performance. HRD newcomers, once through the organization's door, should pay particular and immediate attention to the organization's underlying assumptions about employee development. Examining actual organizational practices and management support will reveal alignment or disconnects between what management espouses and what is actually operating in the organization. Poking at the performance management process through inquiry and observation can get to the underlying assumptions management has about employee development. Further research is needed to build HRD capabilities for that type of inquiry. If the culture is, in fact, unfavorable to HRD functions, practitioners can then make informed choices about the most effective organizational change strategies. If, in the best case, the leadership philosophy, organizational practices, and culture are favorable to HRD functions, then a world of opportunity awaits.

References

Alexander, E. R., & Wilkins, R. D. "Performance rating validity: The relationship between objective and subjective measures of performance." *Group & Organization Studies*, 7 (1982) 485–96.

Becker, B., & Gerhart, G. "The impact of human resource management on organizational performance: Progress and prospects." *Academy of Management Journal*, 39(4) (1996) 779–801.

Bennett, R. H., Fadil, P. A., & Greenwood, R. T. "Cultural alignment in response to strategic organizational change: New considerations for a change framework." *Journal of Managerial Issues*, 6(4) (1994) 1045–3695.

Bernthal, P., Sumlin, R., Davis, P., & Rogers, B. *Performance management practices survey.* (Bridgeville, PA: Development Dimensions International, 1997).

Bretz, R. D., Milkovich, G. T., & Read, W. "The current state of performance appraisal research and practice: Concerns, directions, and implications." *Journal of Management*, 18(2) (1992) 321–52.

Buckingham, M., & Clifton, D. O. *Now, discover your strengths.* (New York: The Free Press, 2001).

Cabrera, E. F., & Bonache, J. "An expert HR system for aligning organizational culture and strategy." *Human Resource Planning*, 22(1) (1999) 51–60.

Chehade, G., Mendes, D., & Mitchell, D. "Culture change for the analytical mind." *Strategic Finance*, 87(2) (2006) 11–14.

Cleveland, J. N., Morrison, R. F., & Bjerke, D. G. "Rater intentions in appraisal ratings: Malevolent manipulation or functional fudging." Paper presented at the First Annual Conference of the Society for Industrial and Organizational Psychology, Chicago. (1986).

Coens, T., & Jenkins, M. *Performance appraisals: Why they backfire and what to do instead.* (Berrett Koehler, 2000).

Cropanzano, R., & Greenberg, J. "Progress in organizational justice: Tunneling through the maze." In C. L. Cooper & I. Roberstson (eds), *International review of industrial and organizational psychology.* (New York: Wiley, 1997).

Deming, W. E. *Out of the crisis.* (Cambridge, MA: MIT Institute for Advanced Engineering Study, 1986).

Ehrlich, C. J. "Human resource management: A changing script for a changing world." In D. Ulrich, M. R. Losey, & G. Lake (eds), *Tomorrow's HR management: 48 thought leaders call for change.* (New York: Wiley, 1997) 163–74.

Folger, R., & Greenberg, J. "Procedural justice: An interpretive analysis of personnel systems." In K. N. Rowland & G. R. Ferris (eds), *Research in personnel and human resources management:* vol. 3. (Greenwich, CT: JAI Press, 1985) 141–83.

Gray, G. "Performance appraisals don't work." *Industrial Management*, 44 (2002) 15–17.

Heathfield, S. "Performance appraisals don't work—what does?" *The Journal for Quality and Participation*, 30(1) (2007) 6–9.

Huselid, M. "The impact of human resource management practices on turnover, productivity, and corporate financial performance." *Academy of Management Journal*, 38(3) (1995) 635–72.

Ilgen, D. R., Fisher, C. D., & Taylor, M. S. "Consequences of individual feedback on behavior in organizations." *Journal of Applied Psychology*, 64(4) (1979) 349–71.

Katz, D., & Kahn, R. L. *The psychology of organizations.* (New York: John Wiley & Sons, 1978).

Kane, J. S., & Lawler, E. E. "Performance appraisal effectiveness: Its assessment and determinants." In Staw, B. M. (ed.), *Research in organizational behavior:* vol 1. (Greenwich, CT: JAI Press, 1979) 425–78.

Kluger, A. N., & DeNisi, A. "The effects of feedback interventions on performance: A historical review, a meta-analysis, and a preliminary feedback intervention theory." *Psychological Bulletin*, 119(2) (1996) 254–84.

Kozlowski, S. W. J., Chao, G. T., & Morrison, R. F. "Games raters play: Politics, strategies, and impression management in performance appraisal." In Smither, J. W. (ed.), *Performance appraisal: State of the art in practice.* (San Francisco: Jossey-Bass Publishers, 1998) 163–205.

Langan-Fox, J. "Images of a culture in transition: Personal constructs of organizational stability and change." *Journal of Occupational and Organizational Psychology*, 70(3) (1997) 273–93.

Larson, G. E., & Rimland, B. *Officer performance evaluation systems: Lessons learned from experience.* (San Diego, CA: Navy Personnel Research and Development Center, 1984).

Miles, R., & Snow, C. "Designing strategic human resource systems." *Organizational Dynamics*, 13 (1984) 36–52.

Mohrman, A. M., & Lawler, E. E. "Motivation and performance appraisal behavior." In F. J. Landy, S. Lydeck, & J. N. Cleveland (eds), *Performance measurement and theory.* (Hillsdale, NJ: Erlbaum, 1983) 173–89.

Morey, N. C., & Luthans, F. "An emic perspective and ethnoscience methods for organizational research." *Academy of Management Review*, 9(1) (1984) 27–36.

Murphy, K. R., & Cleveland, J. N. *Understanding performance appraisal: Social, organizational, and goal-based perspectives.* (Thousand Oaks: SAGE Publications, 1995).

Nickols, F. "Performance appraisal: Weighed and found wanting in the balance." *The Journal for Quality and Participation*, 30(1) (2007) 13–16.

Pierce, J. L., Kostova, T., & Dirks, K. T. "Toward a theory of psychological ownership in organizations." *Academy of Management Review*, 26 (2001) 298–310.

Pike, K. L. "Etic and emic standpoints for the description of behavior." In Smith, A. G. (ed.), *Communication and culture.* (New York: Holt, Reinhart, and Winston, 1966).

Rasch, L. "Employee performance appraisal and the 95/5 rule." *Community College Journal of Research and Practice*, 28 (2004) 407–14.

Reilly, R. R., & McCourty, J. "Performance appraisal in team settings." In Smither, J. W. (ed.), *Performance appraisal: State of the art in practice.* (San Francisco: Jossey-Bass Publishers) (1998) 244–77.

Rheem, H. "Performance management: A progress report." *Harvard Business Review*, 73(3) (1995) 11–12.

Rogers, R. W., Miller, L. P., & Worklan, J. *Performance management: What's hot, what's not.* (Pittsburgh: Developmental Dimensions International, 1993).

Sackmann, S. A. *Cultural knowledge in organizations: Exploring the collective mind.* (Newbury Park: Sage Publications, 1991).

Schein, E. "Organizational culture." *American Psychologist*, 45 (1990) 109–19.

Schein, E. H. *Organizational culture and leadership.* (San Francisco: Jossey-Bass, 1992).

Schneier, C. E. "Capitalizing on performance management, recognition, and rewards systems." *Compensation and Benefits Review*, 21 (1989) 20–30.

Schwartz, H., & Davis, S. M. "Matching corporate culture and business strategy." *Organizational Dynamics* (1981) 30–48.

Semler, S. W. "Systematic agreement: A theory of organizational alignment." *Human Resource Development Quarterly*, 8(1) (1997) 23–40.

Stoker, J. I., & Van der Heijden, B. I. J. M. "Competence development and appraisal in organizations." *Journal of Career Development*, 28 (2001) 97–113.

14
The Link between Culture and Succession Planning

Lori Fancher

Today's organizations are faced with many multifaceted executive leadership challenges. These include competing in a more globalized work world, combating breaches in ethical and moral decision-making, retaining and developing talent, and leading within a more diversified structure. Furthermore, organizations realize that to maneuver these turbulent, deep, and unknown waters, they must have an experienced and qualified captain at the helm. Yet, the process of succession planning can create a situation that is tricky, extremely expensive, and disruptive, particularly in terms of performance and morale (Charan, 2004, 1994). Charan and Colvin (1999) as well as Conger and Nadler (2004) suggest that the problem is not in the plan itself, but in the execution of the plan. Execution problems may exist as a result of our underestimation of the importance of organizational culture and the role of members, top management, the incumbent, and the board (Cannella Jr & Lubatkin, 1993; Denis, Langley, & Pineault, 2000; Kets de Vries, 1988; Schein, 1992).

The succession planning process, including executive development, is the most important responsibility that HRD leaders have when contributing to strategic business success (Cabrera & Bonache, 1999). However, the current lack of research surrounding organizational culture and the succession process can potentially lead to the recruitment of talent that does not meet the needs of the organization, development strategies that may not adequately prepare high-potentials for executive roles, a talent pool that is too large or takes too long to grow, or possible organizational decline.

We know that the organizational founders and CEO shape culture (Schein, 1992). They make decisions to perpetuate the organizational culture by hiring and promoting others like themselves, often subconsciously (Hansen & Kahnweiler, 1997; Kets de Vries, 1988). Therefore the process of succession planning is not likely to be understood without an insider's point of view.

HRD practitioners as "insiders" in this study were seen as responsible for upholding the "psychological contract" (a term used by one participant) between the organization and its employees. HRD can and should be largely responsible as facilitator of organizational culture through the implementation of policies, procedures, and processes. Within this study, most participants stated that the biggest challenge to a viable succession planning process lies in influential HRD-related processes of: (1) leadership development; (2) talent retention; and (3) communication.

Succession planning: Trends and implications

Literature on succession planning suggests that a key performance indicator of an organization's capability is whether it can produce a viable (executive) heir-apparent (Charan & Colvin, 1999). Although most traditional successions in American organizations have been a result of the "relay process" or through lengthy, internal development and selection of candidates, we are now seeing a trend toward the recruitment of outsiders, a development that some have found alarming (Charan, 2004). The suggestion is that a company's failure to grow its own quality "heir apparents" in an effective and timely manner has led to the need to search elsewhere, with often unsuccessful results. However, if organizations are not able to recognize internal talent and retain it, competitors are apt to benefit (Cappelli, 2000).

More than 37 percent of the Fortune 1,000 companies are run by external recruits (2004). However, 55 percent of outsider CEOs who left their positions in 2003 did so by forced resignation by their boards compared with 34 percent of insiders. Succession frequency is on the rise not only because of the increase of mergers and acquisitions, but also the purchase of smaller, founder-owned and run companies (Wasserman, 2003).

Many researchers suggest that the problem lies in the planning (formal and informal) of a succession. A recent study entitled "Assuring Ethical and Responsible Leadership" (Scott, 2004) surveyed and interviewed board members and CEOs in 120 publicly held companies. It found unsettling results. Of those who participated, only 53 percent said that they have an effective succession management plan in place. In a survey of 500 organizations conducted by Caudron (1996), only 22 percent responded favorably to the statement, "My organization has a well-developed management succession system." In either case, Karaevli and Hall (2003) report that companies are moving away from traditional approaches by shifting from formal succession plans to informal plans or vice versa.

Over ten years ago, Kesner & Sebora (1994) presented a model that provides the most comprehensive literature review of succession planning to date. They defined the succession process as "calculated, systematic and political", yet we know little more today about the specifics of the process than this (Kesner & Sebora, 1994; Pitcher, Chreim, & Kisfalvi, 2000). To help others understand what makes up the succession process, their model was formed by grouping variables identified through succession research into one of four categories: (1) succession antecedents; (2) succession events; (3) succession consequences; or (4) contingencies that serve as mediators or potential predictors to succession process outcomes.

Using this model, Kesner & Sebora (1994) list organizational culture as a "contingency," placing it under the realm of organizational issues that can affect the other three categories of succession: antecedents, event, and/or consequences. However, upon further investigation, the term "culture" may have been misconstrued, as it appears organizational climate, organizational context (the impetus or the degree of need for change), and shared beliefs manifested in consensus and politics make up the category termed "culture" in this model. Therefore, perhaps the best way to understand succession processes is by looking at studies of how leaders shape organizational culture.

Executives are organizational heroes (Deal & Kennedy, 1982), who are symbolic (Pfeffer, 1981). They create, change, embody, and integrate organizational culture consciously and unconsciously (Deal & Kennedy, 1982; Schein, 1992; Trice & Beyer, 1993). Even though they may facilitate cultural change, the change will not endure without qualified successors to further their visions.

The succession planning process used in an organization is learned over time as a result of successful outcomes (Haveman, 1993). The succession process might even be viewed as an artifact within an organization (1992). Like other processes in the organization, it becomes an important vehicle to communicate values and beliefs among employees as to what is necessary to be promoted and ultimately to lead the organization. Schein (1992) suggests that initial selection decisions for new members (new management orientation), followed by the criteria applied in the promotion system, are powerful mechanisms for embedding and perpetuating the culture, especially when combined with socialization tactics like high-potential designation and leadership development programs designed to teach cultural assumptions. Basic assumptions are further reinforced through the performance criteria of who does or does not get promoted.

Organizational culture

Culture is a complex phenomenon and there remain many competing views of the definition of organizational culture (Martin, 2002). One researcher (Smircich, 1983) suggests the problem may lie within the attempt to combine the term "culture" with the term "organization." Another (Mead, 1949) describes culture as the ethos of an organization, much as personality is the ethos of an individual. Culture, as representative of ethos and personality, suggests a complex and dynamic system rather than a static, organized one.

Although there remains a lack of consensus about a singular definition of culture, arguably the most widely cited in organization research is that of Edgar Schein (1992). Schein states that organizational culture is

> A pattern of shared basic assumptions that the group learned as it solved its problems of external adaptation and internal integration, that has worked well enough to be considered valid and, therefore, to be taught to new members as the correct way to perceive, think, and feel in relation to those problems.
>
> (p. 13)

More importantly for this chapter, Schein (1992) proposes that founders have a profound influence on the creation of culture through creation of values that are subsequently proven successful in actions taken by employees, which lead to desirable results. Over time, these actions and behaviors become more deeply rooted in subconscious, basic assumptions. These basic assumptions are difficult to change and therefore long-lasting, even to the detriment of the organization. In addition, Schein states that leaders perpetuate existing culture and have the ability to change it by what they pay attention to, measure, and control on a regular basis. Leaders can also perpetuate and/or change culture by using certain organizational systems, processes and procedures, technology, rites and rituals, stories, and so on.

Although most leadership and organizational culture studies acknowledge the importance of the role of the leader in sustaining and managing the organizational culture, some suggest (Martin, 2002) that this approach underestimates the role of other organizational members such as competing subcultures including functions, professional affiliations, religions, social class, and educational backgrounds, and the external environment including industry, market, regulatory change, and so on (Campbell, 2004; Kell & Carrott, 2005; Meyerson & Martin, 1987; Sackmann, 1991; Schultz & Hatch, 1996).

Organizational culture and succession planning

Much of what follows in this chapter is based on a case study that was conducted to understand better the relationship of organizational culture and succession planning within an organization. Sackmann's (1991) qualitative research methods were adapted to understand the cultural knowledge held by various levels of management within it.

The study site was that of a large publicly traded Fortune 500 company within the transportation industry. The company has a rich and lengthy history in package delivery and logistics support. There are multiple offices nationwide as well as a global presence. Drawing upon Sackmann's (1991) typology, which answers questions related to defining the process—describing how it occurs, describing how it should occur, and making assumptions about why it is done the way it is— qualitative ethnographic data were collected from managers at various levels through ethnographic interviews and focus groups. Additional qualitative data were collected through participant observation and related organizational documents.

Those managers who were interviewed had significantly more to say about how the succession process occurs and what should occur than defining what succession planning "is" and why it is done the way it is. As explained later, these findings provide evidence that managers operate on deeply rooted organizational values instilled by the founder, which they may or may not be consciously aware of.

Furthermore, consistent with Schein's theory of leadership of culture, the interviews and focus groups showed us that the founder's "philosophy of management" (decentralized authority, managers as partners and owners, truth found in consensus, and so on) and early policy of "promotion from within" underlay the decision-making behind the succession planning process either consciously or subconsciously. Employees were able to describe what *should* occur rather easily based on these founding principles. The plethora of data gathered that described *how* succession planning occurred was much more descriptive and challenging. Through a process of discovery, the interviewee was able to recount an informal succession process when asked to tell a story of how they had been successful or how others had made it to the top. Story-telling is an important tool for HRD practitioners and organization researchers when conducting ethnographic interviews (Hansen & Kahnweiler, 1993, 1997). Interestingly, participants had more difficulty defining *what* succession planning is because they could not readily see it as separate from the *how* (promotion from within) of the promotion process. "Promotion from within" was viewed as a core value and crucial HR policy instilled by the founder. It was originally created as a reward for all management members who diligently served in the company's core operation of package delivery. Distinguishing this process as one that differs for performing managers from one used for "high potentials" poses problems.

It is perhaps no surprise that the participants had difficulty describing *why* the succession planning process happens the way that it does, separate from the reasoning, "because we've always done it this way." Not unlike the American military, promotion is largely viewed as synonymous with succession in this organization, at least among the tenured, middle managers. Furthermore, like the military, organization members are rewarded with promotion based on their humbleness, hard work, and loyalty.

In summary, this study found that the informal succession planning process serves to perpetuate the organizational culture. Furthermore, cultural values associated with this process are so entrenched and subconsciously held among the organization's managers who are responsible for the execution of the plan, that it is difficult to make any kind of change.

Implications for the company studied

Founders and top executives tend to have their own prescribed theories of how groups should work. They usually select colleagues and direct reports based on who they believe will think and act like them (Hansen & Kahnweiler, 1997; Kets de Vries, 1991). The things these founders pay attention to, measure, and control are intricately woven throughout traditional organizational processes involving succession planning, technology, structure, staffing, skill sets, rites and rituals, values, and physical space. If the former are not aligned, then the latter will be ignored or become a source of conflict among organizational members. Figure 14.1 illustrates the relationship between the founder, the organizational culture, and the role of decentralized authority among member relationships in the succession planning process in this study.

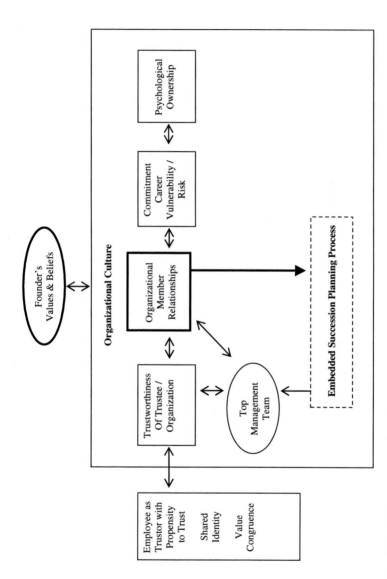

Figure 14.1   Embedded succession planning process.

HR processes perpetuate and/or change the alignment of the founder's values and beliefs of the organization through formal and informal communication about shared values, identity, trust, commitment, and psychological ownership.

In the case study, the founder's "Philosophy of Management," characterized by decentralized authority with managers as partners and owners, truth by consensus, and "promotion from within," as basic assumptions, consciously and subconsciously enforced the execution of the succession planning process as well as the leadership development process. Formal and, more importantly, informal communication plans about these processes perpetuated the founder's core values surrounding leadership and management.

The findings demonstrate the necessity of examining basic assumptions as they are realized in the behaviors of those responsible for implementing HR processes. For example, forces that ensure a tightly woven alignment of culture and process, in the case of the organization studied, were perpetuated by informal communication, decentralized authority in the form of relationships, value congruence, organizational trust, commitment, and psychological ownership. These elements were found to be critical to the traditional means of selection and retention of recognized talent and the overall execution of the succession planning process. In this organization, informal and secretive *identification* was viewed as formal *selection*; the two were not separate components of the process. Titles such as "high potential" were avoided, and communication about one's status as a potential leadership candidate was rarely openly discussed. Managers, viewed as "partners," perpetuated an organization of egalitarianism, circumventing attempts to reassure talent formally of their status as future potential.

However, where communication was scant, HR practices like leadership development and promotion served to reinforce individual trust and organizational commitment. Leadership development opportunities were not communicated before taking place. Participants were often asked to travel or relocate, they were given little notice, and their families followed weeks or months later. Often they were unsure of their next assignment and/or their next promotion; yet the trust in the process and their individual commitment remained high.

Many of these development opportunities were extremely challenging ones that allowed for little or no preparation. The test was to see if the person would be able to leverage relationships to get the work done. Furthermore, many of the developmental tests or opportunities that required travel and/or a move were conducted in locales in which the "high potential" was evaluated, often covertly, by other corporately trusted members of the organization. These tests of leadership were used to verify organizational fit. Promotion was never guaranteed. Work accomplished through these decentralized relationships and "truth" about performance were validated by consensus, based on values instilled by the founder, and remain part and parcel of the succession planning process today.

It is important to understand that people vary in their willingness to trust based on their individual developmental experiences, personality types, and cultural backgrounds including subcultural influences (Hofstede, 1980). The participants in this study stated that they identified with the organization early in their careers. They found a cultural fit or value congruence with the traditionally blue-collar work ethic of the organization and that which they acquired from their largely blue-collar parents while growing up. The company was seen as an American institution. This image also contributed to shared identity and trust in that it stood for familiar values of good, clean, wholesomeness, predictability, dependability, reliability, quality, and pride. Furthermore, the strength of this identity was evidenced as white-collar as well as blue-collar workers found themselves willing to do whatever it took to achieve membership in this tightly knit familial organization, as was evidenced by their humble beginning as college-educated loaders, sorters, car washers, drivers, and so on. Although organizational commitment was high, promotion from these positions was never guaranteed. The findings from this case study provide support for the role played by membership in subcultures like Protestant work ethic/religion, blue-collar social class, and education in the succession planning process. Employees identified with the organization and therefore willingly put their careers at risk as a result of the presumed trust that they had in the organization as a whole.

These findings suggest that, over time, decentralized organizational member relationships facilitate the movement from initially negotiated identities to a deeper identity that is the alteration of one's self concept to include that of the collective. In turn, these deep, collective identities lead to value-based rather than exchange-based commitments. These identities also serve to meet the basic needs of motivational factors such as self-esteem, security, and perceived connection.

Throughout the succession planning and promotion processes, employee commitment was tested and challenged with the desired result of continued loyalty. Relocations, family hardships, career moves, and an almost "blind trust" in the organization mediated by decentralized organization member relationships served to reinforce both commitment and identity. As a result of their value-based commitment to the collective, their perceived vulnerability, and their renewed trust, participants as experienced managers acquired a sense of psychological ownership to the organization and its practices (Pierce, Kostova, & Dirks, 2001). Psychological ownership was important in this study as participants demonstrated that they had a sense of ownership in the succession planning process and in the candidates they chose to succeed them. Managers were in control of the process as each played a significant role in the identification, development, and promotion of those around them as a result of the "promotion from within" policy. The organization relied on each manager's input as verification and proof of the viability of a potential candidate for promotion and eventual succession. These decisions are often rooted in what has been described as a "gut feeling." This "gut feeling" is, in turn, rooted in the subconscious organizational values that, like decentralized authority and truth by consensus, are instilled by the founder and held by the organization's members.

Managers feel personally responsible for those that they choose for succession. They are supportive of each other throughout their careers and maintain lifelong relationships within and sometimes outside the organization. These managers often pick those who are like themselves either personally or professionally to succeed them; therefore successors or "high potentials" become extensions of themselves (Hansen & Kahnweiler, 1995, 1997). One participant suggested that "escape routes" are built in to the promotion of a personally recognized "high potential" and that commitment to their career is a lifelong one. These "escape routes" are used when the potential for success during a developmental rotation has been thwarted for a variety of reasons.

Lastly, the safety and security of the manager's position is ensured by the promotion of those whom they have known. Those who succeed another are seen as "part of them," and their success is attributed in part to those who play a role in their development. Professional and functional subcultures such as engineering and finance foster these enduring value-based commitments to high-potential candidates. These findings support evidence of the tremendous role that professional subcultures and other organizational memberships play in the succession planning process.

The presumed trust in the organization is not only visible in the HR-related organizational processes such as succession planning but also in leadership and the top management team. As Schein (1992) reminds us, the culture of the organization is sustained and maintained by the leadership. It is therefore important for organizational members to view the top management team as extensions of themselves. The identification with the top management team furthers the trustworthiness of the overall organization and its subordinate processes. Therefore, the importance of fit in HR policy and organizational culture is key to the retention of talent and to the future of the organization.

In summary, organizational culture provides a necessary context for the evaluation of organizational practices such as succession planning. In this study, the values of the founder embedded within the organizational culture served to create and perpetuate a "Philosophy of Management", which was a key factor in how the work got done. The execution of the succession planning process cannot be effective if it discounts competing subcultures, the role of organizational managers and key members, their relationships, technology, and "promotion from within" as secondary mechanisms to further the founder's original intent.

Broad implications for HRD practitioners

HRD is largely responsible as facilitator of organizational culture through the implementation of policies, procedures, and processes. Within this study, most participants stated that the biggest challenge to a viable succession planning process lies in: (1) leadership development; (2) talent retention; and (3) communication.

The survival of traditional means of leadership development through relocation and rotational assignment in this company are being tested in the same way that they are in other organizations (Karaevli & Hall, 2003). Questions are being asked by the study's participants about whether these components still fit the needs of the organization and whether they remain cost effective. However, the culture of the organization perpetuates the process of rotational assignments and relocation because of its founder's philosophy of "truth by consensus" and a decentralized approach to management. Furthermore, the "succession planning process" as defined by this organization can be viewed as a process that mirrors and parallels the "promotion process;" the former for the high performer, the latter for the high-potential leader. Therefore, this process cannot be readily changed simply by applying tools related to organizational development such as business process redesign and structure change. Furthermore, the succession planning process cannot be changed by any HRD intervention without considering the role, situated context, and alignment of organizational culture.

Talent retention of a younger and more professional workforce surfaced as a problem resulting primarily from the limitation of development opportunities, a slow promotion process, and compensation. Cultural values instilled by the founder foster such lengthy development processes by placing a primary importance on complicated networking relationships and trust, often without formal communication. Egalitarian, Protestant, and blue-collar work ethics instilled by the founder prevent early designation of high potentials, and rewards are based on loyalty and commitment for hard work rather than only results.

Communication, seen as a factor impacting both of the above challenges, would most likely have the biggest impact on the commitment and trust of those who are relatively new within the organization. However, consistency in the succession planning process and communication of what is necessary to continue to be promoted became more difficult as the organization grew and became more diverse. This was because of culture-enforcing processes such as leadership development through rotational assignments and relocation, which were lengthy and informal.

Decentralized authority within the organization as a result of the leader's "philosophy of management" appears to have worked against many attempts to centralize corporately the processes of talent management and succession planning. Technology was used to improve visibility of the talent and improve communication in a more efficient and timely manner. However, this technology was not used to its fullest extent as it threatened the informal "gut feeling" processes and thwarted the authority of those who felt a sense of pride and ownership in the succession process. Assessments were put in place to test leadership skills. However, in most cases they were dismissed as ineffective or at least tools that should be used with a seasoned manager's discretion. As organizations mature, to ensure future behavior continues to support organizational viability, it is often necessary to abandon some traditional values. Technology offers a tool to accomplish this. HRD can create change management plans that address the implementation of succession planning by considering the role that competing subcultures, key stakeholders, and middle managers have in the change process. Understanding the role that organizational culture plays in influencing this behavior and the alignment of cultural values with HR practices can lead to success. These are all areas in which HRD practitioners can and should play a valuable and strategic role in supporting organizational needs and goals.

HRD practitioners serve two primary customers: the employee and the organization. The challenges faced by organizations (speed, talent retention, capabilities, and so on) and employees (loyalty, trust, identity, and so on) may seem to some to threaten HRD's very existence (Hammonds, 2005). The problem of viability exists and continues to drive the response of scholars and HRD professionals in addressing the strategic role that HRD must play in the alignment of organizational and individual goals. Much of this literature suggests the need to reinvent the field of HRD (Hammonds, 2005; Rynes, 2004; Walton, 2003), whereas others suggest HRD should focus on leveraging its core competencies, including training and development, career development, and organizational development, to enhance organizational capabilities (Ulrich, 1997). Furthermore, the findings of the presented case study and others suggest that a larger impact on the organization may be made with a focus on organizational development, specifically the impact of changing culture on succession planning.

As organizations face ethical issues of leadership, visionary leadership, and pressure for performance, there is perhaps no better time than the present for succession planning to become a key component of sustainability. Successor readiness and development will depend largely on cultural alignment. As this case study revealed, cultural alignment of traditional values with organizational processes can be perpetuated by middle management. The question, then, is one of balance and coordination between corporate *knowledge management* of the succession planning process and the decentralized middle managers who are so essential to process execution.

Conclusion

Succession planning is perhaps one of the hottest topics today. Global organizations faced with fast-paced change can no longer afford the lengthy internal development of an heir apparent. However, those organizations that seek faster, external executive hires have found it no panacea, as organizational culture fit often trumps talent and industry experience. The key to the long-term success of internal successions will depend on the ability of organizations to execute plans (Charan & Colvin, 1999, 2001).

In this day and age of increasing questions about the value of HR and, furthermore, HRD, there has never been a better time to prove a strategic worth. Many organizations are replacing HR executives with legal professionals or those with legal backgrounds as a safety net to preclude unethical and illegal behavior in an effort to treat the symptom rather than the root cause. Cultural alignment of organizational processes such as leadership development, talent management, and succession planning ensures an effect on the root cause in that it serves as a contingency between values, beliefs, and organizational results. HRD practitioners must take a closer look at the organizational culture, why and how succession planning occurs the way that it does, and the role of organizational stakeholders in supporting the effective execution of succession plans.

References

Cabrera, E. F., & Bonache, J. "An expert HR system for aligning organizational culture and strategy." *Human Resource Planning*, 22(1) (1999) 51–60.

Campbell, C. R. "A longitudinal study of one organization's culture: Do values endure?" *Mid-American Journal of Business*, 19(2) (2004) 41–51.

Cannella Jr., A. A., & Lubatkin, M. "Succession as a sociopolitical process: Internal impediments to outsider selection." *Academy of Management Journal*, 36(4) (1993) 763–93.

Cappelli, P. "A Market-driven approach to retaining talent." *Harvard Business Review*, 78(1) (2000) 103.

Caudron, S. "Plan today for an unexpected tomorrow." *Personnel Journal*, 75(9) (1996) 40.

Charan, R. "Ending the CEO Succession Crisis." *Harvard Business Review* (2004) 72.

Charan, R., & Colvin, G. "Why CEOs fail." *Fortune*, 139(12) (1999) 68–78.

Charan, R., & Colvin, G. "Making a Clean Handoff." *Fortune*, 144(5) (2001) 72.

Conger, J. A., & Nadler, D. A. "When CEOs Step Up to Fail." *MIT Sloan Management Review*, 45(3) (2004) 49–57.

Deal, T. E., & Kennedy, A. A. *Corporate cultures: The rites and rituals of corporate life.* (Reading, MA: Addison-Wesley Publishing Company, 1982).

Denis, J.-L., Langley, A., & Pineault, M. "Becoming a leader in a complex organization." *Journal of Management Studies*, 37(8) (2000) 1063.

Hammonds, K. H. "Why we hate HR." *Fast Company* (97) (2005) 40.

Hansen, C. D., & Kahnweiler, W. M. "Storytelling: An instrument for understanding the dynamics of corporate relationships." *Human Relations*, 46(12) (1993) 1391–409.

Hansen, C. D., & Kahnweiler, W. M. "Organizational tension and occupational scripts: Stories from HR professionals and top executives." *Human Resource Management Review*, 5(1) (1995) 25–51.

Hansen, C. D., & Kahnweiler, W. M. "Executive Managers: Cultural expectations through stories about work." *Journal of Applied Management Studies*, 6(2) (1997) 177.

Haveman, H. A. "Ghosts of managers past: Managerial succession and organizational mortality." *Academy of Management Journal*, 36(4) (1993) 864–81.

Hofstede, G. "Motivation, leadership and organization: Do American theories apply abroad?" *Organizational Dynamics*, 9(1) (1980) 42–63.

Karaevli, A., & Hall, D. T. "Growing Leaders for Turbulent Times: Is Succession Planning Up to the Challenge?" *Organizational Dynamics*, 32(1) (2003) 62–79.

Kell, T., & Carrott, G. "Culture matters most." *Harvard Business Review*, 83(5) (2005) 22.

Kesner, I. F., & Sebora, T. C. "Executive succession: Past, present & future." *Journal of Management*, 20(2) (1994) 327–72.

Kets de Vries, Manfred, F. R. "Exploding the myth that organizations and executives are rational." In Kets de Vries, M. F. R. (ed.), *Organizations on the couch*, (1991) 1–21.

Kets de Vries, Manfred, F. R. "The Dark Side of CEO Succession." *Harvard Business Review Management Review* (1988) 23–27.

Martin, J. *Organizational Culture: Mapping the Terrain.* (Thousand Oaks, CA: Sage, 2002).

Mead, M. *Coming of Age in Samoa.* (New York: New American Library, 1949).

Meyerson, D., & Martin, J. "Cultural change: An integration of three different views." *Journal of Management Studies*, 24(6) (1987) 623–47.

Pfeffer, J. "Management as symbolic action." In L. L. Cummings & S. Staw (eds), *Research on organizational behavior:* vol. 3. (Greenwich, CT: JAI, 1981).

Pierce, J. L., Kostova, T., & Dirks, K. "Toward a theory of psychological ownership in organizations." *Academy of Management Review*, 26(2) (2001) 298.

Pitcher, P., Chreim, S., & Kisfalvi, V. "CEO succession research: Methodological bridges over troubled waters." *Strategic Management Journal*, 21(6) (2000) 625–48.

Rynes, S. L. "Where do we go from here? Imagining new roles for Human Resources." *Journal of Management Inquiry*, 13(3) (2004) 203–13.

Sackmann, S. A. *Cultural knowledge in organizations: Exploring the collective mind.* (Newbury Park: Sage Publications, 1991).

Schein, E. H. *Organizational culture and leadership.* (San Francisco: Jossey-Bass, 1992).

Schultz, M., & Hatch, M. J. "Living with multiple paradigms: The case of paradigm interplay in organizational culture studies." *Academy of Management Review*, 21(2) (1996) 529–57.

Scott, A. Ethics and succession studied. *Internal Auditor*, 16. (2004).

Smircich, L. "Concepts of culture and organizational analysis." *Administrative Science Quarterly*, 28(3) (1983).

Trice, H. M., & Beyer, J. M. *The cultures of work organizations.* (Englewood Cliffs, NJ: Prentice Hall 1993).

Ulrich, D. "Judge me more by my future than by my past." *Human Resource Management*, 36(1) (1997) 5–8.

Walton, J. S. "How shall a thing be called? An argumentation on the efficacy of the term HRD." *Human Resource Development Review*, 2(3) (2003) 310–26.

Wasserman, N. "Founder-CEO succession and the paradox of entrepreneurial success." *Organization Science*, 14(2) (2003) 149–72.

Author Index

Subject Index

258   *Subject Index*

258   *Subject Index*